To Defend Ourselves: Ecology and
Ritual in an Andean Village

Latin American Monographs, No. 47
Institute of Latin American Studies
The University of Texas at Austin

To Defend Ourselves

Ecology and Ritual in an Andean Village

by Billie Jean Isbell

Institute of Latin American Studies
The University of Texas at Austin

International Standard Book Number 0-292-78031-1 (paper)
0-292-78030-3 (cloth)
Library of Congress Catalog Card Number 78-620051

The Latin American Monographs Series
is distributed for the Institute of
Latin American Studies by:
    University of Texas Press
    P. O. Box 7819
    Austin, Texas 78712

I affectionately dedicate this book to two women
whose faith and encouragement made its completion possible:
In memory of Dee Furst
and
To my mother, Mildred Richerson

Contents

Figures

Tables

Plates

Maps

Acknowledgements

First, I would like to acknowledge the encouragement, patience, and intellectual as well as moral support afforded me by my family during the various stages of this work. My mother, Mildred Richerson, assumed much of the burden of child rearing and housework to free my time. She accompanied my husband, my daughter, and me to the Andean village under study and proved to be our "survival kit," for only she knew how to slaughter animals, salt meat, and prepare foods as well as administer remedies for our various minor illnesses. Most important, she held my head when I was so sick and drunk from the obligatory ritual drinking in which I had to participate. My daughter, Diana, now thirteen, celebrated her third, fifth, and tenth birthdays in the Andes. She provided proof to the natives that we were not malevolent. My husband, William Harris Isbell, and I have grown together intellectually, and I especially thank him for his stimulation, comments, and criticisms. I consider him my most valuable critic.

Many others have played important roles in my intellectual development. My principal mentor at the University of Illinois has been R. T. Zuidema, who introduced me not only to the Andes but also to structural methodology. Our lively discussions and debates will be cherished for many years. I have had the good fortune to receive guiding criticisms from Jan Brukman, whose assumed role of devil's advocate often made me defend my theoretical and methodological orientation. Joseph Casagrande offered insightful advice concerning field methodology, and F. K. Lehman introduced me to the formal analysis of kinship. All of the above deserve special thanks.

To my colleagues at the State University of New York at Albany I extend appreciation for their support, criticisms, and forbearance while this work was in progress. I would especially like to thank Robert

M. Carmack and Peter T. Furst for critical comments and for useful comparisons with Middle American data. Many helpful discussions resulted from a graduate seminar in kinship and social organization I taught during the spring of 1973. To the challenging students of that seminar I express my acknowledgment of their contribution. Ben Orlove and Glynn Custred helped me tremendously by critically reading chapter 2. Owen M. Lynch provided many helpful criticisms on chapter 8, as did Kenneth David. Olivia Harris carefully read the manuscript and found many weak spots that were either unclear or lacked supporting data. Some of those I have been able to clarify; others will have to wait for future research. The revisions of this book have been greatly facilitated by critical comments of graduate students at Cornell preparing to do fieldwork in the Andes.

Of course, I could not have conducted my fieldwork without the able assistance of Justa Vilca, Alejandro Mora, Eugenio Vilca, Cirilo Tucno, Pablo Alcocer, Fredy Roncalla, and Dario Carhuapoma. I would also like to express my sincerest appreciation to my compadres and the entire village of Chuschi for allowing me to reside with them for a total of twenty-eight months. My presence often demanded patience and understanding on their part. Among my Peruvian colleagues, I would like to thank the anthropologists, Sergio Catacora, Edmundo Pinto, Salvador Palomino, and Ulpiano Quispe, with whom I participated in the Pampas River project. I would especially like to thank Salvador Palomino and Fredy Roncalla for clarifying many Quechua concepts for me.

The Museo de la Cultura Peruana extended Peruvian sponsorship for my research. I would like to thank Dr. Rosalía Avalos de Matos, director of the museum, for the assistance given me through her personal attention to my many requests. I would also like to thank the staff of the Direction of Peasant Communities for making available preliminary reports on Chuschi and the Cangallo region, thus saving many hours of tedious fact-finding. Support for my field research was provided by a National Institute of Mental Health doctoral dissertation grant and post-doctoral research grant, the Social Science Research Council, and the Ford Foundation.

The final preparation of the book was accomplished with the help of many skillful hands. Florence Sloane and Jan Townsend prepared the figures and assisted in the tabulation of demographic data. My husband, W. H. Isbell, drafted two of the maps. He also took several of the photographs during our first field session. Betty Kruger and Joann Somich of the State University of New York at Albany had the thankless job of transforming my draft into an expertly typed finished product. Editing and critical readings were provided by the capable assistance of Elizabeth

K. Hewitt, Dee Furst, Judy Leon, and Mercedes López-Baralt. Marge
Ciaschi and Denise Everhart of Cornell retyped much of the manuscript.
To all of these people I express warmest thanks. Needless to say, all
interpretations and analyses are my own, and only I am responsible for
possible errors.

GUIDE TO THE PRONUNCIATION OF QUECHUA

Consonants (those in parenthesis are borrowed from Spanish)

	Labial	Alveolar	Palatal	Velar	Postvelar	Glottal
Voiceless stop	p	t	č*	k	q	
Voiced stop	(b)	(d)		(g)		
Fricative	(f)	s				h
Nasal	m	n	ñ			
Lateral		l	ĺ*			
Simple trill		r				
Multiple retro-flexive trill		(ř)*				
Semi-vowels	w		y			

*Orthography: /č/ ch, /ĺ/ ll, /ř/ rr

Vowels

	Front	Central	Back
High	i		u
Mid	e		o
Low		a	

To Defend Ourselves: Ecology and
Ritual in an Andean Village

1. Introduction

1.1 My Fieldwork in the Andes

1.1.1 A Confession

Clifford Geertz (1968: 551) has said that "all ethnography is part philosophy, and a good deal of the rest is confession." The introduction to this ethnographic study of a south-central Andean community begins with a confession: I not only changed the design of my doctoral research while in the field and then further refocused my analysis after returning to the United States in 1970, but I also reoriented my professional direction after my Andean experience. This chapter is an attempt to document the process of change in emphasis and orientation that began in 1967 with my first experiences as an undergraduate residing for seven months in a south-central Quechua-speaking Andean village and has culminated with the completion of this book after two return trips to the same village in 1969-1970 and again in 1974-1975. The first part of chapter 2 was written in 1976, as was the postscript.

1.1.2 My Introduction to the Andes

In February of 1967, my husband and I were two of five students from the University of Illinois sent to Ayacucho, Peru, to study with R. T. Zuidema, who was conducting research and teaching at the University of Huamanga. He had begun a project with students from Huamanga on seven villages in the drainage basin of the Pampas River that have been a political and social unit since Inca times. The region was chosen because of the excellent documentation available and because the relative isolation of the villages provided a greater degree of stability of traditional customs. Several significant publications have resulted from the Pampas River project: Zuidema

1966; Zuidema and Quispe 1968; Catacora 1968; Earls 1968; B. J. Isbell 1972a, 1972b, 1974a, 1974b, 1976, and 1977; W. H. Isbell 1970a, 1970b, and 1972a; Palomino 1970, 1971, and 1972; Pinto 1970 and 1972; and Quispe 1969.

After two weeks of orientation in Ayacucho, my husband, another archaeologist named Tom Meyers, and I journeyed on March 2, 1967 to the district capital of Chuschi, 120 kilometers southwest of Ayacucho. We traveled Andean style, in a commercial truck. I fortunately got a seat in the cab along with two other passengers. The back was packed with people and their possessions, produce, and animals. During the eight-hour trip it rained intermittently, which is not unusual for that time of year, and three times men had to clamber out of the truck to pull the vehicle out of mud holes, using chains. On arriving, we were able to get one small room in the "hotel," a row of rooms with dirt floors and no windows behind one of the village stores on the plaza, but only after assuring the owner that we would stay a week or two. Although six or seven trucks arrived with market vendors aboard for the weekly market the next day, we were told the market was smaller than usual because of heavy rains and the poor condition of the road. (See plate 1.)

For ten days the three of us made ourselves as conspicuous as possible, which was not difficult. We sat in the village plaza and attempted at least to exchange looks with the indigenous villagers, who shyly averted their eyes and did not speak. However, outside of the village on the trails, people would greet us as they passed. This was a puzzle until in 1969 I discovered Chuschinos' concepts of space and ecology (discussed in 2.8). My notes read like a forlorn soliloquy. One entry: "Well, I sat on the plaza most of the day again, and like yesterday, none of the Quechua-speaking villagers acknowledged my presence. I desperately need an interpreter. At least Bill and Tom can do an archaeological survey, but here I sit, quietly being ignored." I am sure our presence generated a lot of curiosity, but people simply pretended we were not there. Rumors ran that we were really looking for gold and silver or that we were spies. Their suspicious and cautious attitudes also meant that we could not rent a house. There were several houses vacant in the village, but we would track down the owner through the municipal mayor only to hear that the owner was away or that possessions were being stored in the house and therefore it could not be rented. After three weeks of such discouraging efforts, we rented a house from a mestizo family, one of the descendants of the first schoolteacher who had arrived in Chuschi four generations ago. His descendants are still considered "foreigners." Why are such persons considered foreigners after four generations of continuous residence in this village? What are the Chuschinos' conceptual categories of social classes? What are the criteria for membership in their community that exclude these people? Questions abounded in those first weeks, but all one could do was

Plate 1. On the Way to Chuschi. A landslide on the road from Ayacucho after a rainstorm.

observe from a distance and wonder. Finally, we had a stroke of ethno-graphic luck.

1.1.3   A Breakthrough

During our third week in Chuschi, while I was sitting in the plaza as usual, two men left the church carrying a large silver cross, a wooden litter, a black shroud, a drape with skull and cross bones, and a container of holy water. The night before, the church bells had tolled the mournful death peal. We learned that a man from Upper Barrio had died of *mal aire* (harmful air). From the description of his symptoms, we decided he had died of lockjaw— hence the belief that "the evil in *mal aire* had attacked him and caused his mouth to clamp shut." I decided that we should follow the men carrying the funeral paraphernalia; the worst they could do would be to chase us away. Reluctantly, my two archaeologist companions accompanied me.

We followed the two men to the house of the dead man, where a wake was in progress. The body was displayed on a table in the three-sided portal area of the house, and the widow sat at his right wailing a high-pitched song. There were close to twenty people present, and everyone was drunk. As we paused in the outer entry to the patio, an old man came forward with a bottle in his hand and motioned us to enter. We took off our hats and stood uncertainly, wondering what to do next. Almost immediately the old man poured himself a shot and raised his glass in the direction of Tom Meyers, who nodded acceptance. The old man downed the drink in one gulp, poured another shot, and extended the glass to Tom, who raised it to Bill before drinking. Tom drank and poured a shot full for Bill but did not swallow, while a strange look came over his face. Bill received the proffered drink, raised the cup to his lips, and said, "This isn't cane alcohol, it's kerosene," as he smiled, toasted me, and drank. I took the cup in my hands, wondering what kerosene would do to one's stomach, toasted a woman sitting on the floor, and drank, then poured her a shot. She raised it to her lips and, look-ing surprised, shouted excitedly, but all we understood was the word *kerosene*. Snatching the bottle from my hands, she berated the old man drunkenly sit-ting on the floor and leaning against the wall. He shrugged his shoulders and said nothing. The woman pointed to the bottle in her hand and then at another bottle beside him on the floor. She exchanged the bottles, poured herself a drink from the second, toasted me, and clapped me on the back, laughing. Everyone laughed: the gringos had drunk kerosene and had not even complained. Then we were offered seats and real trago, or cane alco-hol. Remaining through the day, we accompanied the cadaver to the ceme-tery and participated in the *pichqa,* a divination and purification rite involving washing the deceased's clothing and cutting and burning the funeral participants' hair. Being ritually treated in the same fashion as the other participants, we had broken through the initial barrier at last.

After our uninvited intrusion into a Chuschino wake, we were informed whenever someone died and were invited to participate. I attended at least fifteen funerals during my seven-month sojourn in Chuschi during 1967. Jokingly, R. T. Zuidema and my fellow students asked whether I was going to open a Quechua funeral parlor. Slowly, the reserve of the Quechua-speaking comuneros diminished to the point that people began to greet us and even stop and visit.

During the first week of April, we moved our two-year-old daughter, Diana, and my mother, Mildred Richerson, into the village. The rains were abating somewhat and trucks reached the village every Thursday evening, albeit with difficulty. Our second trip into Chuschi was even more eventful than the first. Initially we had secured a place in the cab of a truck for my mother, but a comadre of the owner-driver arrived and my mother was refunded the extra fare for a cab seat and bumped to the rear. Priority is always given to one's compadres, one's spiritual relatives.

Twenty kilometers from Chuschi, a landslide blocked the road, necessitating our spending the night huddled together in the cold with the almost forty other travelers under a decidedly leaky tarp. My husband abandoned the crowded confines of the truck to sleep in the rain with a waterproof ground cover and sleeping bag; soon he took refuge under the truck. Inside we heard a peculiar scratching and thumping noise as Bill tried to scale the high sides of the truck to rejoin us. Someone finally helped him in. Soaked and unable to find a spot big enough to lie down, he crouched and tried to doze. It was a miserable night for all of us; the natives kept encroaching on our space, and, unwise in Andean ways, we were unable to defend ourselves.

The next morning, when people vacated the truck, we discovered that our boxes of belongings had been flattened and broken as if a stampede had run over them. Many items were missing and the remainder were filthy and wet. An infant had had an attack of diarrhea on my mother and on some of our bedding and mattresses. The retrieval operation was very depressing, as was the prospect of getting into the village. Bill walked six kilometers to a village and rented two horses and four donkeys; the owner accompanied us. On one horse, without reins, I carried my two-year old on my lap, my mother rode the other, and Bill walked, guiding the loaded donkeys. We arrived in Chuschi in the late afternoon and installed our family in our three-room adobe house with no windows, no furniture, and dirt floors. Earlier I had felt optimistic when we finally negotiated the rental, but at that point I asked myself, "What are we doing here? This is insane."

These same thoughts occurred again when we tried to persuade the carpenter to build us a bed. He made it clear that he owed us nothing and that he would build one as a favor to us. After waiting three months we were confronted with an apparatus resembling a double-width ladder rather than a double bed. When we left in 1967, we sold the bed. Returning in 1969, we found it being used more logically as a clothes rack for drying laundry. The same preference for social debts over cash meant that we could not hire someone to work for us; therefore we did our laundry in the irrigation canal, maintained our own food animals, and generally spent a lot of time keeping body and soul together.

Establishing a family residence in Chuschi was one of the wisest moves we made. The monolingual Quechua speakers began to bring us gifts of produce or come to just sit on the floor for hours and watch us. We kept a continual pot of soup cooking for our stream of visitors. It would have been interesting to collect their impressions of us during those first months. They began to see we had a family, an extended one just like theirs, so, bit by bit, interaction opened up and people began to joke not only about us but with us. During Santa Cruz, the harvest feast, Bill was initiated into the civil-religious prestige hierarchy as if he were a young single boy. I was treated sometimes as if I were a man, sometimes like a child, and sometimes like a woman, which turned out to be a great ethnographic advantage. They took special delight in holding and talking to our daughter, for they had never had such close contact with blond, fair people before. My mother was considered a marvel for her snow-white hair, an indication to them of extremely advanced age; also, her ability to ride a horse impressed them greatly. People would appear at our door asking for white hairs (to be used in certain rituals) from the *abuelita*'s (little grandmother's) head.

1.1.4 A View through a Kaleidoscope

Slowly we became more and more accepted. But the event that gave us social existence in the community was the acquisition of godchildren and the special compadrazgo relationship this establishes with the children's parents. When we left Chuschi in August of 1967 we had acquired ten godchildren and all the rights and duties these relationships imply. Compadrazgo relationships provided our initiation into the social fabric of the village. Our ignorance of appropriate behavior provided an excellent vehicle for ethnographic investigation. It was viewed as natural that we should ask how to perform our assigned ritual roles and social duties. Both mestizos and indigenous villagers requested our sponsorship. At the end of our 1967 stay, we sponsored a wedding that did not conform to comunero ideals: a village girl married an outsider, a "foreigner," and we, as foreigners, were considered the most logical godparents. This case is reported in 5.6.11.

Even though we had been accepted to some degree, there were, of course, cultural rules we never learned, others we discovered rather late, and areas of investigation that remained closed to us. One of the cultural rules that we realized rather late was the rule of drunkenness. In our culture we value "holding our liquor," but Chuschino culture values getting drunk and passing out. The success of a ritual is gauged in part by how many people pass out. Consequently, they pass out with much less to drink than we do. I have never become so drunk, nor gotten so sick, as I did during those first months in Chuschi before realizing I was not playing by their rules. At one ritual forty-two people were asleep at four o'clock in the afternoon from drinking and I was awake but not at all sober. That I too should "pass out" early in the course of events finally dawned on me.

One episode will illustrate my lack of understanding of Chuschino drinking patterns. At a fiesta sponsored by one of our compadres, I passed out after two days of continuous drinking and very little to eat. The participants decided to place me on the built-in bed made of adobe that traditionally is found in the portal area of the house. They lugged and pulled on me, but finally we all fell in a drunken heap and they just covered me up with alpaca skins and left me to sleep. Awakened by the smell of soup as someone passed a bowl under my nose, I vomited. Now, one may urinate in public, but one does not vomit in public while at an Andean fiesta. They realized I was in a "bad condition" and again let me sleep. The next morning, on awakening, I refused the formalized offer of more alcohol, another breach of appropriate behavior. My compadre and comadre solicitously had bought a bottle of sweet port and offered it in the belief that one must "clear the head" by drinking after heavy festivities. I knocked the cup from my comadre's hand— shocking behavior in their eyes, but my anthropological relativity had dissolved in many cups of cane alcohol and the native corn beer, chicha. I apologized, and my comadre and I embraced. Even so, our relationship was strained for several weeks, an indication that total forgiveness was not so easily obtained.

The areas of Chuschino life that have remained closed to investigation center predominantly on land tenure and herding, because of the fear of taxation. A tax is imposed per animal. The other effort that utterly failed was an attempt at a household census. Again, the formalized procedures frightened Chuschinos because they resembled the procedures of the dominant national bureaucracy. Resistance was very subtle. A request to bureaucratic officials of the village elicited the response that they would see that a traditional authority accompanied us during census taking. We were to meet at six o'clock the following morning to begin the census. For five consecutive mornings I waited, but no one appeared. An explanation from the authorities was never given. They were always cordial, and the broken appointment was their polite manner of saying that a census should not be taken.

I was fortunate to retain the services of two excellent interpreter assistants during our 1967 fieldwork. Pablo Alcocer was the son of a native Chuschino; he worked only two weeks for us but his presence opened many doors. He has since studied linguistics at the State University of New York at Buffalo. The other, Alejandro Mora, was an art student at the University of Huamanga who had a warm and patient way with informants. He worked for two months during 1967 and six months during 1969.

In July of 1967, he, with our daughter on his shoulders, was bitten by a rabid dog. He and Bill rode a half day on horseback to Cangallo, the province capital, in search of vaccine, only to find enough for four shots out of the required thirteen. He journeyed to Ayacucho for the medicine and returned to Chuschi, where the series was applied by the governmental health officer. Rabies is common during the dry season, and we were told that several years ago a man died, "frothing at the mouth and crazed with the disease. He was tied up and died like an animal." One fear that remained with us constantly was of serious illness or accident and the possibility of not being able to get out of the village for medical attention. Mr. Mora's frightening experience made the dangers even more vivid.

My introduction to the Andes resulted in preliminary reports on funeral practices (after attending fifteen); the harvest festival, Santa Cruz; and the traditional, civil-religious prestige hierarchy. But my picture of the Quechua culture was sketchy and incomplete, as if I had been looking through a kaleidoscope in a dimly lighted room. However, with time and a return trip in 1969-1970, I was able to "shed light" slowly on my kaleidoscopic view of the Andean world. Perhaps the most interesting ethnography anthropologists could write would be about ourselves as we experience the process of enlightenment, resulting in the construction of models and explanations.

Much of the ethnographic enterprise is doing what Geertz (1973: 3-30) calls "thick description," which involves interpreting what he calls the web of signification. As ethnographers, we not only record the web of cultural significance in which we find ourselves—we experience it. And, in doing so, we construct models and explanations in order to sort out our experiences and make sense of them. Geertz calls this sorting "process-analysis" and goes on to say "that what we call our data are really our own constructions of other people's constructions of what they and their compatriots are up to" (ibid.: 9).

Each chapter of this book is such a construction, manufactured by me as

I experienced the cultural web of significance manufactured by Chuschinos in their day-to-day interaction.

I have come to think of each chapter as a turn of an Andean kaleidoscope through which we view and interpret Chuschino reality. I have used the metaphor of "a view through an Andean kaleidoscope" because of the processes of my own reflections as I constructed an orderly presentation of my data. I found that one of the major principles of construction that Chuschinos use is duality, and therefore a tactic I found useful was to discover the variations on the theme of duality. I found several. For example, the notion of phenomena as being mirror images of one another is a strong organizational principle in Chuschi. The village moieties are thought to exist in such a mirror relationship. The members of the traditional prestige hierarchies, serving the moieties, act out their ritual duties simultaneously in space in such a way as to give one the impression of kaleidoscopic movements of mirrored images. It is hoped that this metaphor will become clearer as readers look through my Andean kaleidoscope for themselves.

Another major structural principle I found useful is the notion of complementarity in the sense of one entity's being relative to another entity. For example, sexual complementarity is perhaps the most pervasive concept used to classify cosmological and natural phenomena. It also symbolizes the process of regeneration. Phenomena are conceptualized as male and female and interact with one another in a dialectic fashion to form new syntheses, such as new cycles of time and new generations of people, plants, and animals. I have described this dialectic elsewhere as the concept of "the essential other half" (Isbell 1976).

Another organizing principle based on duality is that of symmetric relationships, most clearly expressed in social relations. The basic ideology of Chuschino marriage exchange is to perpetuate equal, and therefore symmetric, relations between two kindreds. Nevertheless, complementary to symmetric patterns are asymmetric, or unequal, patterns in the Andean kaleidoscope.

The most powerful of these is what I have termed the basic opposition into which Chuschino society is polarized: the foreign dominators versus the indigenous members of the community. The major concern of this book is to explore the structural defenses the indigenous population has constructed against the increasing domination of the outside world. The major conflict is between the communal members' ideology of self-sufficiency and the increasing pressures toward cultural and economic incorporation into the nation. The stronger the pressures, the more intensified are the Chuschinos' efforts to defend themselves. I have captured only a small portion of the dynamics of social life and social change. All ethnographies are incomplete. I would now like to explain how I came to my present perspective. In the process of peering through my constructions, that is, my kaleidoscope, I changed my anthropological focus and orientation. Such is the nature of fieldwork and subsequent analysis and interpretation that we learn to see new things as we attempt to communicate what we have experienced.

1.1.5   Another Change of Focus

The return to Chuschi in 1969 was the antithesis of our 1967 arrival. My ten compadres and godchildren greeted us as "their family," which we are—their spiritual family. Because I had written prior to arrival, it was all arranged that I rent part of a house. One compadre provided a bed on loan, another provided a couple of chairs, and I was able to get a table made. My husband and I arrived on motorcycles from Lima, but when traveling by truck I now had the status to deserve a cab seat, and during the few journeys spent in the back of the truck I pushed and kicked and cursed like the other women to protect my space and my belongings. I had learned to defend myself.

My 1969-1970 research was greatly facilitated by the return of Alejandro Mora from Ayacucho and by three Chuschinos: Cirilio Tucno and Eugenio Vilca, who helped copy civil records, and Justa Vilca, a young woman who had migrated to Lima to work and study, provided excellent assistance. Without their collaboration, this study could not have been accomplished.

I returned to Chuschi armed with two intensive language courses in Quechua, which enabled me to communicate on about the level of a four-year-old-child, and a research proposal funded by the National Institute of Public Health to investigate "Andean Reciprocity in Two Peruvian Contexts." One context was to be the complex of reciprocal exchanges I had observed in the village, and the other was to be the mutual aid with which migrants had invaded private property in Lima and established a community. On the return to Chuschi in 1969, however, I found that all reciprocity was kin-based and that it was necessary to understand kinship before one could analyze reciprocal exchanges. Therefore, my second residence in Chuschi was spent in concentration on kinship.

The analysis in chapter 5, "The Structures of Kinship and Marriage," begins with one simple question: "What is the structure of the basic opposition 'my group' versus the 'other group'? " I found that the concept of "my group" can be defined in various ways, depending on the context. For example, the Quechua-speaking traditional members of the community refer to themselves as *comuneros*, members of the commune, as opposed to *qalas,* the foreigners or literally "peeled or naked ones" (chapter 3). For marriage exchanges, "my group" is defined as *ayllu,* a bilateral kindred with sexual bifurcation and genealogical distance as principles of organization (5.2). For reciprocal exchanges, "my group" encompasses a wide network of consanguineal, affinal, and spiritual relatives known as the *kuyaq* (7.2), "those who love me." A comparison of seventeenth-century marriage records with a sample of modern records reveals that the village of Chuschi is more closed in upon itself, more village endogamous, today than during the seventeenth century (5.8.1). Consequently, the concept of "my group," which is more narrowly defined today, provides the major means for Chuschinos to defend themselves against the encroachments of the outside world.

The change of focus from reciprocity to kinship was accompanied by the collection of genealogical data as well as of statements about how various kinsmen should behave—their rights, duties, and obligations vis-à-vis one another. In other words, I constructed the typical anthropological ideal model of Andean social structures, attempting to get at the basic logic underlying the structures or, to borrow from linguistics, to enumerate the minimal number of rules operating. However, this led to an idealized, static view of social life, a depiction of a social mechanism in equilibrium and without change.

Furthermore, this ideal view of Chuschino social structures was diametrically opposed to what I saw happening: change was the reality, and the image of stability was the fiction created by the Chuschinos themselves. This fiction was perpetrated through ritual performers. Leach (1965: 16) has said that "if anarchy is to be avoided, the individuals who make up a society must from time to time be reminded, at least in symbol, of the underlying order that is supposed to guide their social activities. Ritual performances have this function for the participating group as a whole; they momentarily make explicit what is otherwise a fiction." Monica Wilson (1954: 241) believes the essential constitution of human societies can be understood through the study of rituals. She also believes that rituals, taken as a complex, express the central concerns of a people. In chapters 5 and 6, descriptions are given of five rituals performed in Chuschi in which the central concerns expressed are fertility, reproductivity, and regeneration of social and cosmological order. In addition, embodied also in the ritual performances are concerns for bounded ecological zones incorporating the notions of civilized ("my group") versus savage ("foreigners"). The expression of distinct, bounded ecological zones (2.8) correlates with the closed corporate nature of Chuschino society (6.5). Sexual bifurcation is a structural principle of organization that not only is assigned to supernatural deities and powers but that also underlies the organization of the Chuschino cosmology. Along with genealogical distance and generation, sexual bifurcation permeates Chuschino structures of kinship and is the most salient feature of all social interaction.

The ten ritual steps toward marriage dramatize the concern of the marriage congregation (1) to "give birth symbolically to a new kindred" (5.6.8), (2) to redefine the relationships of the marrying couple and their respective kindreds, and (3) to establish a new social order. The newly defined social order specifies that the relationships between the two kindreds interacting as groups be symmetric, while the relationship of the individual affine who has married into the kindred is defined as asymmetric. The affine is considered subordinate to the kindred into which he or she has married (5.4.1 and 5.4.2). Chuschino ritual activity is the temporal process in which meaning is constructed through the manipulation of symbols whose potential is multiple, but specific referents emerge unambiguously in the ritual drama. I found these symbols to center on the major concerns of reproductivity and fertility.

None of the rituals described could be enacted without a wide mutual aid network. Chapter 7 deals with the types of reciprocity in Chuschi and gives a specific example of the reciprocal aid given to one of the highest prestige authorities (7.2); it also provides a view of the strategies available to various categories of kin in a given concrete context. Having moved far afield from my original proposals, on returning to the United States in 1970 I moved even further. Proceeding with the analysis of my data, I became concerned with the interaction of ideology and activities. Robert F. Murphy's *The Dialectics of Social Life* (1971) was a great influence on my final reorientation.

1.2   The Dialectic between Structures and Activities

While I was in the field, genealogical data became convincingly more interesting for what people could *not* specify about their genealogies than for what they could. The genealogical amnesia of a society is perhaps just as revealing as the genealogical information itself, for it gives us clues to the reinterpretation of actual biological events. I was able to uncover some of the fictions fabricated by Chuschinos concerning biological relationships by paying attention to what they did *not* tell me. For example, males could readily enumerate ascendants to the fifth or sixth generation, but women rarely could remember past the third. This leads me to hypothesize that there exist for Chuschinos distinct male and female ideologies of kinship. If proven correct, this hypothesis is logically consistent with other principles of sexual bifurcation found in the ideologies of inheritance (3.5 and 3.6), naming (5.3), and affinal relationships (5.4). It is also mirrored in many of the ritual steps toward marriage (5.6).

More concretely, I found instances of fictionalizing to avoid the primary marriage prohibition, which states that one cannot marry a person sharing one's two surnames, the paternal surname of one's father and the paternal surname of one's mother. I found cases of name-changing to circumscribe this negative rule. In these cases, the actual genealogical information in the village demographic records contradicted genealogies collected from informants. Another instance I found interesting was the practice of fabricating a genealogical link or redefining a person as a near or distant relative (5.2) so that specific types of interaction would be acceptable. It appears that real activities motivate the restructuring of ideology. Near relatives are descendants of one's grandparents, distant relatives are descendants of one's grandparents' siblings. I found instances in genealogical data in which a distant relative with whom an informant interacted on a day-to-day basis, often because of residential proximity, was called a near relative and genealogically reckoned to be a descendant of the informant's grandparents. A genealogical fiction was constructed to conform with day-to-day activities.

As I proceeded with my analysis, I became increasingly aware of the discrepancies between the reality of events and activities and the shared ideologies purported to serve as a guiding model for activities. A close examination of rituals pointed out these discrepancies most strikingly. Although the major concern of Chuschinos reflected in the three rituals discussed in chapter 6 is productivity and fertility, reality is often the reverse in that scarcity prevails during half of the year. And while the relationships between two kindreds are dramatized ritually as respectful, reality is often conflict-ridden. Furthermore, one's affines are the key members of one's *kuyaq,* "those who love one," from whom the lion's share of reciprocal aid is expected (7.2); nevertheless, strife and infighting often occur. Ideology and activity are often opposed to one another, and one without the other gives a skewed picture of a culture.

Murphy (1971: 189) states:

The informants' models (rules, ideologies) are not totally illusory. They represent the real situation in part, but at certain critical points they are inversions of that reality. The ethnographer's task is to discover these contradictory relations and to perform a countertransformation on them. The level of empirical reality provided by the folk sociology serves as a base line, but it must be transcended; the ethnologist goes beyond it, so to speak, to derive another structure that is at once contradictory of the informants' model and capable of explaining the raw behavioral data gathered in the field. The ethnologist's model, i.e., the social structure, is not, however, wholly derived from the latter information, for it must move to a level of generality that is incongruent with statistical reality. One might say that the ethnologist's model, which corresponds to the unconscious model of the society, stands midway between the conscious model held by the members of the society and the data of actual relations.

I have tried to get at the base line of Chuschino folk sociology by examining the society's rituals, and I have compared the ideologies and concepts communicated in rituals with actual events and relationships, being firmly convinced that only by this process can we begin to understand the dynamics of change. It is through the dialectics of ideology and activities that a dual process occurs, resulting in the reinterpretation of events to conform to ideologies or, conversely, the transformation of ideologies by the power of events. As stated by P. Maranda (1972), the shared mythic conceptions and structures of a culture function to abate and negate the entropic effects of history. Chapters 4 and 8 are analyses of the struggles between ideologies and the events of history. Chapter 4 is an analysis of changes effected in the traditional prestige hierarchy in 1970. Currently, a struggle is being waged between the traditional ideology of social space and the transformed concepts of returned migrants from Lima. Chapter 8 and the postscript, chapter 10, offer predictions of the outcome. The rapid events and experiences associated with migration provide an excellent laboratory in which to examine the dialectics of ideological structures and activities. I have made steps toward the study of transformations, believing such a study to be one of the tasks of anthropology. Nevertheless, the success of a culture depends on the ability to perpetuate a way of life—or, as Andean people say, "to defend ourselves."

1.3   A Structuralist's Perspective

Before presenting my structural kaleidoscopic view of Chuschino culture and society, I would like to acknowledge my intellectual debts. Jean Piaget (1971: 5) defines structure as a self-regulating transformational system. Furthermore, he states that a structuralist approach is clearly profitable in the social sciences and that the study of social groups, kinship systems, and myths has resulted in many structuralist theories (ibid.: 97). I have applied a structuralist methodology to the study of traditional concepts and, more important, the transformation of those concepts. Roland Barthes (1972: 148-154) has described the structuralist activity as dissection of reality to discover discrete units and then the rearticulation of reality to discover the relationships operating between the discrete units. The structuralist operation makes intelligible that which eluded explanation before the operation was performed. I have "taken apart" the natives' models of social space (2.7), authority (chapter 4), kinship (chapter 5), and ritual (chapter 6) and put them together again in such a way as to clarify facets that were unintelligible at the outset. Each of these chapters represents a turn on the structural kaleidoscope, revealing structural relationships and principles that render the Andean world meaningful.

I have also examined rituals to determine the central concerns and idealized values of the Chuschinos. A ritual can be defined as a series of formalized actions that are obligatory and standardized. Such actions form a pattern of symbols (Leach 1964: 14) that dramatize important shared values and beliefs (M. Wilson 1954: 241) concerning the natural and social environment in which the participants operate (V. Turner 1969: 6).

A symbol can be defined as a motivated entity, such as a word, an image, an object, or an action, that has a complex of meanings shared by a collective. Symbols are perceived as having inherent value separable from that which is symbolized. An icon is a representation that stands for an object by virtue of likeness or analogy. Symbols are utilized in rituals to unambiguously construct concepts basic to, in this case, Chuschino interaction and activity. One notes, however, in the multivocality of symbols utilized in any given ritual, the logical construction of comparisons, opposition, and analogies. One aspect that has fascinated me is the inclusion of logical opposites in Chuschino symbolic expression, as if the logic must include the obverse to construct the totality of a concept (for examples, see chapter 9). A concept is defined in the Random House Dictionary as "an idea of something formed by mentally combining all its characteristics or particulars." I have attempted to get at the components of symbols by examining the process of combination effected in ritual. Finally, I am interested in the transformation of concepts due to activity and experience. Of course, much has eluded me, but I believe I am beginning to ask the right questions: not simply, "What are Chuschino society and culture like?" but rather, "What is the dialectic between society and culture?"—a perspective necessary for understanding the dynamics of social life, which are ever in motion just as the bits of glass in a kaleidoscope are ever changing alignment.

2. The Village in the Context of a Changing Nation

2.1 Peru—A Land of Paradoxes

2.1.1 The Paradox of the Majority as a Cultural Minority

This book describes and analyzes the structural mechanisms of defense whereby traditional closed corporate communities (see 2.4) in the Andes have attempted to retain autonomy and self determination. Their major strategy has been to maintain social and economic closure. That is to say, they have chosen not to participate in the national economy, preferring subsistence self-sufficiency. When national policies impinge on such closed communities, their concern has been to protect their control over their territory. These types of nonparticipating Peruvian communities have for centuries characterized the majority of the Peruvian population—the mass of Andean Quechua-speaking peasants.

Many scholars argue that these communities have become internal colonies, which are ethnically and territorially distinct and dominated economically and politically. Furthermore, these communities have become increasingly differentiated legally (Cotler 1970, Fuenzalida 1970a and 1970b, Quijano 1971, Van den Berghe 1974).

This chapter briefly discusses: the historical process by which the communities constituting the numerical majority have become internal colonies; the role played by the Peruvian landscape in maintaining territorial separation as well as economic and political domination; some of the dynamics of migration (2.2); the impact of the 1969 Agrarian Reform Law (2.3); and, finally, Peru's peasant communities (2.4). With this all too brief discussion of some of the factors responsible for the rapid changes taking place in the nation, we will turn our attention to the dynamics of social life in one Andean community by taking a hypothetical bus trip to Chuschi. The route chosen is the one taken by migrants who travel weekly back and forth between Chuschi and Lima. At the present time, migration is perhaps the single most important factor responsible for cultural changes in Chuschi. A constant flow of people, goods, and information is maintained between Lima and the once isolated community. With this flow come new ideas and aspirations and new strategies for realizing these newly acquired goals (see chapters 8 and 10).

The current processes of changes, effected by members of the ethnic internal colonies who have gained mobility into the dominant culture, are in some ways similar to the processes that began during the early colonial period. The segment of the indigenous population that mediated between the colonial Spanish society and the indigenous masses was, however, the indigenous elites. Today, the impetus for change in peasant communities is coming from the members of Peruvian society who are partially integrated into the national culture and at the same time maintain leadership roles in their communities (Quijano 1965b, 1967, Cotler 1970, Handelman 1975). These individuals are often called cholos, a term that is sometimes used in a derogatory fashion to refer to upwardly mobile people who have neither become fully integrated into the dominant society nor fully shed their peasant identity. The migrants, with new links to the urban social sectors, are ideal cultural brokers and peasant mobilizers. Thus we shall see that the process of mediation between the two major segments of Peruvian society, which began with the emergence of a powerful commercial class of indigenous elites, can be viewed as parallel to the present emergence of a new mediating class, the cholos, who have important roles in peasant mobilization movements. However, the major difference is that current changes are being generated from the bottom of the urban class structure, whereas, during the colonial era, changes were generated by the indigenous elites.

Studies of the historical processes after the conquest have been expertly summarized by Spalding (1974), who has analyzed the transformations of the indigenous Andean society in her book *De indio a campesino* (From Indian to Peasant). She describes Peruvian society during the first part of the colonial period as heterogeneous in terms of both ethnicity and access to resources. The Incas dominated this variable society less than a century before the conquest by the Spanish (ibid.: chapter 2). An excellent description of ethnic and economic diversity during the early colonial period has been formulated by Duviols (1973). During this period Peruvian society was a typical colonial one in which the dual dichotomy of the conquerors and the conquered predominated. Nevertheless, Spalding argues that the Indian chiefs, the *kurakas*, emerged as a powerful commercial class with elite status in both societies. The *kurakas'* mediating role between the "two republics," the Spanish one and the indigenous one, functioned in such a way that the indigenous chiefs mobilized production and tribute from the Indian masses for the benefit of the Spanish. These activities were in sharp conflict with the demands of the kinship-based, self-sufficient indigenous communities. Spalding's major question is, why, then, did the *kurakas* become the leaders of the rebellions that shook the eighteenth century? The greatest rebellion (in 1780-1783) was led by Túpac Amaru—baptized José Gabriel Condorcanqui—one of the greatest merchants of that century (ibid.: 53). Her hypothesis is that the economic role of the *kurakas* became converted. In addition to collecting the production and tribute from communities, the *kurakas* also became commercial distributors of products produced outside of the communities.

A continuous decline of the *kurakas*' power occurred during the later colonial period, caused in part by the imposition of Spanish authorities in the various regions of Peru and also by the incredible decimation of the Indian population. Their legal status was finally abolished in 1825, and Spalding hypothesizes that they became absorbed into the commercial class of Peru.

The experiences of indigenous communities during the colonial period were dominated by the exploitation of their labor and production by the dominant Spanish society. Moreover, due to the reduction of the Indian population, the Spanish rationalized the reduction of land controlled by the reduced Indian population. Indigenous communities were pushed to less productive regions by the continual reduction of their lands. The end result has been the creation of a suspicious, alienated, and subjugated majority, culturally and linguistically separated from the dominant society. This brief and all too inadequate historical background has been provided to help the reader understand the defense mechanisms of Chuschi, a peasant community whose historical memory has taught its members to protect themselves from the outside world by closing in upon themselves as much as possible.

With the absorption of the indigenous elite into the Spanish mercantile class, many indigenous communities were left with dual authority systems that are reflected in the present authority structures of Chuschi (see chapter 4). The traditional one functions to insure their self-sufficiency by maintaining ecological and cosmological order. The national bureaucratic one functions to exercise centralized control over the community.

Thus we see an interesting parallel with Spalding's historical analysis and the modern emergence of a new mediating class, the capitalistically oriented migrants (see 2.2 and chapters 8 and 10). They find themselves in the most paradoxical position of all. They identify with both the national culture and the traditional one. They argue for the incorporation of their peasant community into the national market, and yet they strive to protect the autonomy of the community at the same time. Often these goals are at odds with their own desires for upward mobility and personal success.

The migrants who crowd into urban centers from isolated communities like Chuschi are the greatest paradox of all. They are on the bottom of the urban class structure but dominate the direction of social change in their communities. They are responsible for the increase in education and, in some cases, better health care; for the expansion of the market system; and for the magnitude of the peasant mobilization during the 1960s (Quijano 1965, 1967, Cotler 1970, Handleman 1975). However, they often find themselves in conflict with their communities. As the migrants gain new aspirations, their goals at times conflict with those of the peasant majority of their community, who are attempting to defend their land and resources. At other times, mutually acceptable strategies for change are effected. Interestingly, Cotler (1969: 184) has argued that change is more rapid in areas of the Andes where extensive hacienda domination is absent. It is also clear that the development of roads and railways into remote regions of the Andes is changing the character of Andean communities. Van den Berghe (1974: 129-130) offers a geographical formulation to generalize about class and ethnicity in the southern Peruvian Andes. He argues that the range of local situations is sufficiently great to require empirical research. Generally, the more remote a community is from urban centers or means of communication with urban centers, the more forcefully will ethnic distinctions operate, resulting in clear differentiation between mestizos and Indians. Conversely, "the closer one gets to larger urban centers and their interconnecting main roads and railway, the more the processes of cultural hispanization and the extension of bilingualism tend to blur ethnic distinctions, and give more salience to class differences" (ibid.: 129). In other words, class differentiation will develop among mestizos, who are hispanized and bilingual and who identify with the national market and culture.

Small communities along main roads and railways are ethnically ambiguous. They are neither mestizo nor Indian, but rather occupy the ambiguous status of cholo, and, like the migrants discussed above, are not fully integrated into either ethnic or class structures. These regions are more complex. Therefore, it is profitable to discuss briefly the Peruvian landscape, given the fact that communication routes play such an important role in the transformation of ethnic populations.

2.1.2 The Paradoxes of Geography

Peru has one of the most difficult and demanding landscapes in the world. Less than 2 percent of Peru's land is arable, whereas 19 percent of the land in the United States, 40 percent in Germany, and 7 percent in Chile, Peru's southern neighbor, can be cultivated. In South America, only Brazil, with its massive tropical forest, has a lower percentage of arable land—1.6 percent. Due to the misfortunes of geography, Peru occupies the lowest position among fifty nations in amounts of land capable of supporting cultivation (De la Puente Uceda 1966: 115). Problems of adequate arable land are intensified in Peru by the diversity of the three distinct geographical regions: the arid coastal plain, the snow-capped Andean chain, and the lush tropical forest.

Peru is a land of geographical paradoxes. Rainfall is almost nonexistent on the coast, overabundant in the tropical forest, and extremely variable in the highlands. Paradoxically, the arid coastal plain, with a mere annual precipitation rate of only 20 to 30 millimeters, is the most productive region in the nation. This long, narrow desert strip, 90 kilometers wide and 1,800 kilometers long, produces 45 percent of the country's annual production on only 27.8 percent of the total cultivatable land. The government plans to develop large irrigation projects to increase further the productivity of the coast.

In comparison, the heavily forested tropical region with its overabundant rainfall of 1,200 to 3,500 millimeters per year produces only 17 percent of the nation's annual production (Alcántara and Vásquez 1974: 42). In addition, the Peruvian coastal waters have some of the richest marine fauna in the world due to the cold, upwelling Humboldt current. Fish meal is one of the most important exports, used throughout the world as fertilizer.

The reason for the paradoxical success of the coastal plain's agricultural production is that the desert is cut by some fifty rivers that drain the Andean chain into the Pacific Ocean. As much as 1,226,000 liters per second rush off of the western slopes of the Andes (De la Puente Uceda 1966: 109). The river valleys lie like green snakes on the drab desert. The region produces the majority of Peru's two most important export crops, cotton and sugar. Cotton accounts for 50 percent of exports, sugar for about 20 percent. The productivity of the coastal river valleys is due to the high degree of mechanized, intensive farming developed in large part by foreign capital (see 2.3).

The highlands present an incredible complexity of microzones. Briefly, the eastern slopes facing the continent are moister than the western slopes along the Pacific coast. Also, the northern highlands are higher in humidity than the southern region. However, temperature and moisture are complicated by altitude, so that high grasslands are wetter and colder than the lower valleys. For an excellent explication of the highland environments see Troll (1958) and the recently published *Atlas histórico-geográfico* published by the Instituto Nacional de Planificación (1969).

To get a feeling of the variability of the Andes, imagine a one-day trip in which one leaves the coast, immediately climbs upward, and within three or four hours crosses passes of over 4,000 meters in altitude. Snow-capped peaks reach 6,000 meters, with freezing-cold glacial moraines and puna in the highest altitudes. Rainfall can vary between 400 and 1,000 millimeters annually, depending on altitude and latitude. In this variable and vertical world, the Andean peasant has adapted well by trying to control as many of the microenvironments as possible in order to diversify crops and spread the risks of agricultural failure. Some communities have been restricted to only a few ecological microzones, but communities like Chuschi control a full range from above 4,000 meters to below 2,000 (see 2.4.3 and 2.7). Recent studies are beginning to document human adaptation in the various Andean microenvironments (Brush 1973, 1976, 1977, Concha 1975, Custred 1974, Flores Ochoa 1968, 1975, Fonseca 1972, Mayer 1974, Mitchell 1977, Orlove 1977).

Although population statistics are generally less than reliable in Peru due to the difficulties in collecting adequate censuses, the following figures provide a general picture of population dynamics in the Andes. The highlands population made up 61.7 percent of the nation's population in 1950, 51.1 percent in 1961, and 47.0 percent in 1970, and has been projected to fall to 38.0 percent by 1980 if current migratory trends continue (Instituto Nacional de Planificación: 1969).

2.2   The Push and Pull of Migration

Like most of the developing nations, Peru has a rapidly growing and mobile population. Since the 1961 census, population growth has been 2.9 percent annually, excluding the tropical forest population that remained inaccessible to the census. In 1961 the total population was calculated to be almost ten million; for 1972 the figures rose to over thirteen and one-half million (Oficina Nacional de Estadística y Censos 1973: 6). The metropolitan area of Lima is growing at an annual rate of 5.8 percent. It has been estimated that during 1970 about 100,000 migrants arrived in Lima, the center of government, banking, and industry (ibid.: 13). Over 70 percent of the nation's industry is located in Lima, a major attraction for the rapidly growing population. The National Office of Statistics and Census estimates that close to 40 percent of Lima's population are migrants primarily from the highland departments.

Furthermore, the proportion of the population under nineteen years of age has been estimated at 55.3 percent in 1970 (ibid.: 5). Population growth, estimated at 2.1 percent annually in 1970, is greater than economic growth (Alcántara and Vásquez 1974: 25). In 1972 there were 200 persons economically inactive for every 100 with employment (ibid.: 27). Arequipa's population exceeded 300,000 in 1972, and 37 percent were migrants. Likewise,

Puno-Juliaca, Cuzco, and Huancayo are experiencing growth due to migration. The recent petroleum exploitation in the tropical forest has stimulated the growth of Iquitos at the phenomenal rate of 6.2 percent annually (ibid.: 13-16). Therefore, a clearer picture is that the major population shift in Peru is from rural to urban centers, with Lima receiving the heaviest burden of migrants. Julio Cotler (1970: 539) argues that the arrival of migrants in cities cannot be attributed to a reduced demand for agricultural labor or to an increase in the demand for industrial workers. Rather, identifications and aspirations are being altered by increased consumption. These cultural changes are reaching traditional sierra regions and causing other changes in social relations and economic life. Such changes began after World War II when trade with the United States increased. The explanation certainly fits the migration history of Chuschinos.

In the recent government publication cited above, population projections were: 1980, eighteen and one-half million; 1990, twenty-five million; and 2000, in excess of thirty-three million (Alcántara and Vásquez 1974: 28). Faced with this phenomenal growth and with the shift from rural to urban centers, the government has formulated long-range plans to industrialize and stimulate Peru's internal market. It states that it will accept foreign investments but will gradually reduce dependence on foreign capital by developing petroleum exploitation and independent industries. The other major plan is to stimulate agricultural production through the formation of centrally controlled cooperatives aimed at increasing regional production.

2.3 The 1969 Agrarian Reform—A Structure of Cooperatives

The military government, under General Juan Velasco A., moved to nationalize large foreign capitalistic holdings. The first move of the regime was to nationalize the International Petroleum Company, now Petro-Perú, and six years later the foreign-controlled mines at Cerro de Pasco were nationalized.

The second move of Velasco's regime was to take control of the sugar haciendas on the coast. Before the reform, eleven coastal haciendas represented one-sixth of all foreign investment in Peru (Alcántara and Vásquez 1974: 64). The expressed aim of the government was to retain the size and technological production of the sugar haciendas while creating cooperatives to promote social justice. The government's slogan is, "The land belongs to those who work it." The sugar haciendas were reorganized into Cooperativas Agrarias de Producción Social—CAPs. Statistics vary somewhat, but it has been estimated that by the end of 1974 over 348 CAPs, with a total of 1,800,000 to 2,000,000 hectares and 87,000 families, had been formed. The

CAPs represent 38 percent of the total land adjudicated under the 1969 reform (*Marka* 1975: 16-20, Alcántara and Vásquez 1974: 72, Harding 1975: 220, Knight 1975: 362).

The CAPs vary greatly in size, degree of technology, and productivity, and there has been some controversy about them. Because each cooperative operates as an independent unit, with the participating members dependent upon the success of the production, the fate of the participating families also varies. In a critical article, the Peruvian leftist journal *Marka* (1975, 1, no. 5: 16-20) argues that at the Pomalca cooperative the mean salary in 1972 was 1,511 *soles* a month (about 35 dollars), whereas at another sugar cooperative, Paramonga, the mean salary was twice as high for the same period. In addition, the authors note that managers and technicians who control the means of production earn 30,000 to 50,000 *soles* (about 800 to over 1,000 dollars). Workers have organized strikes for higher salaries and better working conditions. The authors argue that the workers are alienated from decisions, that redistribution of wealth has not occurred, and that private capitalistic managers have replaced governmental ones.

The article goes on to point out that all members accrue capital investment while working in the cooperative, at an annual rate based on salary, and, on leaving, the worker or manager can take his investment with him. A technician earning 50,000 a month accumulates 300,000 *soles* in six years (almost 7,000 dollars) but a worker earning 3,000 *soles* a month would have to work 100 years to accumulate the same amount. The authors note that members of the sugar cooperatives prefer private and individual accumulation over collective accumulation. The government made the decision to retain the capitalistic structure of the sugar haciendas, maintaining highly paid technicians and managers to prevent production from falling. In fact, production has increased since 1969. The government hopes to reduce the discrepancies in production in the various sugar cooperatives by increasing technology. Furthermore, the long-range plan is to increase the capacities of the workers for control and management.

The above criticisms by the leftist journal *Marka* argue that the corporate structure of the cooperatives has not changed but rather has only changed hands. This argument is in agreement with that of Greaves (1972: 67), who points out that the cooperative members have remained rural wage earners working for a corporate enterprise. In addition, the cooperative structures continue to exploit non-members as a temporary labor force during transplanting and harvesting. The economic position of these seasonal workers is extremely precarious.

The other major effort of the government to stimulate production has been the formation of enormous cooperatives dedicated to cattle production in the highlands. Beef is in short supply in Peru and is sold legally only fifteen days out of every month. The short supply of beef was intensified by the decapitalization of production just prior to the implementation of the reforms. As hacendados and wealthy peasants became aware of impending reforms, they converted their herds into cash (or consumed them) to avoid expropriation, causing a drastic drop in the number of cattle and sheep. Thus the government was faced with a double problem of creating cooperatives while at the same time increasing production rapidly for national consumption. These gigantic production centers are called Sociedades Agrícolas de Interés Social—SAISes.

An example is the SAIS Túpac Amaru near the mining center Cerro de Pasco in the central highland department of Pasco; it comprised fourteen expropriated haciendas and fifteen surrounding peasant communities covering an area of 377,000 hectares on which lived a total of 17,000 people in 3,000 families. As of 1975, there were 50 SAIS conglomerates covering 2.25 million hectares and incorporating over 55,000 families, or 5.3 percent of the rural labor force. More than 1,715,000 head of cattle have been expropriated since 1968. By 1972 these cattle-producing SAISes represented 35 percent of all the land adjudicated under the 1969 Agrarian Reform Law. Under government management the SAISes are expected to increase cattle production and augment the technology of the peasants whose communities have been incorporated. The aim is to increase the productive capacity of the peasant communities to the point that they become an integrated, interdependent part of the national economy (*Marka* 1975b, Knight 1975: 365). "The SAIS is explicitly designed as a transitional form which could lead toward the incorporation of the member communities into an enlarged cooperative, thus creating a CAP" (Knight 1975: 366). It is believed that SAIS membership will break down peasant distrust of the agrarian reform through redistribution of income. However, Knight (ibid.) states that in practice some community representatives form alliances with cooperative technical and managerial personnel to hold down workers' incomes.

According to Plan Agropecuario, almost 12 million hectares of land have been adjudicated by the Peruvian government since 1969—truly the most massive redistribution of land in the history of South America (Alcántara and Vásquez 1975: 46). This far-reaching reallocation of land is a response to the inequality of distribution that characterized Peru's agricultural sector before the reformist military regime assumed power. The 1961 census demonstrated that 0.4 percent of all land-holders held 76 percent of all farms over 500 hectares, while 83 percent of the nation's agriculturalists held small plots of 5 hectares or fewer (ibid.: 38). The Agrarian Reform Law of 1969 is an effort to increase production by transforming the large capitalistic haciendas on the coast and the highland haciendas into cooperatives; to stop the fragmentation of peasant farms; to increase technology, especially among peasants; and to draw the peasants into the national economy and culture.

By the end of July 1974, just under 5 million hectares had been allocated to 196,523 families mainly organized into CAPs and SAISes. The original agrarian reform plan was to transfer some 11 million hectares of land to 340,000 families by 1976 (Harding 1975: 220). Obviously the government has fallen short of its goals.

In the introduction to an excellent collection of articles, *The Peruvian Experiment,* that analyze these measures from various perspectives, Lowenthal (1975: 15-16) concludes that the reforms are as noteworthy for their limits as for their advances. The great majority of Peruvians will not obtain land, because there is not enough to go around. The redistribution of income after implementation of the laws will not even affect three-quarters of Peru's population, and those without steady jobs will not receive improved social security benefits. The majority of school attenders drop out before the sixth grade, and therefore will receive only limited benefits from the educational reforms. The military regime is distributing resources and rewards in a more equitable way to those Peruvians able to make their demands felt.

Julio Cotler (1972 and 1975) has summarized some of the criticisms of the military government's policies. He argues that the urgent need of capital for rapid industrialization, the decolonization of the export sector, and the creation of an internal market counters the possibility of a redistribution of income. The success of state-controlled capitalistic developments depends on internal national peace. The government states that it seeks to insure harmony and reduce tensions between classes in order to create a unified nation. Cotler (ibid.: 9) argues that such a policy amounts to depoliticization of the popular masses. Government spokesmen counter that the polarized dichotomy between those who owned the majority of the land and those who owned nothing has been abolished through the expropriation of lands from the landholding elites and the formation of cooperatives. The government argues that therefore these two classes no longer exist. Furthermore, it argues that government policy is not to control the masses but rather to unify the classes in order to realize a participating social democracy. Cotler (ibid.) states that such policies will cause the dominated popular classes to lose their autonomy and class consciousness. As the popular classes face rapidly rising inflation and bureaucratic assistance programs (instead of redistribution of income), violence will result.

As evidence that governmental policies are designed to raise class consciousness and transform ethnic groups into production sectors, official spokesmen point to the nationalization of the newspapers, whereby different presses were designated to different segments of society. The agricultural sector, the industrial sector, cooperatives, and even the intellectuals were named as proprietors of the different national newspapers. In theory these sectors of society will have a voice in a participating democracy. The experiment is heralded by some as "giving the people a voice" and opposed by others as an oppressive measure.

Caught between these divergent views on how to effect social change are the majority of the Andean popular masses, the peasants: As we will see below, a wide range of variations of economic and socio-political structures exists in recognized peasant communities. At present, Andean peasants are faced with pressures unbeknown to them before from both the government and its critics. The responses by peasant communities to these pressures will be determined by the degree to which they are "open" to incorporation or, conversely, the degree to which they are attempting to maintain social closure and nonparticipation in the national culture. What I will argue below is that Andean peasant communities exist along a continuum between the two extremes of open participation in the national economy and culture and direct opposition to such incorporation (see 2.4.2).

2.4   Peru's Peasant Communities

As of 1960 a total of 1,568 indigenous communities were registered and recognized out of 4,600 population centers censused. These communities are concentrated in the highland departments of Junín (276), Lima (236), Cuzco (215), Ayacucho (162), Huancavelica (147), Ancash (108), Huánaco (83), and Cajamarca (46), and 12 are found in Lambayeque (which is marginally defined as sierra). However, one is found in the tropical forest department of Loreto (Fajardo 1960).

A peasant community is a corporate land-holding body with legal and jural status by virtue of a series of laws beginning with a supreme decree of 1821 abolishing tribute and the hated labor grants, the *encomiendas*.

Beginning with the 1920 constitution a series of laws directed toward Indian communities was passed. Davies (1974) has compiled a list of the major Indian legislation from 1900 to 1948, which is appended to his book. A great flurry of laws was passed between 1925 and 1940, beginning with the recognition of Indian communities in 1925; subsequent laws granted Indians citizenship and guaranteed the integrity and inalienability of the indigenous communities' lands. Laws were passed prohibiting the intervention of national bureaucratic authorities in the administration of communities' lands, and in 1938 procedures were established by which the indigenous communities were registered with the Ministry of Labor and Indigenous Affairs. The 1938 law also

established an autonomous three-person governing junta, headed by a personero, to be elected by the heads of households of the community for non-
renewable two-year terms. The law stipulated that the elections were to be
ratified by the ministry to ensure that the junta members met the requirements of the law—membership in the community, literacy, and military
service.

2.4.1   Abolition of the Old and Institution of the New

The Agrarian Reform Law of 1969 (Decreto Supremo No. 1776) abolished the personero and the junta, replacing them with a vigilance council
and an administrative council, each with a president, a secretary-treasurer,
and delegates (Mayer and Palmer 1972). The 1969 law abolished private
property and established two statuses for membership in a peasant community: (1) full comunero—one who resides at least six months of the
year in the community, derives 50 percent of his income from agricultural
activities, and complies with the membership criteria set up by the community, usually birth and inscription; and (2) associate comunero—one
whose income is equally from agriculture and some other enterprise and who
resides in the community. Both statuses have usufruct rights to all lands held
by the village. In the case of inadequate land for all members, the law provides for a lottery system to allocate usufruct plots.

The Agrarian Reform Law has as specific goals (1) to increase technological
production, (2) to avoid fragmentation, and (3) eventually to organize the
communities into cooperative production units for the national economy.
The law changes the name of the communities from indigenous to peasant
communities, which implies that they shall become a part of the national
political body as well as become incorporated into the national economic
structure (articles 1, 3, and 15). Article 118 stipulates that the dominion of
lands cannot be directly transferred except to become incorporated into a
SAIS or other recognized cooperative. Communities may have usufruct of
the land in accordance with the communal or cooperative organization, and
the land must be worked directly by the members of the community. A
member cannot hold plots in a different community and furthermore has
usufruct to one plot near or adjacent to his residence.

The reform law attempts to achieve clear interdependence between the
agricultural sector and the industrial, public, and financial sectors.

Article 119 specifies that lands that became the property of individuals
after January 18, 1920 shall revert to the community without altering possession, except that these lands cannot be alienated or transferred either by
contract or by inheritance. On the death of the holder, the land shall revert

permanently to the community. Article 120 provides for the recuperation of abandoned lands, and article 121 nullifies all sales or transfers of land that took place after January 1920, with indemnification to the previous owner. In addition, the law establishes a lottery system for allocating land in communities where land is insufficient for all members.

According to article 124 a special statute will be passed to specify the organization and functioning of peasant communities. However, as of 1975 the statute had not appeared; the government is still studying the organizational structures and economic capacities of the diverse peasant communities throughout the Andes.

2.4.2 *"Open" and "Closed" Peasant Communities*

Richard N. Adams (1962: 427-428) has stated that "corporate communities are characterized by a defense action to protect their members from a threat. In so far as we can tell from ethnohistorical reconstruction the communities come into being when they are in fact restricted or excluded from access to resources." This statement clearly holds for Peruvian peasant communities, which through time have been pushed continually into more marginal and less productive regions of the Andes. We can think of highland peasants as the marginal agricultural majority. A peasant community must always be considered as part of a larger social unit, such as the nation, that has impinged upon its agricultural producers.

However, another important dimension must be considered, and that is the degree to which a community is either "open" or "closed" structurally. Eric R. Wolf (1955) defines a peasant as an agriculturalist whose major aim is subsistence and who retains control over the land. He further differentiates between seven types of Latin American peasantry. For our purposes here, the most important distinction made is between the "closed corporate community" and the "open community." The former practices intensive cultivation on marginal lands, utilizing primitive technology. It is a closed corporation because it discourages influences from the outside and because the members of the community do not identify themselves as members of the larger culture. The corporate structure is maintained through control over communal lands as well as through restrictions against selling privately-held holdings to outsiders. In Peru, membership in the many communities demands active participation in the civil-religious hierarchy, whereby a member expends wealth and achieves status through service to the community in a series of ranked offices (see 4.3). Economically, this type of closed corporate community does not participate significantly in the cash economy. Most production is for subsistence, and when cash crops are produced they are used to buy goods from the outside. Exchange and reciprocity are common (chapter 7), and the accumulation of wealth is not tolerated. Wealth is expended in civil and religious displays of generosity.

Wolf characterizes "open communities" as the type common to the vast, humid tropical forest lowlands. But we shall discover that open *corporate* communities are found also in the highlands of Peru. According to Wolf, an open community has continuous interaction with the outside world, and members are encouraged to identify themselves with the national whole. Their participation in the cash economy of the nation accounts for 50 to 75 percent of their production, and furthermore they reinvest to improve production rather than expend their wealth on the structural organizations that maintain closure, such as the civil-religious hierarchies. Nevertheless, open communities, like closed ones, have been pushed to marginal areas, and technology remains relatively primitive. However, they differ from the subsistence-based closed corporate communities in that their economic and social fate depends more heavily on the stability of the nation.

Wolf (ibid.: 463) states that open communities lack formalized corporate structures. However, Keatinge (1973: 40) points out that in Peru at least thirteen of the forty recognized peasant communities surveyed by Dobyns (1964:22) have been characterized as culturally mestizo. That is, members of these recognized corporate peasant communities identify themselves with the national culture and have not maintained the degree of social and economic closure characteristic of closed corporate communities; nevertheless, they are corporate entities controlling land and perpetuating rights and membership. Muquiyayo (Adams 1959) and Sicaya (Escobar 1968) of central Peru in the Mantaro Valley, Hualcan (Stein 1961) and Huaylas (Doughty 1968) in the northern Callejón de Huaylas, as well as Chinchero (Montalvo 1965) in Cuzco (which still maintains a civil-religious hierarchy) and Moche (Gillin 1947) on the north coast, are only a few examples of mestizo corporate communities that maintain a mixed (subsistence-cash) economy and identify and interact with the national culture, thereby maintaining open rather than closed social structures.

An illustrative example is the recognized open corporate peasant community of Huanchaco, located eleven miles from the north coastal city of Trujillo. It was studied by Gillin in 1947 and restudied by Keatinge in 1973. Keatinge found that 37 percent of the community's 2,000 population are fishermen; only 10 percent farm their land directly, while 71.8 percent sharecrop. Furthermore, this peasant community of monolingual Spanish speakers increased from 700 in 1947 to 2,000 in 1973. After the 1969 Agrarian Reform Law was passed, 32 share-croppers petitioned to form a cooperative, claiming that the law states that the land they worked belongs to them. As

Keatinge (1973: 38) rightfully points out, many of the communities studied thus far by anthropologists are open corporate peasant communities "which can play a dynamic role in the process of national integration if the flexibility inherent in the structure of these communities is fully recognized and utilized by those directing the course of national development."

It is perhaps more fruitful to visualize communities in the highlands along a continuum between "open"—becoming incorporated into national economic participation—and "closed"—maintaining the structures that slow the process of incorporation. Van den Berghe (1974) argues that the actual location of communities in relation to communication routes has a great deal to do with the degree of incorporation and culture change evident. If we were to extend Van den Berghe's argument we would expect class relations to predominate over ethnic relations in "open" communities, and the reverse to be true in ideal "closed" communities. For communities experiencing change, a complex mixture of class and ethnic relations and identifications will be present. Chuschi is such a community undergoing rapid change, and change has greatly increased since a road connecting Chuschi with the department capital was completed in 1966. Migration has increased; more consumer products reach the community, and, as we would expect, new aspirations and expectations arise.

Along with these changes, however, I have documented the efforts of the community members to defend their communal holdings and their ethnic identity. Two very dramatic examples will illustrate. In 1970, the apex of the traditional civil-religious hierarchies was abolished (4.5) by communal vote. The same organization was reinstated in 1972 in response to efforts by migrants to form a cooperative. The cooperative was closed (10.3) and ethnic identity was strengthened.

Class structures are being developed in the urban invasion settlement in Lima (10.4). But one can see ethnic relations functioning as a means of expressing group solidarity for both urban and rural members of the community when common dangers are perceived. Migrants helped organize an invasion of hacienda lands (10.3.3) claimed by the community. The action greatly accelerated the bureaucratic procedures for reviewing the case. The migrants play an important role in breaking down the social closure of traditional communities. However, these migrants often have priorities that are at odds with government planners. These and other problems of incorporating peasants into the national culture will be discussed below.

2.4.3 The Problems of Incorporating Peasant Communities into National Economic and Social Systems

The aim of the military junta of Peru is to transform the peasant masses into economically productive agriculturalists for the national market. What is needed to effect this transformation is information on the economic systems of peasant communities. How many are closed corporate subsistence systems utilizing primitive technology with few or no cash crops? How many are dependent on herding? Are their economic activities directed toward the national market system? Furthermore, what is the nature and extent of economic activities other than farming and herding that propel peasant communities toward "open" national incorporation?

Unfortunately, such information is perhaps most difficult to obtain in closed corporate communities such as Chuschi because they perceive economic dependence on an outside market system as a serious threat to their continued independence. In addition, centuries of taxation based on production, and most recently taxation calculated per head of cattle, make systematic investigation of economic activities extremely troublesome. In Chuschi, my efforts to obtain economic data were further thwarted by the passage of the Agrarian Reform Law during my investigations in 1969. Members of the community understandably were more reluctant to divulge information that might place them in a disadvantageous position with authorities. Given these difficulties, I have provided examples of types of exploitation strategies (chapter 3) and the dynamics of migration (chapter 8) to illustrate the process of change occurring at present.

Fortunately, other investigators have been more successful in obtaining information on Andean economic systems, especially of mestizo communities. Adams's study of Muquiyayo (1959) provides excellent data on the historical dimensions of a peasant community's emergence into the market economy; and other studies, such as Escobar's (1968) of Sicaya, Stein's (1961) of Hualcan, and Doughty's (1968) of Huaylas, describe the impact of hacienda domination, agricultural techniques, the growing scarcity of land, the decrease in traditional reciprocal exchanges, and the commercialization of farming.

More recently, examination of the exploitation of various microecological zones by modern communities has been stimulated by John V. Murra's (1967, 1968, 1972, and 1975) "archipelago" model of verticality in the Andes, which argues that economic success in the Andes was achieved by pre-Incaic kingdoms by effectively controlling production and redistribution from diverse ecological zones often dispersed over large distances in the vertical and variable Andean chain. Important studies are emerging that allow us to compare the exploitative techniques and strategies of pastoralists and agriculturalists from different regions of the Andes.

Flores (1968) has studied the high-altitude pastoral community of Paratía in the province of Lampa, department of Puno, and describes the strategies of alpaca specialization. Custred (1974) describes how the community of Alccavitoria, in the province of Chumbivilcas, Cuzco, is restricted to altitudes of 3,920 to 4,890 meters. This community produces only potatoes six months out of the year and exchanges some of the products from its herds, such as dried meats, wool, hides, and woolen goods, for agricultural products from lower altitudes in direct barter relationships. However, Custred points out that the larger part of wool and meat production is destined for sale at the local market in order to procure cash to buy salt at a mine, or sugar and peppers at the market as items for barter.

Long-distance exchange relationships between a small lowland coca-producing community in the department of Huánuco with other communities in higher altitudes have been described by Burchard (1974). He has demostrated that the traditional exchange relationships are wide-ranging in territory and stable. The coca producers exchange their product for food-stuffs, and even labor, with communities in the mid-altitudes of the region as far as 200 kilometers away.

One of the most interesting aspects of Burchard's study is that he provides information on the temporary migration of a community of 400 Quechua-Spanish bilinguals. This community, situated some 64 kilometers from the capital of Huánuco, controls land at altitudes between 2,700 meters and 3,054 meters. Although agricultural exploitation is diversified, it is by no means self-sufficient. Of 58 families censused, half had members who had worked in Lima; 30 percent of male heads of households, as well as a number of women, had migrated to the Cerro de Pasco mines. Most of the population had worked at some time on haciendas, and some were even seeking wage employment as agricultural laborers in other peasant communities.

Perhaps most significant is the fact that 92 percent of the families had members who had migrated to the coca fields over 200 kilometers away to seek temporary employment (ibid.: 222-223). Both Burchard's and Custred's studies demonstrate the growing importance of cash in traditional exchange relationships.

In contrast, the community of Q'ero (Webster 1973) in the province of Paucartambo, Cuzco, controls a continuous territory including grazing land extending above 5,000 meters in altitude, agricultural plots in the intermediate zones, and tropical forest plots below 2,000 meters. The community's ceremonial center is situated in the intermediate zone at 3,300 meters, and other dwellings are maintained in both the high pasture lands and in the lowlands. Exploitation of these various zones is achieved by family units, but the community authority structure controls crop rotation (Webster 1973: 118-119).

Orlove (1977) argues that in the province of Espinar, Cuzco, the trans-humance cycle is controlled by the availability of pasture; agricultural activities are secondary. We are beginning to understand the diversity of economic techniques in the Andes. According to present data summarized by Lambert (1977), one universal seems to be that "households based on nuclear families control productive resources and allocate consumer goods. . . households strive to attain self-sufficiency, either through exchange or by securing direct access to land in several zones. Such vertical control also enables the group to utilize the labor of its members most efficiently, and provides it with some insurance against the disruptive effects of localized frosts, hailstorms, and excessive rainfall."

Mayer (1974) has contributed important information on subsistence activities, crop rotations, and exchange relationships of the community of Tangor, located in a narrow intermontane valley in the province of Daniel A. Carrión, Pasco. Mayer states that this village retains an economic system that is a vestige of islands of exploitation known as "archipelago" (after Murra) because its territory is interrupted by the holdings of other communities. Its grazing lands are located beyond other communities' lands.

Mayer differentiates between four named microzones: two for potato production and two for corn. Every family has access to land devoted to potato production and to pasture lands, but along the river valley, where corn can be grown, land is less evenly distributed.

Tangor and other communities in the narrow valley are nucleated at mid-points between the upper and lower microzones. This same settlement pattern is common on the Pampas River, where Chuschi is located, as well as along the Apurímac (Orlove 1975). Fonseca (1972), in a detailed comparison of vertical exploitation in the northern, central, and southern highlands, argues that this is a common strategy in the Andes, with the names for ecological zones referring not to fixed upper and lower levels but rather to different microenvironments in relation to a mid-point where nucleated settlements are found (ibid.: 318-324).

Exploitation of the various zones is accomplished by household units utilizing various forms of labor exchanges. One of the most common forms implies returned labor of equal value and is restricted to close and distant kin of the household work force.

Mayer (1974: 144) points out that "governmental community development agencies have since 1960 pushed cooperative ventures assuming that because peasants tend to exchange labor that they would therefore readily accept cooperative forms of organization." Mayer demonstrates that reciprocal labor exchanges are for very specific short-term tasks and are contracted on an individual basis. Even if the reciprocal contract is with formal institutions it is conceived of in the same manner.

I have taken a different perspective and have distinguished between private and public reciprocity (chapter 7), the former between private individuals for short-term tasks, the latter between the civil-religious hierarchy and the entire community, the government, and the church on a continuous basis if both parties fulfill their contracts. In both of these forms the most important components of exchange are to secure a supportive network of relationships and to gain prestige through the display of extreme generosity to those who have aided one in specific tasks. As discussed in 7.2, the necessary generous supply of food, drink, cigarettes, and coca that accompany reciprocal labor exchanges often cost more than hired labor. Nevertheless, such exchanges are essential to a closed corporate community such as Chuschi because they guarantee the participation of members and the exclusion of outsiders—one of the principal mechanisms for maintaining social closure. The diversity and complexity of Andean exchange systems have been described in a volume edited by Alberti and Mayer (1974) entitled *Reciprocidad e intercambio en los Andes peruanos*.

It appears that Andean peasant communities do not readily accept cooperatives. Mayer (1974) and Escobar (1968) have shown that the trend is toward commercialization of agriculture and increased participation in the market economy. When this happens, reciprocal exchanges decline and eventually disappear. The ideal strategy in the Andes is to control many plots, however small, in all of the microzones controlled by ones' community. This minimizes crop failure and increases the diversity of one's production, which in turn guarantees economic autonomy.

However, economic autonomy is declining in highland communities. In communities like Chuschi and Tangor, land is not the index of wealth. In Tangor, class stratification is due to differential access to cash through out-migration or connections with migrant relatives (Mayer 1974: 54). In Chuschi, class stratification depends on the number of animals held by a household and the prestige gained through service in the civil-religious hierarchy, which is increasing the demand for cash. Mutual dependence between the subsistence agriculturalists-herders of Chuschi and their migrant population in Lima is developing.

Most of the migrants in Lima retain land and animals in Chuschi. They maintain sharing agreements with their relatives in the village called *mitades* (halves). Those who stay in the village tend the fields and herds, and the migrants provide needed aid, usually in the form of gifts or loans. Migrants often return to oversee and participate in planting and harvest. This strategy provides a type of insurance for both parties: the migrant is able to supplement his or her low cash income in the urban environment with agricultural products, and the villager has a source of cash and aid. One of the most important forms of aid is the assurance of help when one of the household migrates. Also, in Chuschi, a pattern is developing of sending children to migrant relatives in Lima to be educated. The traditional exchange network has been extended to encompass the migrant population in Lima. The rules of reciprocity remain the same, but new elements have been introduced. Migrants function as important cultural brokers, introducing new ideas and products to their rural relatives.

Another important function of migrants is as representatives and intermediaries for their village of origin with the web of bureaucracies in Lima. In the case of Chuschino migrants, wealth and power have become concentrated in Lima to the point that migrants control village politics.

From the point of view of government planners, the fact that permanent migrants retain their land creates developmental problems. They argue that it encourages instability in the population at a time when Peru needs a stable agricultural and industrial population to facilitate development. Furthermore they argue that, after two or three generations, migrant populations lose interest in their agricultural land and do not farm even on a sharecropping basis. Land lies fallow and production drops.

The major problem in reconciling the perspectives of migrants and their rural relatives with development planners is that the arrangements between Andean peasants and their migrant relatives follow traditional rules of reciprocity designed to meet immediate needs. Furthermore, villagers view the political sophistication of their migrants as essential when dealing with bureaucratic agencies. Some villages in the Pampas River basin have voted to inscribe those migrants as comuneros who aid in the legal transactions of the communities with the government offices in Lima. In other words, they have decided that migrants can retain their claim to land as long as they act as intermediaries for the rural community.

A final problem I would like to mention is that of the inheritance of land. The 1969 Agrarian Reform Law abolished private property in recognized peasant communities and has furthermore established a lottery system for usufruct distribution. Many Andean communities have authoritative means of redistributing land, controlling crop rotation, and maintaining communal agricultural land, differentiated from private plots, for the benefit of the community (Mishkin 1963, Matos Mar 1964, Fonseca 1972, Mayer 1974). But many communities, such as Chuschi and others in the Pampas River region, control continuous territories extending from high communal grazing lands to agricultural plots held individually in the river valley. Inheritance, ideally, is parallel, that is, from father to sons and mother to daughters.

The reform law defines usufruct rights for heads of household that would negate the right of land to married and single women and thereby drastically reduce their economic independence. Given the complex nature and diversity of Andean vertical exploitation, it appears that the stipulation of the 1969 Agrarian Reform Law that a peasant have usufruct to one plot adjacent to or near his residence will meet with a great deal of resistance by populations practicing the diversified microzonal exploitation that developed as a successful strategy in the Andes many centuries before the arrival of the Spanish. The geographical distribution and range of variation of vertical exploitation, subsistence, and settlement patterns, as well as inheritance practices and exchange relationships, are beginning to be systematically examined. The government is moving cautiously because it realizes that such information is essential.

According to one source (*Marka* 1, no. 5), only 137 communities had received a total of 476,000 hectares of land as of June 1975. Some communities have been incorporated into SAISes. However, recent complaints by various of these incorporated communities have been registered with the government to the effect that they do not want to be a part of the SAIS structures but would prefer their independence. Other efforts of incorporation include commercial agricultural *empresas*, or enterprises that must earn at least 50 percent of their profits from marketing. As of 1974, 263 such enterprises, called *grupos campesinos* (peasant groups), with 17,000 families controlling 125,000 hectares, have been formed (Alcántara and Vásquez 1974: 75).

In the department of Ayacucho, the National Office of Planning is contemplating forming multicommunity cooperatives directed toward the national market. However, somehow they will have to overcome old rivalries and disputes over land, which are common (see 2.10 for an example).

Mobilizing the peasants of Peru is the stated task of a governmental organization created in 1972 called SINAMOS—Sistema Nacional de Apoyo a la Movilización Social (National Support System for Social Mobilization). This organization has met with some resistance from the peasant sector, notably in Huancavelica and Cuzco and to a lesser degree in Ayacucho. In November of 1973 there were riots in the streets of Cuzco. The SINAMOS headquarters was burned and martial law was imposed for about a month. There were reports of shootings, but news coverage was limited. Rumors of opposition to SINAMOS came from other parts of the country. As of 1974, strikes among the cooperative members on the coast were occurring, and in February of that same year the national police went on strike in Lima for higher wages. The army surrounded the police headquarters, and official reports claimed that six or seven men were killed, but rumors had the numbers much higher. Martial law and strict curfews were imposed, and order was restored. During the first few days of the strike, looting of downtown stores and businesses near the invasion settlements was phenomenal. People were cutting through metal protective doors and carrying off stoves, televisions, and other large appliances, and clothing, foodstuffs, and other goods. The new cultural center was burned. The army conducted a house-to-house search in the invasion settlements for the stolen property. For two months a nervous peace was maintained, but one can see that Cotler's (1972) prediction of violence had come to pass. The military government desperately needs peace and broad-based support from the various sectors of Peruvian society to accomplish its aims.

The name SINAMOS was designed to connote SIN AMOS, without masters. But many critics argue that the organization often uses repressive measures and has become the new master of the highland peasantry. Recently, both the Agrarian Reform Law and SINAMOS have come under governmental scrutiny. Perhaps the bureaucratization of such an organization has resulted in many development workers' losing sight of their original aim of establishing self-determinancy for the Peruvian peasantry and working class in an effort to perpetuate their jobs. In the summer of 1975, the government greatly reduced the number of SINAMOS employees and is currently redirecting their efforts.

Since the reform law was passed in 1969 there have occurred signs of possible cohesion and solidification of the Peruvian peasantry. The government has organized agrarian leagues under the National Agrarian Confederation (CNA). However, a new peasant organization has emerged, with its center of support in Cuzco; it is called Confederación Campesina Peruana (CCP), the Confederation of Peruvian Peasantry.

In a recent interview Hugo Blanco (1975), the Trotskyite guerrilla who was jailed and deported by Belaúnde's regime, states:

> I have returned to Cuzco after 13 years absence, and I have noted great changes. Hacendados have practically disappeared. Nevertheless, one notes that the peasant continues to live in the same misery as before. This is an apparent contradiction. When one converses with peasants, one notices that the form of exploitation has changed. Before, exploitation was more of a feudal type and now it is capitalistic exploitation. Now, the struggle of the peasantry is a struggle against capitalism and against the capitalistic state. . . . it seems to me that the CCP is the greatest and most important centralizing organization that the Peruvian peasantry has had in its entire history. . . We Trotskyites support the CCP for two reasons: it is independent, and this is fundamental. . . . Our fundamental criticism of the CNA is not for supporting the government *but for depending upon the government*. . . . [the second reason we support the CCP] is that it depends upon the masses.

Hugo Blanco is voicing a hope that the masses of Peruvian peasantry will reject capitalism for a form of socialism allowing them solidified independence. However, until we understand the dynamics of Andean vertical exploitation, exchange systems, and strategies preferred by the diverse Peruvian peasant communities, we cannot foretell their choices as they approach degrees of national incorporation. In the remainder of this book I attempt to build toward an understanding of one closed corporate community and outline some of the dialectics occurring as the community is made aware of the rushing approach of the outside world.

2.5 On the Way to Chuschi

Before discussing the geographical location and micro-environments of the village of Chuschi, I would like to contrast briefly the departments of Ayacucho and Junín, the major migratory route for Chuschinos destined for Lima. (See map 1.)

Junín has the greatest number of recognized peasant communities (Fajardo 1960), but 60 percent of Junín's population is urban. The city of Huancayo, situated in the beautiful and fertile valley of the Mantaro River at 3,249 meters, is the most important commercial center in the central Andes, with 1,700 established industries producing textiles, cement, and chemicals. Metal refining and exploitation of wood are also of importance. In 1967, the population of the city of Huancayo was almost 84,000 out of the department's total of 521,210 (Instituto Nacional de Planificación 1969: 474).

An analysis of migration to and from Huancayo in relation to Lima for 1961 shows that population movement between the two cities remained balanced at 7 to 8 percent (ibid.: 279).

Not only is Huancayo a principal commercial center, the province is also a leader in agricultural production—over 4 billion *soles* were produced in 1965 (ibid.: 474). The department of Junín plays an important role in feeding the rapidly growing population of metropolitan Lima. The departments of Junín and Lima produce 50 percent of the metropolitan capital's consumption.

In comparison, the neighboring department of Ayacucho is sixth in geographical size and is third in the number of recognized peasant communities after the departments of Junín and Lima. There are 162 such communities (Fajardo 1960).

In 1967 the city of Ayacucho, situated at 2,752 meters in the bend of the Huatata River, a tributary of the Mantaro, was less than one-third the size of Huancayo, with an urban population of 27,000 out of the department's total of 410,000 (Instituto Nacional de Planificación 1969: 404-406). The total

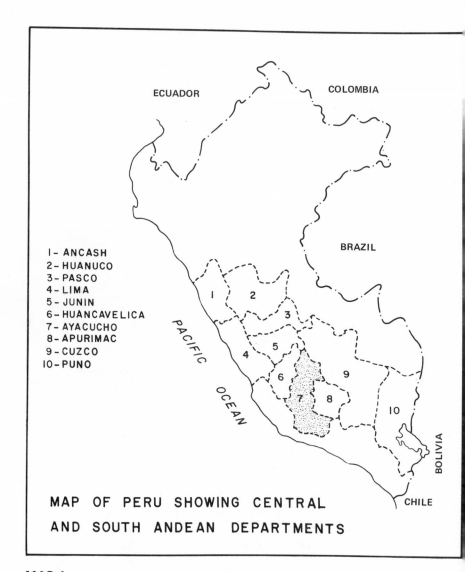

1- ANCASH
2- HUANUCO
3- PASCO
4- LIMA
5- JUNIN
6- HUANCAVELICA
7- AYACUCHO
8- APURIMAC
9- CUZCO
10- PUNO

ECUADOR

COLOMBIA

BRAZIL

PACIFIC OCEAN

BOLIVIA

CHILE

MAP OF PERU SHOWING CENTRAL
AND SOUTH ANDEAN DEPARTMENTS

MAP 1

urban population of the department of Ayacucho does not equal that of the city of Huancayo.

The city of Ayacucho increased only 2 percent in the twenty-year period between 1940 and 1960. This is due to the migratory flow to Lima. The city of Ayacucho lost 8 percent of its population to Lima in 1961, and only 2 percent returned that year. In comparison with the even flow of population to and from Huancayo and Lima, we see that Ayacucho is not experiencing growth (ibid.: 279).

In large part this is due to the lack of industry in the city. Because it is the department capital, its largest business is, of course, government, which employs the largest number of people. The only industry is artisan cottage weaving, knitting, pottery, leather work, and silver smithing. Ayacucho serves a wide region as a commercial center, but it is principally a center for redistribution of manufactured goods that come from Huancayo and Lima. Transportation therefore is another principal business.

Out of the total population of the department, 77 percent depend on agriculture and herding for subsistence (ibid.: 404). Only 13 percent of the department's surface sustains production. The northern-eastern portion of the department is *ceja de montaña* between the Apurímac and the Mantaro rivers. In the extreme south, the snow-capped peak of Sarasara is surrounded by the high table of Parinacochas. Altitudes range from high peaks and cold punas to low temperate and hot valleys.

Corn, grown at middle altitudes, is one of the major products, whereas potatoes, wheat, barley, and other grains and tubers withstand the extremities of the higher altitudes. Fruits, coffee, and cacao are major products of the low valleys. Alpacas, llamas, sheep, and cattle are maintained on the extensive punas. Ayacucho is a melange of diversified microzones where altitude is a major factor. (See plate 2.)

The majority of the department's population lives between 2,500 and 4,000 meters. In the six provinces the population is unevenly distributed. Lucanas in the south is the largest province, covering 40 percent of the department's territory. Only four persons per square kilometer inhabit this large puna-dominated region. In Cangallo, where Chuschi is situated, population density reaches twenty-two persons per square kilometer (ibid.: 403).

Of this predominantly agricultural population, only half speak Spanish and over 40 percent are under sixteen years of age. In addition, 74 percent have never received formal education (ibid.: 403-404).

Ayacucho is a prime example of the two negative extremes of the land tenure system—the latifundio and the patchwork minifundio. The majority of the agricultural population (83 percent) holds farm plots that are less than 5 hectares in size, totaling only 28 percent of the department's arable area,

Plate 2. Exploitation of Andean Vertical Ecology. Aerial view of a typical mid-altitude indigenous community in the department of Ayacucho, with agricultural production above and below the community.

whereas only 17 percent of the agricultural units are over 500 hectares in size and account for 57 percent of the productive land (ibid.: 403-404).

Bourque and Palmer (1975: 213-214) document the events following the expropiation of one of the largest haciendas in Ayacucho. The huge hacienda was utilized primarily for pasture (7,540 hectares), with only 93 hectares for dry farming (mostly potatoes). In October of 1969, this hacienda and twelve others, totaling some 25,000 hectares, were designated as part of a government-organized transitional structure called a PIAR—Integral Rural Settlement Project. This particular PIAR was to specialize in cattle production.

Organized much like the SAIS, the PIAR is visualized as concentrating government technical resources in a given homogeneous geographical area. It guarantees shared profits to its members and assumes that the membership eventually will become part of the Agricultural Production Cooperatives—CAP. However, efforts to cooperativize the traditional peasant sector have not been successful in Ayacucho. Bourque and Palmer (ibid.: 215) state that in December 1971, the scene of the former hacienda was a desolate one. Eighty-eight families had been declared beneficiaries, but those who remained on the land were near starvation. Indiscriminate grazing had ruined the improved pastures; the hacendado had sold the herd of improved cattle, in his eyes to compensate for his loss. No program of technical assistance was organized. And the ultimate irony is that this particular hacienda had been considered a model one. At the time of the expropriation, a plan had been approved to turn a large portion of the land over to the dependent peasants. The owner left Peru, but the peasants remained on the land, their situation becoming worse by the day.

Aside from problems of unequal land distribution, the department of Ayacucho is besieged by problems of high fertility, high mortality, intensive migration, and the uneven distribution of a population that is undereducated and underemployed. These problems are intensified by the lack of adequate systems of communication.

The migrant who leaves Chuschi, usually in search of employment for needed cash, travels by bus for three days to reach Lima. The buses leave Chuschi, which is at the end of the road, three times a week during the dry season and, road conditions permitting, once a week during the rainy season. Travelers crowd onto the buses, carrying produce, animals, wool, and often children to deliver to relatives residing in Lima.

The buses rumble away loaded to the utmost for the long journey, stopping in the nearby villages of Cancha-Cancha and Pomabamba. Then the buses cross the high cold puna of Pampa Cangallo, the home of the light-skinned Morochucos. The ascent continues until the divide between the Pampas and Ayacucho valleys is crossed at about 4,300 meters. Then the buses toil slowly downward to the city of Ayacucho. Although the distance is only 120 kilometers, the journey to Ayacucho usually takes from six to eight hours.

Beyond Ayacucho the route continues north, following the Mantaro River into the department of Huancavelica, where the Mantaro is crossed at its great bend at Mayoc.

In the spring of 1974 the Mantaro flooded and this bridge was destroyed, disrupting the route between Huancayo and Ayacucho for almost a year. A new bridge was constructed farther north along mining roads. Travelers reach the bustling city of Huancayo toward the end of the second day of their journey. From Huancayo, they follow the railway route northwest through the fertile valley to Jauja and on north to the mining town of La Oroya.

At La Oroya both the road and the railway turn westward and climb upward to the pass at Ticlio, almost 5,000 meters, to descend into the Rímac Valley and the industrial, financial, and governmental heart of Peru—Metropolitan Lima. The buses arrive in the major market area of the city called *La Parada*—the stop. From there Chuschinos can walk to the invasion settlement where from 250 to 300 fellow villagers are nucleated.

A week does not pass without seeing several Chuschinos taking this long, tortuous journey either to or from Lima. The flow of goods, people, and information is constant. Chuschinos consider the invasion settlement in Lima an important part of their community, and we cannot fully understand the dynamics of change in this closed corporate peasant village without an understanding of the roles played by the migrants, the important cultural brokers who mediate between the closed, self-imposed isolation of the village, and Lima, the center of rapid cultural change (see chapter 8).

2.6 Location

The village of Chuschi is approximately 120 kilometers southwest of Ayacucho, the department capital, and 30 kilometers from Cangallo, the province capital, via an unpaved road (see maps 2 and 3). Prior to 1961, Chuschi communicated with department and province capitals and points beyond via foot paths and llama trails. Then, in 1961, Public Works of Ayacucho built a road from the department capital to Cancha-Cancha, 10 kilometers from the village of Chuschi. In 1966 the remaining 10 kilometers were completed by public communal labor, called *faena*, which obliges every household to contribute so many days of labor under pain of a fine. The village government provides coca for each laborer.

The completion of this road has facilitated the movement of the traffic to and from Chuschi and has increased the community's importance as a market

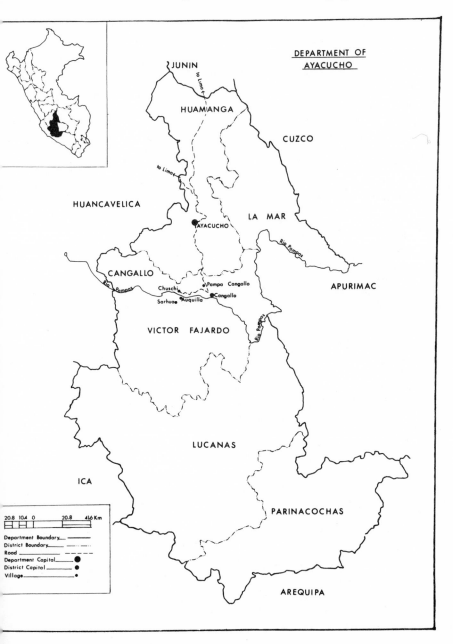

DEPARTMENT OF
AYACUCHO

JUNIN

to Lima

HUAMANGA

CUZCO

to Lima

HUANCAVELICA

LA MAR

AYACUCHO

Río Pampas

CANGALLO

Río Pampas

Chuschi

Pampa Cangallo

Sarhua   Auquilla   Cangallo

APURIMAC

VICTOR FAJARDO

Río Pampas

LUCANAS

ICA

20.8 10.4 0   20.8   41.6 Km

Department Boundary
District Boundary
Road
Department Capital
District Capital
Village

PARINACOCHAS

AREQUIPA

MAP 2

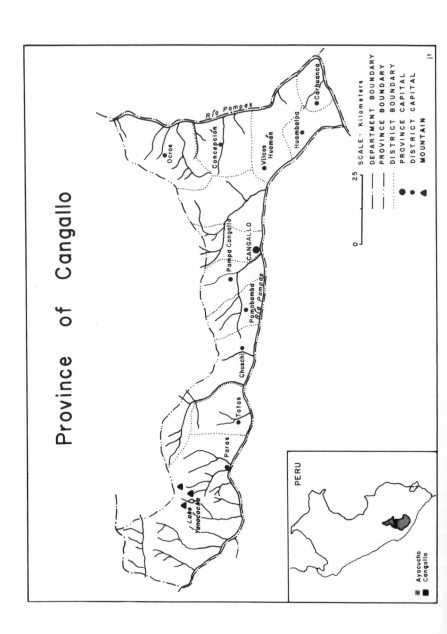

center (see map 4). Bus lines already communicate between the village and Lima, as described above (2.5), and communication with the coast will be further increased when the village completes a road that will connect with the new road, Los Libertadores, that extends from Ayacucho to the old mining center of Castrovirreyna and then descends to the coast at Chincha and Ica. It is expected that this project will take several years to complete through the traditional obligatory communal labor.

The village of Chuschi has been an important market, administrative, and ceremonial center for the surrounding area for at least four hundred years. Once a week, on Fridays, people from distant communities converge on Chuschi to buy the manufactured goods brought in by some twenty to thirty traveling market vendors. The items most in demand are coca and cane alcohol, trago, the necessary elements for any ritual activity. Clothing, aluminum cooking pots, school supplies, dyes, and numerous small items such as needles, thread, safety pins, and decorative costume jewelry are conspicuous consumer items. Some fresh food stuffs are sold also. Wool and cheese are the two products that are produced in any quantity by the peasants. Entrepreneurs (very often women) from the department capital buy wool, cheese, and eggs and sell them to the market vendors in Ayacucho. Occasionally, a peasant, or a community, will sell an animal at the market. Animals are important as ready cash reserves. Pigs, sheep, goats, and cattle are sold. Rarely does one see llamas or alpacas sold in the village market, but occasionally guinea pigs are sold or traded.

Chuschi is also the communication center for llama and mule trains that carry goods to communities beyond the road and bring in goods to the road to be transported by truck. The completion of the road has enabled the few mestizo families holding land in the area to produce for the Ayacucho or Lima markets. However, the greatest impact of the road has been to open up a consumer market consisting of the communities along this part of the Pampas River. People walk one or two days to Chuschi to attend the weekly market. (See plate 3.)

The village is situated in a deep valley on one of the tributaries of the Pampas River, known by several names—Chuschi Mayo, Taksa Mayo, and, in the past, Chocloqocha Mayo. This small river serves as the boundary between Chuschi and its great rival, the peasant community of Quispillaqta, whose central plaza is only 200 meters from the plaza of Chuschi. The conflicts between these two villages will be discussed in 2.7. Directly above the village to the southeast is the mountain peak, Chuschi Urqo, that prevents the sun from warming the village until 8:00 or 8:30 in the morning. The sun disappears behind the mountains at 4:30 in the afternoon, causing a variation in daytime-nighttime temperatures from a warm 75-80 degrees in the

Plate 3. Market Day in Chuschi. The boys' primary school is on the left. The view is to the south,

daytime during the dry season to below freezing after the sun disappears. The daily variation is not so extreme during the rainy season.

Chuschi is dominated physically and supernaturally by the mountain peak, Comañawi (also called Humankiklla), and the powerful mountain deity or Wamani believed to reside there. This peak rises to an altitude of approximately 4,750 meters and is located south of Chuschi across the Pampas River in the province of Víctor Fajardo. The village is the capital of the district of the same name, covering 271.50 square kilometers. The Pampas River separates the district of Chuschi from the province of Víctor Fajardo to the south, and the district of Socos Vinchos borders on the north, María Parado de Bellido borders on the east, and Totos and Paras border on the west (see map 4 and plate 4.)

Since the nearest haciendas are some fifteen kilometers away in the province of Huamanga, Chuschinos have not felt direct hacienda domination. There is one small hacienda in the district that became the object of an organized invasion (see 10.33). Chuschi is an independent peasant community whose status was secured through the efforts of a small group of migrants in 1941. There are two other recognized communities in the district with lands that border on Chuschi's, Quispillaqta and Cancha-Cancha. Not surprisingly, land disputes are a dominant theme in the documents and records of the village.

Chuschi represents one of the negative extremes of land tenure in Ayacucho, discussed in 2.5. Chuschinos hold on the average one and one-half to two hectares of agricultural land per household, relegating Chuschi to the bottom of the minifundio extreme. Furthermore, the maximum of two hectares held by the average household is usually dispersed throughout the community's diverse ecological zones in as many as fifteen or twenty tiny fields.

2.7 Ecology and Agricultural Cycle

The village of Chuschi is situated at an altitude of 3,154 meters between the two ecological extremes under its control: the communal pasture land on the high puna reaching above 4,000 meters, and the individual, family-controlled land in the steep valley of the Pampas River below 3,300 meters. The village therefore exploits three distinct zones of what John Murra has termed the "vertical ecology" of the Andes (1967, 1968, 1970, 1972):

1. The *sallqa* or puna—3,300 meters to above 4,000. It is divided into an upper region, beginning at about 3,600 meters, which supports herds of alpacas, llamas, sheep, and cattle, and a lower region, 3,300 to 3,600 meters, where tubers such as potatoes, *ocas, ullucos,* and *mashuas* as well as wheat, barley, and *quinua* are grown. (See plate 5.)

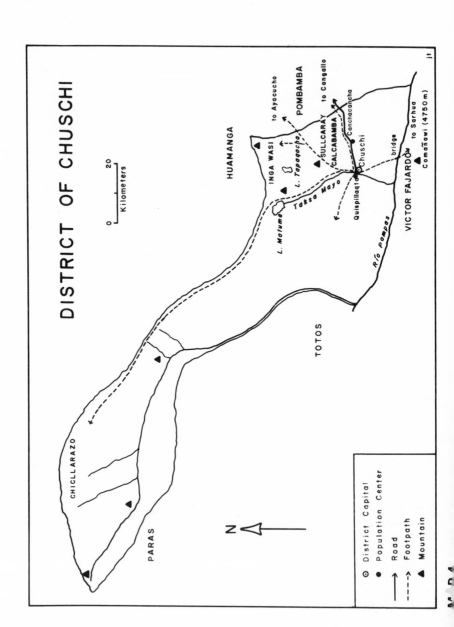

Plate 4. The Pampas River Valley. Courtesy of Servicio Aerofotográfico Nacional, Lima.

Plate 5.   Alpacas. On the *sallqa*, or puna, directly above Chuschi.

2. The *qichwa*—below 3,300 meters. This is the important corn-producing zone, which makes it the most valued of the three. The village is located in the *qichwa* at 3,154 meters. This zone, too, is divided into upper and lower regions; the lower limit is uncertain, but conjoins with the third zone. (See plate 6.)

3. The *mayopatan* or river bottom—2,300 meters. It provides cactus fruit, some tree fruits, and squash. Corn is also produced in this zone.

This pattern of exploitation of vertical zones is ancient in the Andes. Murra (1972) demostrates that vertical control was maintained through the systematic relocation of populations in the various economic zones. This practice has become known as the *mitmaq* system after the Inca practice; however, Murra's document research provides five different cases of Andean groups of diverse political and economic development between 1460 and 1560. W. H. Isbell (1968) argues that this pattern of vertical exploitation dates at least from Middle Horizon times. What is apparent in Chuschi is a pattern of exploitation in which the nucleated settlement is located at about 3,000 meters, which marks the maximum altitude of corn cultivation in the Pampas Valley. The *sallqa* zones above the village as well as the *mayopatan* below the village can be exploited easily. Each member of the community attempts to control land in each of these zones to maximize his success with varied crops as well as to diminish the environmental threats of any one zone. The Agrarian Reform Law of 1969 stipulates that a communal member of a peasant community must reside adjacent to his agricultural land or at least nearby. The law also stipulates that such a member shall have usufruct right to one agricultural plot, not various small ones. This stipulation is an effort to diminish the unproductive minifundio. Strict enforcement of the above could be disastrous to the subsistence farmer who relies on vertical exploitation of various zones for success.

The agricultural cycle is determined by the two distinct seasons. The rainy season begins in late September, and planting is officially begun by the ritual cleaning of the irrigation canals at that time. The dry season is ushered in by the harvest festival in May. Often rains continue into May, but the major rains occur during the months of November through April. During the rainy season the village is often cut off from the outside world due to landslides and impassable roads.

Corn fields are irrigated before the initial planting in late September through November. After planting they are irrigated again, and if rainfall is sufficient, further irrigation is not necessary. Corn is harvested in June, after which herds are brought down off the high puna to feed on the stalks remaining in the fields. Potatoes are planted in November and December, but irrigation is not essential to potato cultivation.

Plate 6. The *Qichwa* Zone. A family plants a corn field, the women sowing seeds, the men plowing.

Division of labor in agriculture is sex-based. Women must always place the seed for planting. They also select the seed after harvest and reserve it for the next planting. At a wedding ceremony the female relatives of the bride and groom donate seed for the couple's first planting. Men operate the plow and the native hoe, the *lampa*, while women place the seed and help with weeding and mounding earth around the young plants, which is performed twice during the growing season. Both men and women harvest in the following order: *ocas* are first; then potatoes, *mashua*, wheat, and barley; finally the corn fields interspersed with broad beans.

When the first corn field is planted, a celebration is observed in which the man and woman invite their compadres to plant the field, and a special chicha (corn beer) is prepared with toasted ground *quinua* (an indigenous high-altitude grain) sprinkled on the top. This drink is called *machka*. Planting and harvesting require communal labor, with relatives and compadres reciprocally aiding one another. When someone requests labor, he is calling together a *minka*, and those who respond to his request are giving *ayni* and expect repayment. Such reciprocal labor is essential to the subsistence agriculture of Chuschi.

2.8 The Natives' Conceptualization of Their Ecology

The vertical zones of Chuschi's ecology are conceptualized onto space through the delineation of boundaries between each of the zones and their subzones. The boundaries are demarcated by the location of chapels housing crosses. The focal point of the conceptual scheme is the village, which mediates between the high puna, *sallqa*, and the river bottom, *mayopatan* (see map 1). The village itself is divided into two localized barrios, one to the north called *Hanay* (Upper) Barrio and the other to the south called *Uray* (Lower) Barrio. Thirteen chapels are said to belong to the barrios, seven to Lower Barrio and six to Upper Barrio. The chapels, all housing crosses, radiate out along three access trails from two matrix chapels located within the boundary of the village. In chapter 6 we shall see that the chapels are the locales of fertility and harvest rituals. The organization of space is essentially conceived of concentrically, with the mirror halves of the village, Upper Barrio and Lower Barrio, at the center. The village is said to be civilized, whereas the term *sallqa* literally means savage. The agricultural zone is located between the nucleated village and the savage tundra. We can consider the *mayopatan* as part of the agricultural zone. Therefore, disregarding the accidents of geography, the conceptual pattern of Chuschino space is concentric, with the civilized village at the center opposed to the savage puna, the *sallqa*. (See map 5.)

The dual opposition of civilized versus savage is dramatized during Corpus

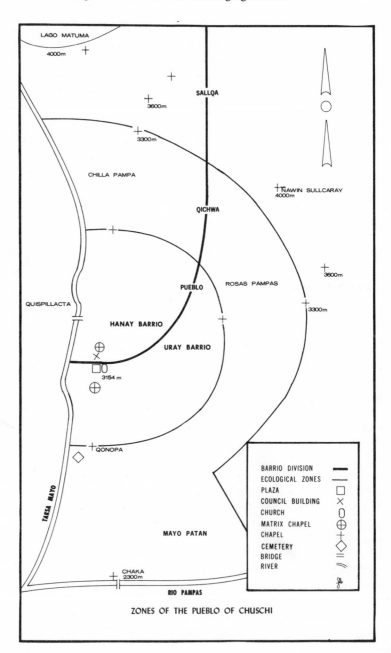

LAGO MATUMA
4000m

SALLQA

3600m

3300m

CHILLA PAMPA

ÑAWIN SULLCARAY
4000m

QICHWA

3600m

ROSAS PAMPAS

PUEBLO

3300m

QUISPILLACTA

HANAY BARRIO

URAY BARRIO

3154 m

QONOPA

TAKSA MAYO

BARRIO DIVISION	▬
ECOLOGICAL ZONES	—
PLAZA	□
COUNCIL BUILDING	×
CHURCH	○
MATRIX CHAPEL	⊕
CHAPEL	+
CEMETERY	◇
BRIDGE	=
RIVER	≈

MAYO PATAN

CHAKA
2300m

RIO PAMPAS

ZONES OF THE PUEBLO OF CHUSCHI

MAP 5

Christi in May or June when the *sallqaruna,* or "savage men" of the puna, depicted by herders on horseback, descend on the village and enact savagery by defiling the Virgin Mary and insulting anyone they encounter. Also, the *sallqa* is where sexual acts not permitted in the village, such as incest and other illicit encounters, occur. Young single people arrange group rendezvous in the *sallqa*, which begin with marathon dancing and drinking and terminate in indiscriminate sexual intercourse. Such behavior is not tolerated within the boundaries of the village, where the traditional authorities, the *varayoq*, patrol and arrest anyone engaging in such activities within the civilized zone.

The puna, or *sallqa*, begins above the altitude of corn cultivation at about 3,000 meters. This zone is delineated by chapels at its lower and upper boundaries. The upper *sallqa* begins at about 3,600 meters and continues to well above 4,000 meters. The highest regions of the tundra are the domains of the mountain deities, the Wamanis.

As owners of all plants and animals, the Wamanis are the most powerful indigenous deities of the Pampas region. Their residences are the highest mountains and puna lakes, which villagers never approach alone. A sickness called *puqyo unqoy* may be inflicted on anyone who walks beside a puna lake at night or who neglects the necessary rituals and offerings. The Wamanis must be placated with ritual payments to insure personal safety and the fertility of one's animals. If angered, the Wamanis can devour the hearts of men and cause miscarriages and infant deaths. Ritual payments are made by individual families twice a year, during August and February, when the earth is "open" and the Wamanis are especially receptive to offerings.

The most powerful Wamani of the district of Chuschi resides in the lake, Yanaqocha, at an altitude of 5,095 meters northeast of the village in the communal puna lands called Chicllarazo (see maps 4 and 5 for locations of entities discussed). This particular Wamani commands the other Wamanis of the district, just as the highest military official commands those under him. He is also believed by many to communicate directly with the national president in Lima in Chuschi's behalf. Two subordinate Wamanis reside in the mountain Ontaqarqa and in the lake Tapaqocha, both located in the high puna.

The Wamanis preside over territories and have an organizational hierarchy likened to provincial governmental structure. They are described as tall, white, bearded males who dress elaborately in western dress. Their palaces, located inside the mountains and lakes, are sumptuously furnished in gold and silver. The Wamanis transform themselves into condors and are associated with crosses and chapels. A group of children whom I asked to draw pictures of Wamanis depicted them as (1) richly dressed men (often bearded) living inside a mountain, (2) condors flying over the peaks, or (3) simply as mountain peaks and lakes with crosses located nearby. Palomino (1968) argues that the cross of the Andes is a prehispanic concept that reflects the indigenous symbolism of fertility and abundance. An examination of Chuschi's complex of crosses and the rituals associated with them supports this view.

The communal grazing lands of Chuschi—Inga Wasi, Chicllarazo, and the church's Cofradía de Buena Memoria—are located in the upper *sallqa*. The communal lands are said to belong to the village as a whole, and there are chapels with guardian saints at Inga Wasi and Chicllarazo. These two *santas menores*, as they are called, are cared for by the *sallqa varayoq*, who also dedicate a year to the tending of the church's 250 head of cattle and 1,500 head of sheep. The two *santas menores* are small replicas of Mama Rosa and Mama Olimpia in the village church. Twice a year, in June and December (during the solstices), the "daughters" (the small replicas) descend from their *sallqa* chapels and visit their "mothers" in the village church, where they remain until the ritual cleaning of the irrigation canals, the Yarqa Aspiy (6.2), which takes place around the time of the equinox in September.

Within the civilized village, the matrix chapels in the barrios are the meeting places of the dual prestige hierarchies, the *varayoq* of the Upper and Lower Barrios. Their principal tasks are twofold: the care of the chapels and other sacred places and the care of the dual irrigation systems. Residence in one of the moieties determines eligibility in the *varayoq* structure.

The concentric spatial pattern is repeated within the village itself. Upper and Lower Barrios are a basic dual pattern that is disturbed by the penetration of political and religious domination in the center of the village, represented by the church and the bureaucratic government. The Quechua-speaking communal members speak of these institutions as belonging to the category of foreigners associated with the threatening outside world that impinges on their closed corporate universe. We can conceptualize the organization of the ecological zones thus:

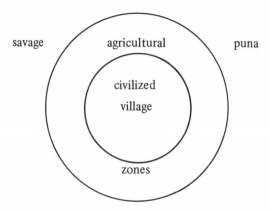

The civilized village and its two barrios are positive forces; the agricultural zones mediate between the civilized village and the savage part of the world, the *sallqa* or puna. Likewise, the spatial organization of the village itself is concentric; the foreign, dominating outside world has penetrated the center of the village in the form of the church and the bureaucratic government, while the indigenous moieties maintain the traditional way of life. The *qalas*, or foreigners, have the opposite perspective; they see themselves as occupying the (positive) center of the village oriented to the outside world. From their viewpoint, the moieties are negative.

COMUNEROS   QALAS

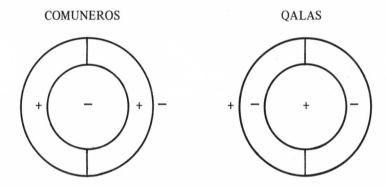

2.9 A Note on the Prehistory of Chuschi

The prehistory of the region is little known. Recently archaeological work has been initiated in the Pampas River Valley with focus on San Miguel in the province of La Mar (W. H. Isbell 1973). The survey was begun in the Chuschi-Sarhua area in 1967 (see W. H. Isbell 1968, 1972a; also Raymond and Isbell 1969). One of the most interesting aspects of the 1967 work was the recovery of a classic Tiahuanaco artifact eroding from the wall of a circular platform mound called Plaza Pata, located below the modern village of Chuschi toward the Pampas River. The circular platform is constructed of rubble-filled fieldstone typical of the Middle Horizon site of Wari. The platform is forty-two meters in diameter across its flat top, which is under cultivation. The height of the platform varies from two to four meters, with variation due in large part to agricultural modifications. A ramp appears to project from the north-east side of the structure.

The artifact is pictured in Bonavía (1972: 55) and is discussed in Raymond and Isbell (1969). Burned llama bones were found in association with the vessel, which is called a *puma incensario* and features a modeled feline head projecting from an open body with a scalloped rim. This Middle Horizon style, dating to about 700 A.D., had never been found previously this far north of Lake Titicaca.

W. H. Isbell (personal communication) is of the opinion that the vessel is a copy of classic Tiahuanaco, indicating some form of direct contact with a classic Tiahuanaco site, such as trade or political hegemony. Another Middle Horizon site, called Pillawa, is located across the Taksa Mayo River outside the modern village of Quispillaqta. This site had larger and denser occupation than Plaza Pata. W. H. Isbell (personal communication) suggests that Pillawa was a village site and Plaza Pata a ceremonial center.

There are numerous hilltop sites around Chuschi, with simple brown or red ceramic assemblages including *ollas* with low, slightly flaring collars and sub-hemispherical bowls (W. H. Isbell 1972c). There is disagreement as to the interpretation of these sites. Lumbreras (1959) proposes that they represent Late Intermediate occupation by the Chanca Confederacy in the Pampas region. We know from documentary sources (Rowe 1963: 188) that the Chancas centered in the province of Andahuaylas. They began an expansion by conquest about the same time as the Incas. The Chancas almost destroyed the Inca Empire at the end of Viracocha's reign (ibid.: 189). Since there is no evidence that the Chancas ever inhabited the Pampas region, the counter view to Lumbreras's is held by W. H. Isbell (in Bonavía 1972), who argues that these sites represent a population that had been in the Pampas since Middle Horizon times or earlier. He further hypothesizes that Quechua speakers occupied the Pampas Valley and represent the expansion of maize farmers from the northeastern Andes southward into available low valleys with ample rainfall. This expansion was effected by the simple adaptation of slope cultivation utilizing semiterraces and dry farming. His argument maintains that the Pampas region was penetrated by these Quechua-speaking maize farmers continuously from at least Middle Horizon times or before and that the Inca expansion represents one of these waves.

2.10 A Brief Historical Sketch

During colonial times Chuschi was the administrative center for seven villages known as the *Curato de Chuschi:* Chuschi, Quispillaqta, Cancha-Cancha, Huarcaya, Tomanga, Auquilla, and Sarhua.   Today the political division of the district of Chuschi is different; the latter four villages are now in the province of Víctor Fajardo (see map 4). When asked how Chuschi is divided, informants still say "into seven parts" and name the original seven villages of the *curato,* for which Chuschi serves as the market center. Even though the district of Chuschi was created in 1857 covering 271.50 square kilometers, a reduction of the area of the colonial *curato,* Chuschi remains the market center—and to a lesser degree the administrative and ceremonial center—for the seven villages. The latter point is evidenced by the fact that some of the villages still send *santas menores* to "visit their parents" in the Chuschi church; this symbolizes their subordinate status to Chuschi as an administrative and ceremonial center. With the restructuring of the provinces, Chuschi lost its place as the official center for the seven villages, but some hierarchy may still exist among the indigenous prestige officials, the *varayoq,* as a vestige of the political structure of the colonial era.

Chuschi was recognized as an indigenous community, under present law called a peasant community, in 1941 as a result of the efforts of a small group of migrants residing in Lima. The other two principal villages of the district, Quispillaqta and Cancha-Cancha, are also legally recognized peasant communities, which means their large expanses of communal grazing lands cannot be alienated from the community directly controlling usufruct rights.

The earliest historical documentation pertaining to the village of Chuschi is a portion of the official report of an inspection in the province of Vilcas Huamán by the *visitador* Juan de Palomares in 1574, discovered by R. T. Zuidema. There was an earlier *visita*, conducted by Damián de la Bandera, but the report has not been found. (See Zuidema 1966 for a discussion of the ethnohistory of the Pampas River area). Palomares recorded the various land boundaries of the indigenous communities in the province.

From this document we know that Chuschi belonged to the labor grant (*repartimiento*) of Juan de Mañueco, a resident of the department capital, Guamanga (modern Ayacucho), who had been granted the Aymaraes Indians of Chuschi, Cancha-Cancha, and Moros. The Aymaraes were resettled in the Pampas by the Incas after the Chanca defeat. In a later document (1593), the Aymaraes Indians claim that they were relocated from the Apurímac by Topa Inca Yupanqui. According to John Rowe's calculations (1963: 203), Topa Inca Yupanqui reigned from 1471 to 1493, which places the founding of the village during the late fifteenth century.

The principal chief (cacique) of the Aymaraes of Chuschi, Cancha-Cancha, and Moros was Antonio Astocabana, who succeeded the first principal chief named by Damián de la Bandera. This chief, called Guacra, had died, leaving no heirs. Antonio Astocabana, declaring that he was ill and had no sons willing to assume the office, petitioned that his brother, Juan Astocabana, succeed him in the office of cacique of the Aymaraes of Chuschi, Cancha-Cancha, and Moros.

Juan Astocabana declared that the Aymaraes of these three villages possessed forty-five llamas, eleven sheep, and twenty-three male and seventy-three female alpacas. There is no mention of population size for any of the villages. However, some idea of the ethnic complexity of the region is clear.

The province of Vilcas was totally repopulated by the Incas with tribes from various regions of the empire. Besides the Aymaraes from the Apurímac region and the fierce Angaraes from Huancavelica, as well as Incas of privilege, the Chillques, and Yungas Indians from Canas south of Cuzco and from Muchic (Zuidema 1966: 71), Palomares also mentions Quichuas, Condes, Papres, Cañares Quitos, and finally the Tanquiguas, who are said to be the only original inhabitants of the province of Vilcas Huamán (Jiménez de la Espada 1965: 219). The Tanquiguas had their headquarters in the *curato* of Guambalpa. Palomares mentions a boundary between the Tanquiguas and the Aymaraes near the lake Yaguarcocha, which is near the source of the Pampas River, the lake Choclococha.

The next major ethnohistorical source is Jiménez de la Espada's publication of the *Relaciones geográficas de Indias—Perú* (1965). The *relación* of Vilcas Huamán was written by the *corregidor* Pedro de Carbajal in 1586. It describes briefly the *curato* of Chuschi, which was composed of four villages: Chuschi, nearby Cancha-Cancha, Sarhua, now in Víctor Fajardo, and Moros. The first three still exist, but the fourth, a *reducción* across the Pampas River, was abandoned during the colonial period. The *relación* (1965: 204) states that the Incas maintained 30,000 troops in Vilcas Huamán as an administrative and defensive center. In 1586 the capital of Vilcas was depopulated; the Indians of Vilcas had been diminished greatly, largely through service in the mines and as servants and herders for the Spanish, and the *relación* states that the Inca subjects went back to their original provinces.

   In pre-Inca times, each ethnic population of the region was subject to its own chiefs and owed them personal service, such as house building, weaving, and agricultural and herding duties. The general language was Quechua, and each village had its own gods (ibid.: 207).

   After the Inca conquest, the area was depopulated except for the Tanquiguas and repopulated by the Inca *mitmaq* resettlement policy. As stated earlier, this resulted in ethnic diversification, with groups from as far away as Quito and Cañares in Ecuador, the Yungas south of Cuzco, the Apurímac, and Muchic on the coast. Aymará was spoken in addition to Quechua throughout the province. The Incas imposed their own gods, the sun and the moon, as supreme deities. The *relación* states that the old sacred objects, the *huacas,* were destroyed; however, if present-day Catholicism is an example, it is likely that the ethnic populations brought their own religious concepts with them and added the sun and the moon to the pantheon.

   The *relación geográfica* does not mention Quispillaqta, the neighboring village of Chuschi. However, Palomares states that in a deep ravine, half a league from a plain called Calcabamba, two villages have been settled, one called Chuschi, populated by the Aymaraes Indians of Mañueco, and one called

Locroca, belonging to Pedro de Rivera (written Rribera); both villages are surrounded by many corn fields, and they are separated by a small arroyo. This description corresponds to the location of modern Chuschi and Quispillaqta. Furthermore, the document describes the location of modern Cancha-Cancha, also populated by Aymaraes Indians of Mañueco (see map 4). However, Palomares mentions a village on the banks of the Calcamayo River called San Bartolomé de Calcabamba. The latter does not exist today, either on the Pampas River or its tributaries.

The modern oral history maintains that Chuschi was relocated from the plain of Calcabamba to its present location after three consecutive disappearances of a small effigy of El Dulce Nombre de Jesús (The Sweet Name of Jesus) from the Calcabamba chapel. The effigy of Jesus as a boy was found three times at the site of modern Chuschi. This theme of three disappearances and encounters of a religious statue as a origin myth is common to neighboring villages as well. The pampa of Calcabamba does have a chapel, but there is no evidence of house structures or refuse indicating a nucleated village.

The third important early source from the village archive of Quispillaqta is a copy of a decree, dated 1593, by the *corregidor* Blasco Núñez de Vela in Vilcas Huamán. (See Appendix.) Two Indians, Antonio Astocabana, principal chief of the village of Chuschi and all the Aymaraes of Juan Mañueco, and García Yanqui Tanta, also a *principal* from Chuschi, appeared before the *corregidor*. They claimed that the Canas Indians were usurping land alloted to them by Topa Inca Yupanqui with the aid of Negro slaves belonging to Diego de la Rivera. The Canas Indians produced an *auto* prepared by a previous *corregidor* of Vilcas, Damián de la Bandera, that stated they had been relocated from Canas, south of Cuzco, by Wayna Cápac. Blasco Núñez ruled that the Canas had legal claim to 10 *topos* of land to the west of the river. They have remained and expanded as the Chuschi population has declined.

In 1602 another dispute between the Aymaraes of Chuschi and the Canas Indians, now of Luis Rivera, Diego's son, comes before the *corregidor* in Vilcas. This document states that there were fifty Indians in the *encomienda* of Luis Rivera at the time. This is the only reference to population that we have. I assume that the reference is to fifty tribute-paying Indians and that we might assume a population of around four or five hundred. Unfortunately, there is no mention of the number of Indians in Chuschi. The reference to a land grant, an *encomienda*, is substantiated by oral history.

The disputes between Chuschi and Quispillaqta have continued through the centuries. The last actual battle occurred in 1959 when the two villages fought over boundaries of puna grazing land. It began with slingshots and stones but culminated in three Quispillaqta deaths by shotgun wounds inflicted by a Chuschino. A few months later a Chuschino was ambushed in the puna in retaliation. The situation between Chuschi and Quispillaqta had reached the point in 1969 that Chuschi attempted to prevent Quispillaqta from receiving piped-in drinking water that originated in the puna of Chuschi. Government technicians prevented a conflict by proclaiming that water belonged to the state, not individual communities. Conflict between the two villages is heightened by the fact that Chuschi's population is declining due to outward migration while Quispillaqta's is increasing.

3. The Social Classes of Chuschi

3.1 A Basic Opposition

Chuschino society is polarized into two social groups: the *comuneros,* or communal members of the village, who participate in the prestige hierarchy, wear traditional dress, and speak Quechua; versus the *vecinos,* or *qalas* (literally, peeled or naked ones), who are Spanish speaking, western dressed, foreign nonparticipants in communal life. This basic opposition is maintained by mechanisms characteristic of ethnic groups. Nevertheless, class differentiation exists in both groups. Mediating this basic opposition of communal member versus foreigner are the migrants, who identify themselves as sons of comuneros. But, at the same time, they have lost full integration in the indigenous culture without having gained integration into the national one. Self-consciously, the migrants are constructing social classes in their urban settlement (10.4). The relations between these groups are complex. The separation between the ethnic groups is maintained rigidly. The class structure within each group is not as rigid: mobility upward and downward is possible. Marriage is one of the major means of achieving upward mobility. For the comuneros, endogamy within the village and ethnic group is ideal: for the vecinos, exogamy outside the village is desirable. The migrants move ambiguously within the ethnic and class structure, but marriage with another Chuschino is most valued. Chapter 8 deals more fully with the migrant community. In this chapter, a construction of the ethnic and class relations is provided by giving examples of each group. The emphasis is on the comunero majority and the terminologies and concepts discussed are those of the community members themselves.

The comuneros are subdivided into three subclasses: the "rich ones," called *apus*; the "orphans" or "poor ones," *wakchas*; and those without land who must depend upon others, the *tiapakuq*. It is conceivable that the vecinos are similarly subdivided; however, my research has focused on the indigenous majority. Before beginning the description of *qalas* and comuneros, let us turn briefly to the current decline in village population and the rise of education.

3.2 Population Decline

While the nation's population increased 61 percent in the period between 1940 and 1961, the department of Ayacucho increased only 15 percent and the district of Chuschi 20 percent. Conversely, the village of Chuschi suffered a population decline during this same period, the 1,310 persons in an estimated 320 households in 1940 dropping to 1,099 persons in 297 households in 1961. The village of Chuschi made up 27.5 percent of the district's population in 1940 but only 17 percent in 1961 (Ramón et al. 1967: 17).

Chuschi's population decline is due to outward migration and reflects what is occurring in the department as a whole. Ayacucho is fourth in the nation in outward migration with 128,000 migrants in 1961. Only three departments had larger outward migration in 1961—Ancash with 175,000, Arequipa with 138,000, and Cuzco with 136,000. Nucleated agricultural communities such as Chuschi are experiencing the heaviest outward migration ever as infant mortality declines and education increases.

3.3 Increase in Education

In 1961 almost half of the district's population was under seventeen years of age, which is comparable to the figure for the department (40 percent). Less than 10 percent of the village was either literate or proficient in Spanish. The rate of illiteracy and monolingualism is higher than for the department's 1961 statistics—74 percent specified no schooling, and over 50 percent were monolingual. The problem of monolingualism has been unofficially handled in the district by teaching one year in Quechua (called "transition") before exposing the children to Spanish. Such efforts at diminishing the shock of encountering the demands of school simultaneously with the demands of Spanish have proven successful, so much so that bilingual education is now an official policy throughout the country.

As of 1970, the district had nine primary schools. The two largest are in the village of Chuschi, with over 200 enrolled in the girls' and boys' schools. However, the boys' primary school is three times the size of the girls', and a girl attends the boys' school if she continues beyond the third grade. In 1970 only ten male students attended the fifth grade—no girls. The figures for 1966 are comparable:

1966, BOYS

	Transition	First	Second	Third	Fourth	Fifth	
Enrolled:	48	37	28	23	17	10	163
Attending:	40	32	24	20	15	10	141

The girls' school had a total enrollment of 55 students in grades transition through third for the same year. The total district enrollment in primary schools in 1966 was 726, roughly 11 percent of the total population; an equal percentage was enrolled in the village primary schools. At that time the district did not have a secondary school, but in 1968 the first secondary institution opened with the first year of instruction, planning to add a year of instruction each year until a complete secondary school was established. By 1970, forty-nine students attended the first- and second-year classes. The age and sex distribution of the secondary school in 1970 demonstrates the motivation of Chuschinos to receive an education. Six of the forty-nine students were females. The age distribution is especially interesting:

> 40 percent—24 to 40 years of age
> 50 percent—15 to 23 years of age
> 10 percent—below 15 years of age

It was not uncommon to see father and children walking to the plaza in the morning, the father to attend the secondary school and his children to attend the primary schools.

According to the investigations of the team of social scientists from the Institute of Peasant Communities, the district of Chuschi had produced the following professionals:

> 1 veterinarian
> 1 lawyer
> 1 investigator for the Peruvian Investigative Police (PIP)
> 1 secondary professor
> 1 *Guardia Civil* (National Police)
> 6 primary school teachers (5 are of third category without
> diplomas)

Students studying outside of the district include:

> 1 with the Investigative Police School
> 1 in officers' school for the National Police
> 2 at the provincial university in Ayacucho
> 1 at San Marcos University in Lima
> Numerous students in secondary schools in Ayacucho

The majority of professionals and students come from the vecinos, but increasingly the younger comuneros are viewing education as an escape from the harsh existence of subsistence agriculture and herding. Education is also seen as one of the avenues leading to integration into the national culture, whereby one loses one's identity as an "indio bruto" (a stupid Indian) and becomes part of the mass of cholos, the upwardly mobile segment of Peru's peasant class. Migration out of the village and district offers the same avenues of escape and the same hope of improvement in class identity and standard of living.

Members of this newly emergent class participate in both the indigenous peasant culture and the national culture but are not fully incorporated into either. This degree of social mobility, provided by new economic opportunities such as truck or bus driver, small-scale merchant, and laborer, has provided this emergent class the means with which to break the rigid, almost caste-like character of Indian-mestizo relationships. The social, economic, and geographic mobility of the new cholo class has meant that they have proven to be the effective leaders of peasant movements (Cotler 1969, Handelman 1975, Quijano 1965a, 1965b, 1967). In a review of the literature, Mayer (1970) rightly points out that mestizo, Indian, and cholo relationships are only definable in relative terms vis-à-vis one another.

In Chuschi, Indians define themselves as comuneros. Mestizos call themselves vecinos, or neighbors, but the comuneros call mestizos *qalas*, or "naked ones." The migrants and the newly educated children of comuneros can be seen as the structurally ambivalent cholos, who often become leaders and agitators for change.

3.4 Vecinos, or *Qalas*

In Chuschi, anyone who does not participate in the communal life of the village is either a foreigner or is emulating foreigners. Such a person is a vecino, a polite term applied to the mestizos residing in Chuschi. They include eight shopkeepers, a health worker, a government agronomist, seven primary school teachers, the priest, and descendants from the first teacher who arrived in Chuschi three generations ago. Quechua speakers also call the vecinos by a derogatory Quechua term, *qala*, which means naked, peeled (*pelado*), or skinned. A Quechua-speaking informant told me that *qala* used to refer to villagers who had gone away and come back wearing shoes instead of sandals. Then, when so many mestizos took up residence in Chuschi, the derogatory term *qala* was applied to them as well, due to the fact that they did not participate in communal rituals and reciprocal exchanges and did not define themselves first and foremost as Chuschinos. One might say that the *qalakuna* have peeled off their indigenous identity.

The outward-looking vecinos identify themselves as Peruvian nationals, not as Chuschinos; they participate in the national economy and government. On the other hand, comuneros participate in the economy to a limited degree. Ramón et al. (1967) estimates that 20 percent of Chuschi's products, primarily derived from the herds—alpaca wool, hides, milk, and cheese—reaches the market through traveling agents from commercial houses in Ayacucho. There are four vecino families whose crops are for the market economy rather than for subsistence, as is the case for comuneros. Two vecinos own trucks and easily transport their crops to Ayacucho or Lima for sale; they also transport produce and animals on a commercial basis.

To hold a district or municipal office, one must read and write Spanish, skills that have traditionally defined the *qala* or vecino group. However, as of 1971, returned migrants began to hold the newly instituted governmental offices for the district. The consequences of this event will be discussed in chapter 8.

Vecinos, without exception, live on or near the village plaza, where all things foreign are located—the municipal and district governmental offices, the stores, the schools, and the church. The church is located in Lower Barrio and the governmental offices in Upper Barrio; nevertheless, these two entities are portrayed as despicable *qalas* during the ritual cleaning of the irrigation canals to be discussed in chapter 6. In contrast, the comunero's residence in one of the two barrios determines his affiliation with the dual prestige hierarchy (see chapter 4).

Comuneros assume that all foreigners are rich, with the exception of lowland tropical forest Indians, the *chunchus*. Wealth is another criterion for vecino membership, and the richest entity in Chuschi is the Catholic Church. Fourteen saints are celebrated annually; each saint "owns" a corn field two or three yugadas in size in the prized lower *qichwa* zone. A yugada is the Spanish term for the amount of land that can be plowed in one day by one pair of oxen. In the context of Chuschino agriculture, this is a relative measure that takes into account the degree of slope, rockiness, or other obstacles to plowing and planting. Ramón et al. (1967: 34) estimate one yugada to be equal to about 250 square meters. Therefore, there are approximately four yugadas to one hectare, and the church's agricultural land totals between 30 and 40 yugadas or 7.5 to 10 hectares of land in plots about one hectare or less in size. The corn that is produced is used for the celebration of the saint's day. The incoming sponsor harvests the field, and the outgoing sponsor plants at the end of his tenure as mayordomo. The sponsor relies on his network of kin and compadres for aid. Both sexes sponsor saints' day celebrations.

The members of the prestige hierarchy are obliged to participate in the planting and harvesting of saints' fields. At one planting sponsored by a woman, ten women and twelve men were present, including four officials of the prestige hierarchy. After the planting, which was the last obligation of her year of service to the saint, she fêted all those present with a meal of grain and meat soup after an all-night vigil in her house. When I attempted to take down the names of all those present to study the relationship between kinship and reciprocity, my efforts were thwarted by a woman who claimed that I was going to make millions of *soles* by selling the list to our army and that all would be taken off to the war (I assume the Viet Nam war). However eventual success led to the findings set forth in chapter 7.

The church is the wealthiest entity of the community not only in land but also in herds. Its 250 head of cattle and 1,500 head of sheep are cared for by a prestige hierarchy—the *sallqa varayoq*—whose members give a year's service in the puna as caretakers under the *sallqa alcalde vara*. The cows do not give milk, having been allowed to revert to almost a wild state, and no improvement through breeding has been attempted. In the future the situation may change. A group of migrants is supported by the office of the agrarian reform in their efforts to convert the church's possessions into a cooperative, although they are still opposed by the priest, who receives one sheep a month and one bull and ten sheep annually. Conflict with the church is discussed further in chapter 8.

The second largest land-holdings are those of four vecino families who are said to own fifty to sixty yugadas collectively (Bolívar de Colchado 1967: 17). These are distributed throughout the three major zones. One vecino family owns eight separate fields; three are three yugadas each in size, two are of about one or two yugadas, each planted in corn, and three are located in the puna, one yugada each. This totals approximately fifteen yugadas, or three or four hectares. A large part of the harvest is for market. These figures contrast sharply with the estimated average for comunero families. In a public meeting in 1967, agrarian reform workers asked for the average amount of land held by comunero families. The assembly responded that the average holding was six to eight yugadas, or one and one-half to two hectares of agricultural land.

The head of the vecino family under discussion has not made his will, even though several of his children are married. He does not operate within the network of characteristic mutual aid; rather, he relies on wage labor. Relationships within his own family are usually on a cash and carry basis. For example, his married daughter paid him twenty *soles* for the use of two teams of oxen to plow a rented field. She also paid two men fifteen *soles* a day to plow and five *soles* a day to a woman to place the seed. Still, the vecinos do perform the first planting ritual, in which one's compadres plant to insure a good harvest. This ritual is accompanied with chicha (corn beer), *machka* (chicha sprinkled with toasted ground corn or *quinua*), and a special meal. Coca is never used. As mentioned earlier, agricultural production is directed toward the market, whereas the comuneros' production is principally for subsistence. Thus vecinos are eager to adopt better agricultural methods to increase production, while little headway has been made among comuneros to change traditional agricultural techniques, which are felt by them to be best.

The vecinos use village exogamy to secure upward mobility. It is desirable to marry someone from the province or department capitals. For the local vecinos, marriage with one of the bureaucrats, teachers, or merchants ensures upward mobility if that person's wealth is equal to or greater than one's own. I witnessed a shotgun wedding one year of a young male teacher and the daughter of one of the vecino families.

Compadrazgo exists among vecinos in Chuschi; however, it is considered more prestigious to have a compadre from Cangallo, the province capital, or from Ayacucho. The comuneros not only marry among themselves and within the village, they also consider it propitious to marry within their particular social stratum. This is also true for compadrazgo ties.

The principal characteristic of *qalas*, or vecinos, is not distinctive dress, language, or an outward orientation to the Peruvian nation; it is the negation of membership in the commune with all of the attendant obligations. Obligatory positions are not held; reciprocal aid is not utilized, but rather laborers are paid with cash. In short, vecinos do not define themselves as Chuschinos, nor do comuneros so define them. Vecinos and comuneros alike were asked to compile a list of foreigners in the village. Agreement was universal. Separation of the two major ethnic groups is carried even to the soccer field. In 1969 the vecinos formed a team of "foreigners" to compete with the local teams from the village. Any new foreigner is obligated to join this team, called *amauta* ("the learned ones"). Social stratification in Chuschi as dramatized on the soccer field is a stereotype of the basic opposition in the village of comunero-*qala*, or member versus nonmember.

3.5 The Rich Ones—*Apukuna*

At the top of the comunero class structure are those known as *apukuna*,
considered the most prestigious, wealthy, and powerful members among the
comuneros. An *apu* has the resources to fulfill several positions in the civil-
religious hierarchy. We can assume that any man who reaches the top of the
hierarchy and becomes alcalde menor of his barrio is *apu*—wealthy by comunero definition. He has held at least five civil-religious prestige positions,
garnering the necessary aid from his consanguineal, affinal, and spiritual kin
to successfully fulfill each of the one-year positions culminating in alcalde
(see chapter 4). In return, he has been obligated to reciprocate appropriately
to those who love him—his *kuyaq* (see chapter 7). However, holding a position in the prestige hierarchy is not a necessary condition for designation as
an *apu*. The one defining characteristic of an *apu* is wealth; he is said to
possess more land and animals than the average comunero. To focus more
sharply on the *apu* class, let us examine one *apu* family in detail. This family
is comprised of a man, his wife, and four legitimate children, of whom three
are married by both church and state. The eldest is a female residing in Lima
with her Chuschino husband and eight children. Their marriage was arranged
by both sets of parents when she was fifteen years old. Her prospective
husband returned to Chuschi to take his wife-to-be to Lima for a period of
trial marriage called *watanakuy*, "having a year together." With no period
of courtship prior to this, they lived together for eight months, after which
they returned to Chuschi to be married. Both families are considered *apu*,
and the marriage is therefore a propitious one.

The second-born is also a female who for several years resided in Lima.
She has four children by a married man who is not a Chuschino comunero.
Her parents are raising one of the children. However, she subsequently entered
into a common-law union with a Chuschino of comunero parents and had
two children by him. They have recently returned to Chuschi, married in
the church, and taken up residence in the village with his parents, awaiting
the house being built for them.

The third-born is a young male in his early twenties married to a fifteen-
year-old Chuschino girl, both residing in the house of his father. Her family
is not considered *apu*, and the marriage is therefore less than ideal. That he
has married beneath his social class stems from the fact that he bears a debili-
tating physical handicap, which in Chuschino eyes diminishes his productivity
and marriageability.

The youngest child is a young woman who at the time of field research
was single and residing with her eldest sister in Lima. She attended the local
primary school and worked part time as a traveling market saleswoman

handling produce and clothing. Her aspirations included finishing primary school and securing a job in a textile factory. Hoping she will marry a Chuschino and settle either in Chuschi or in the squatter settlement, 7 de Octubre, near her sister, her parents have actively tried to arrange marriages for her, but she has resisted. They fear she will marry a non-Chuschino and thereby diminish the possibility of consolidating land and animals with another *apu* family. Marriage with a Chuschino comunero is the strongest preference.

Another preference in marriage is for two families united by one union to exchange siblings (or first cousins) of the principal union. This may take the form of sister (or first cousin) exchange or cross-sex sibling or first cousin exchange. For this particular family, the marriage possibility has not presented itself to allow adherence to this preference. Furthermore, the younger Chuschinos state that this type of marriage is preferred by their elders and resisted by themselves; they want to marry whomever they wish within the traditional prohibition of not marrying anyone who shares one's paternal and/ or maternal last names. This prohibition eliminates all siblings, half-siblings, and first cousins, who are terminologically grouped under the sibling category of brother and sister. The nearest consanguineal relatives that are reckoned eligible are one's second cousins. The latter are termed *karu ayllu,* distant relatives, as opposed to *ayllu,* near and non-marriageable relatives. Marriage potentials from the point of view of the younger generation living in Lima are not as narrowly defined as tradition prescribes; they see themselves as potentially marrying "anyone they like." Only time will tell us whether they will in fact realize their newly acquired preference for nonadherence to traditional marriage alliances.

The wealth of this *apu* family consists of fifteen fields, three houses, and many animals—llamas, alpacas, sheep, and cattle, pastured on communal land. The paternal head of the family inherited twelve fields and the three houses from his father; the three remaining fields belong to his wife, who inherited them from her mother. She does not own a house in the village. However, her eldest daughter took possession in her mother's name of a small plot during the invasion of 7 de Octubre in Lima, where a small, partially constructed house is being occupied by a relative who pays the women fifty *soles* a month rent. This house and the three fields owned by this woman will be inherited by the second-born and last-born, both daughters.

The *apu* man has prepared his will, but none of his offspring has taken possession of his or her inheritance. He is dividing his fields between his eldest child (a married daughter) and his only son. The son is to receive two houses, and the eldest daughter the third house, which has the potential for a small store.

In the above inheritance, we see the operation of two of the principal inheritance preferences of comuneros: (1) a son should receive the property of his father and a daughter that of her mother; and (2) the eldest child should receive special consideration regardless of sex. The first is the primary preference voiced by everyone as an ideal that should be adhered to if possible. The second is of lesser importance. There exists a third consideration concerning inheritance: the child who remains the longest at his or her parents' side, is a hard worker, and shows obedience and love will be especially rewarded. Often this takes the form of receiving the house the parents are residing in and perhaps more animals and land than the other siblings.

The fields of this *apu* family are distributed in the three major productive zones: six are in the high puna where root crops, *quinua*, and some barley are grown; seven are within the corn-producing *qichwa* area around the village; and two are in the *mayopatan* near the Pampas River, where squash, corn, and cactus fruits flourish. It is considered essential to maintain fields in all three zones and thereby produce a wide range of cultigens. Corn is the prestige crop; potatoes and other root crops are of lower status. Corn is necessary for the manufacture of chicha, the essential drink for all rituals. Also, corn is associated with fertility and is used symbolically in rituals to denote fecundity. The *apu* family observed the ritual first planting with one compadre and one comadre, who subsequently loaned them a pair of oxen to plow the larger fields requiring two pairs. At one planting ten people worked; the *apu* man, his wife, their son and his wife, her parents, a compadre and comadre, a maternal uncle of the *apu* man, and the young man's wife's sister. The women placed the seed as the men plowed; none of the women worked with their husbands, but rather with other men; the *apu* family provided a midday meal, chicha and coca, for four coca breaks during the day. They will owe each of the participants repayment in labor; thus operates private, kin-based reciprocity.

The family that cannot call upon this network of kin for aid is poor or orphaned, *wakcha*. Likewise, the family is poor that only has access to communal puna lands for root crops, but of meaner status is the family that cannot mobilize reciprocal aid—its members are truly orphaned, not just materially poor.

3.6 The Poor Ones—*Wakchakuna*

The term *wakcha* literally means poor or orphaned, but generally a social definition is intended that refers to a person who is economically poor and does not have an adequate network of kin and compadres to supply the necessary reciprocal aid to function in the comunero society. The latter is

far more important than economic poverty. An example of a *wakcha* family
will illustrate why its members often speak of themselves as orphans, referring
to their lack of potential aid.

This *wakcha* family is comprised of a man, his wife, two married daughters,
and a son. One of the daughters resides in the Lima squatter settlement, 7 de
Octubre, with her Chuschino husband. The other daughter is married to a
Quispillaqteño and lives in Ayacucho. The youngest child, a fifteen-year-old
boy, is the only offspring living at home with his parents, who bemoan the fact
that they have so few children (several have died). The siblings of both parents
are dead. However, they do have four compadres and comadres.

In 1969 the head of the family left for Lima in search of work, living with
his married daughter during the seven or eight months he remained. As
planting-time approached in mid-September, the father had not returned and
the fifteen-year-old son and his mother prepared to plant the fields without
him. This family owns six corn-producing fields in the *qichwa* zone, and they
have usufruct rights to two fields of the puna communal land. The latter two
are usually planted in barley, wheat, and potatoes and other root crops, such
as *mashwa, ullucos,* and *ocas.* All of the fields belong to the man; his wife
owns a few animals but no land.

In his father's absence, the boy tried to organize the traditional first
planting celebration whereby one's most esteemed compadres plant the first
seed, which is believed to insure a good harvest. The boy approached his
godparents, who said they preferred to wait for his father's return. The boy's
mother, landless and with few relatives, is not valued as a comadre. She
could do nothing to persuade her compadres to come to her aid. She also
has one social failing that is most frowned upon: she drinks alone. While
reciprocal obligatory drinking is an essential part of all rituals and fiestas,
drinking alone is interpreted as evidence of supernatural possession or inti-
macy with the powerful mountain deity, the Wamani. Her antisocial
behavior means that she is not a reliable comadre. Her compadres therefore
try to avoid mutual obligations and keep their exchange of labor, ritual
duties, and favors to a minimum. If the woman possessed a large network
of consanguineal, affinal, and spiritual kin with whom active reciprocal
relationships had been maintained, she could have planted the fields without
difficulty, but she was being ostracized, and her husband's absence accen-
tuated their problems. Perhaps he could have persuaded his compadres to
come to his aid. However, his wife could not convince anyone to lend her
oxen to plow the fields nor to participate in the first planting. Furthermore,
no one answered her call for a communal work day to be repaid in kind, a
negative constrast to the events accompanying the first planting of the *apu*
family. The situation was strikingly different for the *wakcha* family. As

planting time grew short and the rains began in earnest, the fifteen-year-old boy took matters in his own hands—he came to me, the foreigner whom he had helped, and asked for a loan of thirty *soles* (ten for a laborer for one day and twenty for two oxen for one day). He received the loan in return for ethnographic help during a ritual.

The boy has a special interest in his father's lands: in accordance with the preferred mode of inheritance he stands to inherit all six of the titled fields and the use of the two in the puna. His father has not made his will, and when he does he has the option of either giving to his daughters or following the indigenous pattern of parallel inheritance. The son feels that he stands a good chance of inheriting all the land and at least one of the two of his father's houses because he has stayed at his father's side longer than his older, married, female siblings. This is often the case; Chuschinos take into consideration the devotion and service of their children. One informant told me that the son or daughter who "shows his parents more love by residing in their house and working at their side longest stands a good chance of receiving at least the house in which they reside." There is no rule that states that a house must go to either the youngest or the eldest, but chances are that the youngest will receive the house in which he has resided. The poverty of this family is not due solely to the scarcity of their agricultural plots, which is within the average range of six to eight yugadas (one and one-half hectares); the major contributory factor is their extreme inability to mobilize a network of mutual aid necessary for social survival in comunero society. However, they are one rung above the lowest subclass of the comunero social ladder, the *tiyapakuq*.

3.7 Those Who Roost on Land Belonging to Others—*Tiyapakuq*

The root of this substantive is the verb *tiyay,* to sit down or to roost. The construction communicates the idea that the person benefits himself and another party as well. The term refers to landless persons who have access only to communal land or to those who labor for others. The *apu* family described above employs a *tiyapakuq* couple as herders. They are not related consanguineally, affinally, or spiritually to the *apu* family, and there are no reciprocal obligations that bind them together. They receive one sheep a year for their service. The *apu* family also provides enough subsistence products for the couple and their small children. The *tiyapakuq* person also has the right to pasture his own animals with the *apu*'s herds.

The comuneros most likely to find themselves on this bottom rung of the social ladder are those who have been deprived of their inheritance. This can happen if one sibling gains the good will and favor of his or her parents to the exclusion of one or all of the other siblings.

Parents have a great deal of latitude in setting the inheritance of their children. The decision as to *when* their children can claim possession of their designated inheritance is entirely up to the good will of the parents, who have the duty to provide land, animals, and if possible a house for their children. Indigenous parallel inheritance preference is modified by a secondary predilection for the eldest, plus a third consideration already mentioned, namely, that the child who resides the longest with his or her parents and serves them faithfully is likely to be favored. This child runs the risk of receiving little if he or she does not persuade the parents to make their will in his or her favor. Also, the youngest child is affected by another residence preference, than no more than two married sons reside in their father's house at any given time.

Upon marriage, it is customary for a young man to bring his wife to the house of his father until their parents decide to activate their inheritance. The inheritance ideal expressed by comuneros is for men to inherit from their fathers and women from their mothers. They say it is very important to keep possessions within a group sharing a patriname. For patrilineages, this is insured through time by restricting inheritance to male descendants. Women carry the patriname of their fathers in modern Chuschi, but the earliest marriage records in the church archive (beginning with 1660) indicate that a certain percentage of siblings carried the names of their parents of the same sex, that is, boys had the surname of their father and girls of their mother. In other words, the passing of names in 1660 mirrors the stated parallel inheritance preference of modern Chuschi.

In 1969 the notary public in Cangallo, the province capital, informed me that Chuschi and three other villages—Quispillaqta, Ochuri, and Chacoya—persisted in this peculiar parallel inheritance pattern. He stated that he has battled since his arrival in 1921 to teach them that the Peruvian constitutional law requires that all siblings inherit equally. He refused to record wills that did not conform to the law. The notary was especially dismayed by the possibility that women could inherit greater estates from their mothers than their male siblings if the woman was richer than her husband. This can happen and has happened. Villagers simply register a will that complies with the law, return to the village, and institute the traditional inheritance, sealing the agreement with a solemn oath and mutual drinking.

If a female has inherited a considerable amount from her uterine ancestors and if she marries someone of lesser wealth than herself, residence at marriage will be with her parents rather than with her husband's. I know of one case of a widowed woman and her three married daughters living within one household compound. It is the usual practice for no more than two married sons or daughters to reside in the house of their father (or mother) at any given time. Here, a *minka* (reciprocal labor) was called to build the eldest daughter a house, and in this case it was built adjacent to the mother's house, thereby reinforcing the dominant position of the matriline.

One usually enters marriage knowing what one and one's spouse will bring to the marriage in the way of wealth in land, animals, and a house. These details are usually settled by the parents of both parties when the parents of the boy, accompanied by a spokesman bearing alcohol, cigarettes, and coca, go to the house of the prospective bride to ask for her hand in marriage. If, after much drinking, the parents of the girl agree to the marriage, then promises of inheritance for each are arranged by both sets of parents. These promises are very rarely realized at the time of the wedding. Rather, several years of residence in the boy's father's house is required, during which time the girl serves her mother-in-law by performing household duties and the young man works at the side of his father. Setting up an independent household depends on several factors: (1) the wealth of the parents, (2) their need for help, and (3) the marriage and co-residence of other siblings. As stated earlier, it is preferred that no more than two married siblings reside with their parents at any given time, and, as offspring marry, available land and animals diminish as each one agitates for his or her share during the first years of marriage. There is considerable maneuvering among siblings, and a person in disfavor with his or her parents may end up "roosting on someone else's land"—a *tiyapakuq.*

3.8   The Statuses of Illegitimate Children

Thus far we have considered the rights and duties of legitimate offspring from legal unions. The offspring who must carefully plan his or her strategies is the *usupa,* or child born to a couple before they marry. Such a child usually carries the paternal surname of the father but does not inherit from him. Any *usupa* can inherit from the mother. It is not uncommon for a *usupa* child to be raised in the house of the maternal grandparents. Also, if the illegitimate child displays devotion and obedience toward the grandparents, he or she may inherit from them. This social category probably has the least promising economic alternatives of all, but nevertheless there is little or no social stigma in being *usupa.* If grandparents wish to do so, they can refer to their adopted child as *uywasan,* literally the child they have raised.

Another type of illegitimate child fares much better with regard to inheritance. If a married man or woman has a child by someone not his or her spouse, that child is referred to as an *hijo político,* or in Quechua simply as a child, *churin* (man's child) or *wawan* (woman's child). Such a child has inheritance rights but is expected to receive less than legitimate siblings.

It is interesting to note that the comuneros' major concern seems to be not so much with legitimacy as with children before marriage (*usupa*) as opposed to children after marriage. This correlates with the comuneros' attitude that one becomes an adult and full participant in communal affairs only after marriage. Therefore, a child born to unmarried persons is considered the issue of socially immature non-participants. The *usupa* child is difficult to categorize because the parents are still considered children. Such a child may carry the father's name, but is incorporated into the mother's agnatic household and inherits from the mother or her parents and not from the father or his parents.

4. The Political Structure of Chuschi

4.1 Dual Systems of Authority

We have seen that dual structures and concentric dualism are basic to the organization of comuneros' conceptualization of physical (2.8) and social (3.1) space. Dual opposition is likewise central to the political systems of the village. The basic opposition follows the comunero-*qala* distinction: a traditional prestige hierarchy characterizes comunero status and membership, while nomination to bureaucratic governmental office has been restricted to Spanish-speaking *qalas*.

After a description of the bureaucratic governmental organization, we will then concentrate on the prestige hierarchy of the comuneros. Two periods of fieldwork, 1967 and 1969-1970, provided two distinct experiences that resulted in two different analyses. Contrasting the two by giving the findings that resulted from both will provide a better understanding of the 1970 abolition of the prestige system that had been the apex of the indigenous hierarchy in 1967.

4.2 The Bureaucratic Authorities in 1967

Before the enactment of the 1969 Agrarian Reform Law, the village of Chuschi possessed a bureaucratic government characteristic of legally recognized indigenous communities throughout Peru. The village is also the seat of the government for the district. Both systems will be discussed. For the village, the highest bureaucratic official is the municipal mayor. Prior to the 1968 military takeover, the mayor was elected by all village residents, both males and females. Comuneros maintain that a person cannot vote unless he or she is married. Marital status, not age, determines the local electorate, which correlates with the concepts of illegitimacy and legitimacy discussed in

3.8. The military government suspended all elections in 1968, and thereafter all bureaucratic positions were to be appointed. However, in 1969 I witnessed the election of one of the most important political bodies in Chuschi, the junta comunal.

4.2.1   The Junta Comunal

The junta comunal constituted perhaps the most important body in the village bureaucracy; they were the guardians of the village communal lands. The highest position, that of trustee or personero, the legal representative of the village in all land disputes, was one of extreme responsibility, consuming a great deal of time and energy because of the frequency and seriousness of boundary disputes. A personero was assisted by a six-man committee, elected like him for four-year terms. For the election I observed in 1969 the list of candidates had been compiled by the migrant organization in Lima, the Progressive Society of Santa Rosa of Lima, an organization whose stated purpose is to further and protect the well-being of the village. Members take it upon themselves to audit the accounts of the village, compile lists of candidates and supervise elections, raise funds, and represent the village legally. This last function was the original motivation for forming the society, which gathered the necessary documentation and petitioned for legal comunidad status for Chuschi in 1941.

4.2.2   The District Authorities

District authorities, consisting of a governor and a lieutenant governor, do not have the power of those discussed above; rather, they insure communications between the district and its members and the subprefect in the province capital, Cangallo. They are primarily responsible for law and order in the district, taking orders directly from the subprefect. Until 1970 the governor had as subordinates one of the prestige systems, the varayoq mayores, also called the hatun varayoq. However, the village voted to abolish the mayores, leaving a dual system for each barrio and a separate organization representing the puna.

4.3   The Indigenous Prestige Hierarchy in 1967

During seven months of 1967 almost the entire period of field investigations in Chuschi was dedicated to the indigenous prestige hierarchy. I encountered three interrelated systems encompassing the essential social mechanisms of reciprocity and expressing the structural principles of the comuneros' conceptualizations of space and ecology. The prestige hierarchy functions to reinforce these concepts and to maintain the closed corporate status of the village. Social mechanisms include the complex of reciprocal aid that is necessary for the completion of a position in the hierarchy. Another mechanism embodied in the prestige system is the concept of gaining prestige through service to the community. Such service is costly in material wealth and demands that one control wealth as well as command a large network of kin. In other words, men who successfully climb the ladder of hierarchically arranged positions and retire from public service are *apu,* or wealthy. When one retires from the prestige hierarchy, one acquires the prestigious status of *señor cesante,* literally, retired lord.

In 1967, ascension to the status of *señor cesante* required the completion of at least fifteen hierarchically arranged positions representing fifteen years of civil-religious service to the village. Such a man was indisputably *apu,* rich in wealth, kinsmen, and prestige. In chapter 7 we will see that the successful completion of the higher positions in the hierarchy requires the expenditure of at least three years of surplus.

Each position in the hierarchy is signified by a staff of office called a *vara.* The higher the position in the hierarchy, the more elaborate the decoration and adornment of the staffs. The highest positions are delineated by a staff made of a black, dense tropical forest wood, *chonta,* and adorned with silver. These staffs command respect, and it is common to see one of them at a ritual celebration displayed for all to see. One informant told me that a relative had loaned him the staff during the celebration of a saint's day that he had sponsored. He said, "See that staff. When that staff is in my house, I command and everyone has to obey." A senior member of the prestige hierarchy complained that "everyone used to tremble at the sight of the staff, but no more. We have lost our authority and no one pays us proper respect as they should." The staff is the traditional symbol of authority, and a member of the hierarchy must carry it at all times. While he sleeps, the staff is propped vertically against the wall—the staff of authority must never be placed horizontally on the ground. Another staff is carried on ritual occasions; it is a six-foot tree branch painted with red and green spirals. In 1967 these staffs were carried by members of the two systems associated with the village, the *hatun* (great) and the *taksa* (lesser), but not by the *sallqa* herders of the third structure.

Within each prestige organization a strict ranking order was observed. The ultimate authority, the alcalde, commanded those below him; he in turn was subordinate to the specific bureaucratic official above him. Section 4.3.1 presents a diagrammatic sketch of the bureaucratic and prestige structures in hierarchical relation to one another. The three *hatun* and *taksa* alcaldes were each served by two subordinates called regidores (a Spanish term meaning aldermen), who were referred to as the "arms" of the alcaldes. Regidores in turn commanded those on the bottom of the hierarchy, the alguaciles. The dual structures that represented the moieties were mirror images of one another, and the lowest position, the alguacil, was the point of entry into the prestige hierarchy for young single boys. In 1967 I found that the competing demands of school attendance on two boys named as alguaciles resulted in their fathers' performing their duties, and this custom had been occurring for several years. Moreover, infants had been named, a solution deemed most satisfactory: boys could attend school and progress up the hierarchy at the same time if their fathers performed their duties. Then when they married they would be eligible for the next position in the hierarchy, *hatun* alguacil. The obligatory progression in the hierarchy in 1967 is shown in figure 1.

FIGURE 1
OBLIGATORY PROGRESSION IN THE PRESTIGE
HIERARCHY (1967)

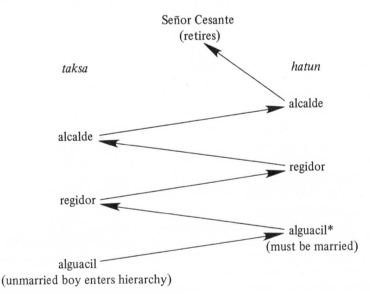

taksa

hatun

Señor Cesante
(retires)

alcalde

alcalde

regidor

regidor

alguacil*
(must be married)

alguacil
(unmarried boy enters hierarchy)

*Owners of animals entered the organization of herders, the *sallqa varayoqkuna* (4.3.4), after holding the position of *hatun* alguacil.

In 1967 there were 27 men serving in the *hatun* and *taksa* organizations of the village, and the interrelated structures formed a pyramid (see figure 2).

FIGURE 2
THE CIVIL-RELIGIOUS HIERARCHY (1967)

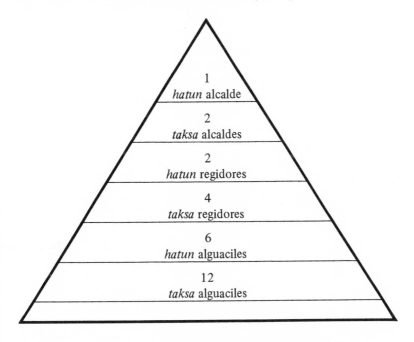

In addition to the six levels of the pyramid, the village prestige hierarchy was articulated with the herding organization under the priest and the complex of celebrations dedicated to the fourteen saints revered in the village. A man could not become *hatun* alcalde without having sponsored at least one saint's day celebration, a year-long religious obligation involving planting and harvesting the saint's corn field and publicly observing the saint's day by paying for the mass and decorations and preparing corn beer for all the devotees. A man wishing to become *hatun* alcalde also must have served in the herding organization, the *sallqa* structure.

Within each of the structures, a ranked hierarchy prevails, with deference behavior displayed by subordinates. For example, the *hatun* and *taksa* members meet with their respective alcaldes, who provide cane alcohol and coca for each subordinate. The regidores buy kerosene for the lamps of the alguaciles, who in turn show extreme deference; they carry their superiors' hats and staffs and are generally responsible for their comfort. Seating and ritual drinking order always reflect ranking order, as does the order of entering and exiting a room as well as in religious processions. However, the entire hierarchy is subject to bureaucratic domination.

4.3.1   The Indigenous and Bureaucratic Structures in 1967

Figure 3 depicts the relationships between the bureaucratic authorities and the subordinated traditional prestige hierarchy. The district governor is responsible directly to the bureaucratic authorities in the province capital, Cangallo, and to the prefect in Ayacucho. His job is to maintain order in the entire district and carry out mandates from his superiors. He has at his disposal a portion of the prestige hierarchies of the communities in the district. Until 1970, the *hatun* hierarchy served the governor and the church.

FIGURE 3
INDIGENOUS AND BUREAUCRATIC HIERARCHIES (1967)

DISTRICT	CHURCH	VILLAGE BUREAUCRACY		
Governor	Priest	Personero	Municipal Mayor	Judge
Lt. Governor	Ecónomo	Junta Comunal	Town Council	Assistant

HATUN	SALLQA	TAKSA	
Alcalde	Alcalde	Upper Barrio	Lower Barrio
Regidores	Ovejeros	Alcalde	Alcalde
Alguaciles	Vaqueros	Regidores	Regidores
	Pastores	Alguaciles	Alguaciles

THE SUBORDINATED PRESTIGE HIERARCHY

However, the priest and his comunero accounts-keeper (*ecónomo*) maintain the church's herds through the services of the traditional *sallqa* structure.

Likewise, the municipal mayor is the superior bureaucratic authority over the moiety *taksa* structures. His task is primarily concerned with village affairs. However, the municipal mayor in Chuschi maintains the demographic records for the district, and in terms of power the municipal mayor is superior to the district governor. He also handles the municipal budget allocated to the village by the department. He is in charge of all village improvements and of keeping order.

As of 1968 the holder of this important office was named by the department prefect rather than elected by the village.

The 1969 Agrarian Reform Law abolished the personero and his junta comunal, the autonomous, elected committee in charge of legally defending the communal property of Chuschi. In its place two elected offices with subordinate committees have been instituted—the president of administration and the president of vigilance. These committees have the responsibility of the administration of the recognized community. They deal directly with departmental and provincial bureaucrats as well as report to the migrant community in Lima.

In 1970 these two important offices were occupied by returned migrants (see chapter 8). Therefore, the migrants' political role in the community became legitimized.

The bureaucratic structures represent the presence of foreign domination in the midst of the comuneros' social space. These dominators are localized in the center of the village around the plaza, reminding the members of this closed corporate community that they are subject ultimately to *outside* authorities who are not members of the communal fabric of the village represented by the various structures of the prestige hierarchy. This hierarchy embodies the basic dichotomies of Chuschino social organization:

The Prestige Hierarchy as a Native Construct
of Their Social Organization

Basic Dichotomies	Prestige Hierarchy
Upper Barrio versus Lower Barrio	*Taksa* Organizations
Savage Puna versus Civilized Village	*Sallqa* versus *Taksa* and *Hatun*
Herding versus Agriculture	*Sallqa* versus *Taksa*
Church and State versus Community	*Hatun* versus *Taksa* and *Sallqa*

These basic dichotomies are native constructs of the fundamental opposing forces in Chuschino social and economic organization. These conflicts are dramatized, often comically, in important rituals (see chapter 6).

We will now turn to a description of the organization and duties of each prestige structure as found in 1967, beginning with the apex of the system, the *hatun varayoqkuna.*

4.3.2 *The* Hatun Varayoqkuna

The apex of the hierarchy was dedicated to the church and the center of the village. The members were called *hatun varayoqkuna,* which signifies "those who own the large (high or great) staff." This structure was also known in Spanish as the *envarados mayores,* which signifies the same. In 1967 there were nine members of this organization subordinate to the district governor, who utilized them as messengers to communicate with the provincial and departmental capitals. This traditional role was diminished by the completion of the road and the telegraph lines. The other major role of the *hatun* hierarchy was to publicly observe Easter, Lent, and Christmas and to attend all other religious holidays celebrated in the village. They were required to attend mass and to go in procession, with their high staffs of office, in rank order.

Aside from the ritual duties, the members of the *hatun* hierarchy were required to meet three times a week with their alcalde in his house to discuss and plan their activities. Their most important civil duty was to patrol the village and keep the peace. They had the power of arrest and could bring offenders before the village judge. Offenses included family quarrels, sexual breaches such as incestuous acts, and drunkenness. The provincial government considered these authorities necessary for village law and order, and the provincial prefect drew up the list of new *hatun* members to be installed by the village priest on the first of January every year. Members of this particular system in the hierarchy had to be married, and they could reside in either of the village moieties. In order to qualify for eligibility in the *hatun* structure, a man had to have completed at least one year as a *taksa* (small or lesser) alguacil in service to his barrio.

4.3.3 *The* Taksa Varayoqkuna

Each barrio, upper and lower, had an independent prestige structure that was identical in organization and obligations. Membership in the moiety structures was determined by residence and comunero status. Members of each barrio organization met three times a week in the matrix chapel of the barrio. The alcaldes received orders from the municipal mayor and instructed their subordinates accordingly. Duties included: alternately cleaning the village plaza on Thursdays, the day before market; imposing fines for damages to crops caused by animals; and canvassing house by house when the municipal mayor called a communal work day, a *faena*. Every household was required to supply one male for one day's labor; failure to do so resulted in a fine of ten *soles* collected by the *taksa* regidores. It is interesting to note that communal labor was abolished in 1810 (Fuenzalida 1970: 71) but still functions throughout the Andes. Furthermore, communal labor has become an integral part of Lima squatter settlement development.

Ritual obligations included responsibility for the observation of the ritual cleaning of the dual systems of irrigation canals, the Yarqa Aspiy, which delineates the beginning of a new agricultural cycle in September, and Santa Cruz, the harvest ritual in May. The latter was also the occasion of the installation of *taksa* members for a year of service. (See plate 7.)

4.3.4 The Sallqa Varayoqkuna

The term *sallqa* has a double meaning in Quechua; it signifies the high puna and also means savage or uncivilized. People who live on the puna permanently and do not engage in agriculture in the *qichwa* zone are called *sallqaruna,* savage people. During carnival, the members of the *sallqa* prestige hierarchy descend upon the village on horseback and inflict on the civilized village such savage and barbarous acts as insulting the Virgin Mary, brandishing their whips at anyone crossing their paths, and feigning sexual acts. Everyone is a possible target for their sexual jokes. As mentioned in 2.8, the *sallqa* is the savage part of the world where uncivilized acts such as forbidden sexual activity occur. Villagers believe that incestuous acts occur in the *sallqa,* and people engaging in such acts are condemned to roam the streets of the village at night in animal form with bells around their necks. If such an animal is touched, it will immediately resume human form and plead with its captor to keep its secret. The *taksa varayoq* are charged with patrolling the village streets. If someone reports incestuous activities in the puna, the village prestige authorities must capture the offenders, who are then tied up in the village plaza for all to see. Such individuals must thereafter leave the village.

In 1967 the *sallqa* hierarchy consisted of the alcalde subordinate to the village priest; his accountant, the *ecónomo,* two *ovejeros* (sheep herders), two *vaqueros* (cattle herders), and numerous subordinate herders. All of the members had to live in the puna on the communal herding land and care for the church's 250 head of cattle and 1,500 head of sheep. In order to fulfill their obligations, the *sallqa* members depend on their relatives and compadres to tend their agricultural plots. The alcalde assumes his duties in January, when the *hatun* authorities are installed. The remaining members assume their duties in August or September, when the herds are branded or marked and the Wamanis

Plate 7. The *Varayoqkuna*. An alcalde drinking with his regidores during the ritual cleaning of the irrigation canals.

are paid their offerings during the ritual called the Herranza.

The *sallqa* authorities honor Mama Limpiay (Saint Olimpia) on the eighth day of December, the day of the Immaculate Conception. The other major ritual observed by the *sallqa* is Corpus Christi in June when the herds and the two small female saints, Mama Limpiay and Mama Rosa, who are guardians of the herds, are brought into the village until the Herranza, the branding and marking of the herds in August when the Wamanis are placated with ritual payments. Mama Rosa is honored on August 30.

4.4 Historical Antecedents

In an effort to account for the events of 1970 that resulted in the abolition of the apex of the prestige hierarchy, the *hatun* structure, I interviewed aged men and women and discovered that the prestige hierarchy had undergone a continuous process of reduction. According to various informants, several positions in the hierarchy have disappeared. Among these was an organization called *qichwa varayoqkuna,* or in Spanish *campo envarados,* comprised of an alcalde and two young unmarried boys as his subordinates. Their principal duties were to guard the agricultural zone, the *qichwa.* In order to become a member of the *hatun* structure, a boy was required to complete three lesser positions in the hierarchy as well as a minor obligation called *estandarte del Señor de los Temblores,* standard-bearer of the Lord of Earthquakes. The last involved carrying a banner or standard during the celebration of the patron saint's feast day in July. In 1967 only one position in the hierarchy, *taksa* alguacil, was reserved for unmarried boys, and we have seen that due to school attendance eligible boys were scarce for this position and fathers assumed their sons' duties.

Aged informants insisted that another position has remained vacant for thirty years—inspector of water, responsible for the allocation of irrigation water. In the past the obligatory progression was to complete all of the *taksa* and *hatun* positions, inspector of water, and *sallqa* alcalde, and terminate with *qichwa* alcalde.

Also within the memory of informants was a hierarchical organization of women that mirrored the prestige hierarchy of the men. Their major obligation was to observe the fiesta of Santa Rosa of Lima on August 30. At least five positions were included in the female prestige system, and it is noteworthy that even though this structure has disappeared, Santa Rosa is the patron saint of the migrants in Lima and girls are named as co-sponsors of the celebration.

The best description of all aspects of life in the sixteenth century for Ayacucho and the Pampas River comes to us from a thousand-page letter written to the King of Spain by Don Felipe Guamán Poma de Ayala, an Indian of noble birth. Guamán Poma (1936: 354) describes the *Coya Raymi,* the great feast of the moon, the wife of the sun, as the principal feast observed by women in September, when women "beat their drums and wailed to the moon to provide water." When I read this document to female informants, they claimed that thirty years ago this same ritual was observed during August and culminated with the feast of Santa Rosa, *"La Coya,"* wife of the sun.

Guamán Poma also describes village authorities (1936: 794-802) analogous to those in the structures of Chuschi. He mentions an alcalde mayor (*hatun* alcalde), alcalde campo (*qichwa* alcalde), and alcaldes ordinarios, who were responsible for law and order in the village. The alcalde campo was responsible for the safety of the crops, and the alcalde mayor was the assistant and messenger of the cacique. He also mentiones subordinate regidores and alguaciles.

It is worth observing that the authorities described by Guamán Poma de Ayala and the modern authorities of Chuschi differ greatly from those mentioned in the ordinances passed by Viceroy Toledo in 1575 to institute village governments. Toledo's ordinances declared that on the first of January the retiring authorities would elect two alcaldes from Indians of common birth (Toledo, Francisco de: 1867) to assume duties for two years. Also, a retiring authority could be reelected for another term in the same office (ibid.). Today, it is inconceivable that a man succeed himself in the same office. Reelection would be counter to the principle of obligatory hierarchical progression up a ladder of prestige-giving positions. Another discrepancy in Toledo's 1575 decree and modern practice is in the admonishment against drinking. Toledo instituted punishment and loss of office for all Indian authorities who were found inebriated (ibid.). Today, ritual drinking and drunkenness during fiestas are obligatory for all members of the prestige hierarchy. It appears that the indigenous prestige hierarchy began a process of adaptation and reinterpretation shortly after the institution of foreign laws, superficially acquiescing to each new regime while maintaining traditional patterns in as unaltered a form as was deemed prudent. Guamán Poma probably wrote his famous letter to the king thirty to fifty years after Toledo's ordinances were passed. The adapted form of indigenous authority has survived in spite of a law passed in 1938 abolishing all traditional authorities in Peru (Law No. 605, in Tarazona: 1946). The traditional authority structure in Chuschi was further reduced and readapted in 1970.

4.5   The Events of 1970

On January 1, 1970, the usual date of the installation of new members into the *hatun* structure, the comuneros of Chuschi held a public meeting, voting instead to abolish the *hatun* structure altogether. Furthermore, public

observation of Lent, Christmas, and Easter was no longer to be the responsibility of the traditional authorities. Christmas and Easter have increasingly
come under the domination of the schools. Continued pressure from the
provincial subprefect culminated in an order on July 26, 1970, for those named
as *hatun* authorities to either assume their duties or be jailed. Solidarity prevailed and the entire group of nine were jailed for two days; after a shouting,
fist-waving free-for-all, a compromise of sorts was reached. The bureaucratic
officials claimed that the *hatun* authorities were necessary for law and order to
be maintained. The comuneros claimed that the *hatun* positions were no
longer necessary and cost too much, and that the prestige and respect previously
accorded the *hatun* authorities had all but disappeared. Also, they complained
that it was the wrong time of year to assume office. A sixty-four-year-old
informant said:

> I think we should have them [traditional authorities] without expenditures.
> The harvests are less now, and besides we don't need the *hatunkuna* any
> more. We used to take papers to Cangallo and Ayacucho by foot, and we
> used to patrol with the *guardias* [policemen]. The alguaciles used to serve
> the governor of the district and another served the priest. Even our wives
> used to have to work for *qalas* [mestizos], tending their children and
> cooking. Today everything is different. Now even the priest tells the
> school children that they will have a different life. It is good to have only
> the *taksa varayoqkuna*. They can guard the fields and communicate with
> the comuneros. Now each barrio has an alcalde and his *varas*. That is
> enough.

The resident comuneros refused to accept the staffs of authority. Village
guardias were instituted as a compromise, and four younger men accepted
this duty. They will not carry a staff nor participate in costly fiestas; rather,
they will wear arm bands designating their status as village policemen under
the district governor, and fulfill their commitment to maintain law and order.

After these events, I asked comuneros how one would become a respected
retired elder, *señor cesante,* and speculations included having to occupy such
bureaucratic positions as governor of the district, municipal mayor, or judge,
all requiring facility in spoken and written Spanish. Perhaps as the traditional
structures undergo further pressure, the all-important acquisition of prestige
will be shifted to the bureaucratic system. In chapter 8 we will see that an
urban prestige structure developed in Lima. Other important changes in the
dual authority structures of Chuschi occurred in 1970. The Agrarian Reform
Law abolished the personero and his junta comunal and initiated two administrative bodies—a vigilance council and an administrative council. Due to

the stipulation of the law, migrants have returned and were elected to the above councils in 1971 (see 4.2.2). The remaining barrio *taksa* structures and the *sallqa* organization will probably undergo further pressure. Traditional hierarchies have been reduced to the barest expression of the social and ecological concepts discussed in chapters 2 and 3.

Pressures were apparent in 1967 from the results of a census of twenty-seven retiring members of the prestige hierarchy as compared with seven bureaucratic officials. Three criteria provided a basis for *not* serving in the traditional prestige structures: (1) having worked or lived in an urban center such as Lima or Ayacucho, (2) having attended school beyond the third grade, or (3) having served in the army. All of the above can provide literacy in Spanish and thereby eligibility for a bureaucratic office. All of the bureaucratic officials had completed primary school, and none had progressed beyond the two lowest *varayoq* positions. In contrast, none of the twenty-seven traditional authorities had gone beyond the third grade, none had been in the army, and only two had worked outside of the village. The dichotomy of comunero-*qala* discussed in 3.1 was perfectly mirrored in the bureaucratic and traditional authority structures of the village. In 1970 I observed only one of a series of reductions of the traditional structure and the integration and legitimization of migrants into the political and social fabric of the village. Traditional structures will undergo further reduction and adaptation, probably with the social mechanism of prestige through service and generosity readapted to new social demands. The impact of an urban ideology on a closed corporate village is discussed in 8.6. Migrants are agitating for a takeover of the church's land and animals in order to establish a cooperative in the name of the village. Though the manner in which the cooperative is established will affect the prestige structure, given the history of continual reduction, it appears that the most sensitive structure at this point is the *sallqa* one. The *sallqa varayoqkuna* could be integrated into the structure of a cooperative, or their functions could be defined as not corresponding to an economic production unit. Investigation of the prestige hierarchy from 1967 to 1970 has shown that the hierarchy itself is flexible, but the principle of hierarchical progression is central to the structure. It is very possible that the indigenous prestige structure will one day incorporate bureaucratic positions at the apex. The bureaucratization of the system has already begun with the institution of village *guardias* in place of *hatun* alguaciles. Also, increasing demands of school attendance will probably reduce the number of *taksa* alguaciles from the present six for each barrio.

The ease with which the *hatun* structure was abolished is a reaction to the foreign domination of the church and the district bureaucracy, whereas the retention of the *taksa* moiety and the *sallqa* structures reaffirms the basic dichotomies of:

savage (*sallqa*)	-	civilized (*taksa*)
herding	-	agriculture
outside (savage)	-	inside (civilized)
nonmember (*qala*)	-	member (comunero)

Whatever adaptations are made in the prestige hierarchy, these oppositions will be found in some form. The reduction of the prestige hierarchy in 1970 appears to be an effort on the part of comuneros to preserve their closed corporate identity in the face of increasing pressure. Through the years, they have abandoned the nonessential elements and are faced with preserving and defining that which expresses the basic concepts governing their interpretations of their social and natural environment. The preservation of the basic dichotomies set forth above is the comuneros' major means of defending their way of life. Another line of defense, perhaps the strongest, is the structure of kinship and marriage.

5. The Structures of Kinship and Marriage

5.1 Terms of Address

Chuschino terms of address reflect the organizational principles of generation, sex, relative age, and genealogical distance. These same principles will reappear when we discuss the structure of the kindred's bipartition of near *(ayllu)* and distant *(karu ayllu)* relatives. The behavioral aspects of these principles will become clear in chapter 6, a discussion of three indigenous rituals, and chapter 7, an explication of the operations of reciprocal exchanges. In ritual and reciprocal exchanges, the most important categories are generation mates, both consanguines, or *ayllu*, and affines, called *awra*. Generation mates of the same sex, siblings, and children of parents' siblings—or first cousins— share reciprocal terms; *wawqey*, male to male, and *ñañay*, female to female. Cross-sex generation mates are differentiated: *paniy* refers to "sister," male speaking, and *turiy* to "brother," female speaking. In the marriage ceremony (5.6), the exchanging units are clearly brothers and sisters, and the preferred marriage alliance is to exchange generation mates of a couple, thereby strengthening the affinal ties between two kindreds.

Differentiation by sex is seen in parent and child terminology as well. A woman addresses a boy child as *qari waway*, a girl child as *warmi waway*; a man addresses his children as *qari churiy* and *warmi churiy*. *Wawa*, the term used by women, is a general term for child or baby. Sex of speaker is not a criterion for parent terms; *taytay* and *mamay* are used by males and females alike. Parent terms are used generally to denote respect and deference. Document sources reveal that sex differentiation was applied to ascending generation terms during Inca times (Rowe 1963: 250, Zuidema 1977a) with bifurcate merging terminology for siblings and cousins of parents. Mishkin states that in Kauri, "fathers' brothers are called 'fathers' and mothers' sisters 'mothers' or often 'aunts'" (1963: 452). Likewise, Webster (1977) attests to bifurcate merging terminology in modern Q'ero with the Incaic terms for father's sister, *ipa*, and mother's brother, *kaka*. In Chuschi and the neighboring village, Huarcaya (Catacora 1968), the Spanish terms *tío* and *tía* are used for siblings and cousins of parents. Quechua morphological suffixes and pronunciation result in *tiuy* and *tiay*. These terms, as well as the terms for ego's generation mates, are extended collaterally to the categories of distant relatives such as *karu wawqey* or *karu tiuy*.

An examination of the adoption of Spanish terminology reveals only one set of terms uniformly Hispanicized, *tiuy* and *tiay* and the corresponding *sobrino* and *sobrina* terms for the child of one's generation mates, including the children of siblings and first cousins. This set of terms conforms to earlier Quechua referents and not to correct Spanish usage. All other Spanish terms are unilaterally applied, with alter responding with the traditional Quechua terms. For example, the appropriate address for grandparents and further ascending generations to the fourth generation is the Spanish *abuelo-abuela*. However, alter responds with the Quechua for grandchild, *willkay*.

The same unilaterality is evident in affinal terminology. A man who marries "my child" or "my sister" (including first cousin) is addressed *masay*. Likewise, the woman who marries "my son" or "my brother" is called *llumchuy*. However, both of these respond with the Spanish terms (see table 1). Another instance is in the case of an illegitimate child born to a legally married person; the child is called *hijo político*, and responds in Quechua *mamay-tatay*. *Hijo político* in Spanish usage generally refers to one's son-in-law, not to an illegitimate child. Note that with the exception of the last case, all other instances of Spanish-Quechua ego-alter combinations are instances where the Quechuan word is retained for the subordinate term and the superordinate term is Spanish.

An interesting insight into the ambiguities of the system is provided by an examination of the terminology accompanying joking relationships. A man and a woman jokingly call their spouse's *ayllu* generation mates "husband" and "wife." These are the only two categories of the two *ayllus* not automatically redefined as nonmarriageable during one of the ceremonies accompanying marriage, the *perdón*. If they are single, they do not participate in the ceremony and thereby remain marriageable. Both the sororate and the levirate are practiced. A godparent jokingly calls the godchild "little wife" or "little husband" if he or she is the first born. Like the *awra*, compadres are selected from the marriageable category and are ritually redefined as nonmarriageable.

Grandparents jokingly call their grandchildren "little husband" and "little wife." An informant clarified this relationship by explaining that "grandparents are both *ayllu* and *karu ayllu*." The grandparents' generation contains the crucial collateral link to marriageable *karu ayllu* persons. Descendants of

TABLE 1
AYLLU TERMS OF ADDRESS
A. Ego's Generation

Generation	Ego Addresses Alter	English Gloss	Spanish Gloss	Alter Responds
Ego's Generation Mates	*Wawqey* (male speaking)	Brother—my parents' male child	Hermano	*Wawqey* (male speaking)
		Cousin—my parents' siblings' male child	Primo	
	Paniy (male) speaking)	Sister—my parents' female child	Hermana	*Turiy*
		Cousin—my parents' siblings' female child	Prima	
	Turiy (female speaking)	Brother—my parents' male child	Hermano	*Paniy*
		Cousin—my parents' siblings' male child	Primo	
	Ñañay (female speaking)	Sister—my parents' female child	Hermana	*Ñañay*
		Cousin—my parents' siblings' female child	Prima	
	Mayorniy	Eldest sibling	Hermano, na Mayor	*Sullcay*
		or		
		Eldest cousin	Primo, ma Mayor	
	Sullcay	Younger sibling	Hermano, na Menor	*Mayorniy*
		or		
		Younger cousin	Primo, ma Menor	

TABLE 1
AYLLU TERMS OF ADDRESS
B. Ascending Generations

Generation	Ego Addresses Alter	English Gloss	Spanish Gloss	Alter Responds
First Ascending Generation	*Taytay*	Father—my male parent	Padre	*Churiy*
	Mamay	Mother—my female parent	Madre	*Waway*
	Tiuy	Uncle—my parents' *Wawqen* and *Turin*	Tío	Sobrino, na
	Tiay	Aunt—my parents' *Panin* and *Ñañan*	Tía	Sobrino, na
Second Ascending Generation	Abuelo or *Machuy**	Grandfather—my parents' male parent	Abuelo	*Willkay*
	Abuela	Grandmother—my parents' female parent	Abuela	*Willkay*
Third Ascending Generation	Abuelo, la	Great grandparents	Bisabuelo, la	*Willkay*
Fourth Ascending Generation	Abuelo, la	Great great grandparents	Tatarabuelo, la	*Willkay*

Machuy is still used by some in the village. It also denotes any old man.

TABLE 1
AYLLU TERMS OF ADDRESS
C. Descending Generations

Generation	Ego Addresses Alter	English Gloss	Spanish Gloss	Alter Responds
First Descending Generation	*Churiy* (male speaking)	My child		
	Qari Churiy (male speaking)	My male child	Hijo	*Taytay*
	Warmi Churiy (male speaking)	My female child	Hija	
	Waway (female speaking	My child		
	Qari Waway (female speaking	My male child	Hijo	*Mamay*
	Warmi Waway (female speaking	My female child	Hija	
	Piwiy (female or male speaking)	My first born		*Taytay* *Mamay*
	Paqway (female speaking)	My last born		*Mamay*
	Usupay	My child born to me before marriage		*Taytay* *Mamay*
	Hijo Político Hija Política*	My child born to me by someone not my legal spouse		*Taytay* *Mamay*
	Uywasay	The child that I have raised or my adopted child	Hijo, ja Adoptivo, va	*Taytay* *Mamay*
	Sobrino, na	The child of my *Wawqey, Paniy, Turiy* or *Ñañay*	Sobrino, na	*Tiuy* *Tiay*
Second Descending Generation	*Willkay*	Grandchild	Nieto, ta	Abuelo Abuela

*The general Spanish usage of hijo político is that of son-in-law.

TABLE 2
AFFINAL OR AWRA TERMS OF ADDRESS

Generation	Ego Addresses Alter	English Gloss	Spanish Gloss	Alter Responds
Ego's Generation	*Qusay*	Husband	Esposo	*Warmiy*
	Warmiy	Wife	Esposa	*Qusay*
	Masay	Brother-in-law—the man who has married my *Paniy* or my *Ñañay*	Cuñado	Cuñado, da
	Llumchuy	Sister-in-law—the woman who has married my *Wawqey* or my *Turiy*	Cuñada	Cuñado, da
First Descending Generation	*Masay*	Son-in-law—the man who has married my *Warmi Churiy, Warmiy Waway*, or Sobrina	Yerno	*Suedro, dra* *Tío, a*
	Llumchuy	Daughter-in-law—the woman who has married my *Qari Churiy, Qari Waway*, or Sobrino	Nuera	*Suedro, dra* *Tío, a*
Second Descending Generation	*Entenado, da*	My spouse's *Hijo Político*		Padrastro Madrastra
	Masay or *Willkay*	My *Willkay's* husband		Abuelo, la
	Llumchuy or *Willkay*	My *Willkay's* wife		Abuelo, la
First Ascending Generation	*Suedruy, dra* *Tiuy, a*	My *Warmiy's* or *Qusay's* father, mother, uncle, or aunt		*Masay* *Llumchuy*
	Awray	The *Ayllu* members of a person who has married into my *Ayllu* (see 5.4)		*Awray*
	Masamasiy *Warmimasiy*	Co-inlaws of same sex (*masi* refers to sharing equivalent relationship)		*Masamasiy* *Warmimasiy*

grandparents' siblings are the closest relatives (second cousins) deemed marriageable. Grandparents and their siblings call each other by the same term, and if a relationship is established with grandparents' siblings, the term *abuelo* or *abuela* is extended to them. Thereby lies the ambiguity; grandparents are both *ayllu* and *karu ayllu.*

5.2 The *Ayllu* and *Karu Ayllu:* The Kindred

Ayllu is a general Quechua term denoting relative. A complementary term is used to differentiate near relative *(ayllu)* and distant relative *(karu ayllu).* However, the word *ayllu* is a general term that can refer to many kinds of groups. One informant told me that *ayllu* refers to "any group with a head." He explained that an *ayllu* can be a barrio, the entire village, one's family, or even the district, the department, or the nation. Salvador Palomino (1971 and 1972) has expertly described the various forms of *ayllu* structures as barrios and/or moieties in the Pampas River region. Our concern here will be with *ayllu* as a kin term.

An examination of the kin terms *ayllu* and *karu ayllu* reveals the structure of a sibling-centered kindred, in which the organizing principle is genealogical distance at the second ascending generation. Ego's grandparents' siblings and their descendants are excluded from the *ayllu* and categorized as *karu ayllu. Ayllu* members are not marriageable; *karu ayllu* relatives are marriageable if they do not share one's paternal and maternal surnames. The Chuschino *ayllu* has the structure of a kindred of first cousin range composed of the two stocks of the descendants of two married couples—ego's two sets of grandparents. The most important link for reckoning genealogical distance is at the second ascending generation, whereby siblings of grandparents and their descendants are *karu ayllu.* Figure 4 illustrates the structure discussed above. Note that affines are not considered *ayllu* members.

The diagram in figure 4 has been constructed to demonstrate the relationship existing between naming practices and the principle of genealogical distance through collateral reckoning. Examination of the diagram reveals the operation of the primary marriage rule, which holds that ego cannot marry anyone who shares his paternal and maternal surnames—in our example designated A and G. Anyone else who is not a member of ego's *ayllu* is marriageable. The nearest marriageable relative to ego (a male) is a descendant of his grandparents' siblings, where there has occurred a sex differentiation in the relevant links in the ascending lines or in the collateral line. This is not true for females; a sex differentiation is not necessary in the female line simply because females change their surnames with every

AYLLU-KARU AYLLU

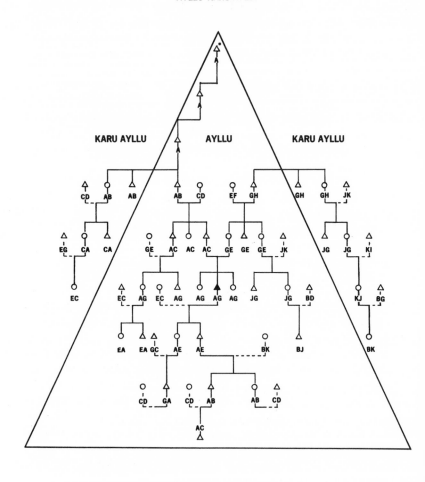

KARU AYLLU   AYLLU   KARU AYLLU

| | Marriage - both parties considered Ayllu
| | Descent
△ Male relative
○ Female relative
| Dotted line indicates nonrelative
Letters (ie.AB) first letter A is paternal name
second letter B is maternal name
▲ Ego

* Female informants usually cannot name Ayllu beyond the third ascending generation whereas males often can

FIGURE 4

generation. However, for every male and female, an unbroken line of male links to the *karu ayllu* member of the same generation deems that person nonmarriageable in that they share paternal surnames. In our example, ego has married his patrilateral second cousin, his father's father's sister's daughter's daughter (FFZDD). She is a member of his *karu ayllu* who does not share his surnames and is therefore the closest relative that is marriageable. This naming practice may be an adaptation to Spanish naming customs; parallel transmission of names is evidenced in the marriage records for 1661-1685 (see 5.3). While parallel transmission of names is not practiced today, the preferred inheritance of land, goods, and animals is parallel. People state that men should inherit from their fathers and women should inherit from their mothers.

A stated marriage preference is demonstrated in the diagram, namely, the practice of exchanging generation mates (siblings or first cousins) between two *ayllus* once a marriage tie has been established. This has been diagrammed on ego's generation and again on the first ascending generation. Further examination of the diagram reveals another feature of the personal kindred of Chuschi. Men have a longer lineal recognition of ascending generations than do women. Male informants could name ascending agnates to the fifth generation. Women could not enumerate ascending agnates or uterines past the third generation. Structurally, this results in different "shapes" of kindreds for males and females. Also, women's surnames are more often forgotten than men's. It would be interesting to determine whether women have more knowledge of their collateral relatives than do men. This would contrast logically with the lineal orientation of males. Such a lineal organization might tempt one to postulate the presence of unilineal descent groups. However, this organization is not a descent group, but an ego-centered—or more aptly a sibling-centered—kindred in which many rights and duties are vested in the male members and passed to male members. For example, it is believed desirable to keep possessions within the group sharing a paternal surname. For males, this produces long-standing inheritance of land, houses, animals, et cetera through male links. This is reinforced by residence, which is virilocal, and by inheritance of pasture lands, which is also generally through males. These rights are passed on from father to son. For women, the perspective is much different; ideally, a woman inherits land, animals, and possessions from her mother. She carries the paternal name of her father, but her children will have a different surname.

Uterine kin change surnames every other generation. She resides in the paternal house of her husband for a period of years before independent residence is established, and her animals are pastured with those of her husband. The bilateral structure of the kindred corresponds to the groups involved in inheritance practices. Fox (1967: 168) stresses the fact that "the kindred is not really a *group* in the sociological sense." We must examine the various groups that function and discover the organizational principles operating for each group. We have discussed the principles functioning within the domain of inheritance above and in 3.5 through 3.8. There are many rights and obligations that are transferred through male links, but unilineal descent is not an organizing principle of the various groups in which these rights and obligations operate. None of the groups described recognize a focal ancestor. There are no named patrilineages such as those described by Vásquez and Holmberg (1966) and by Stein (1961). Furthermore, we cannot assume that the organization described above is a vestige of a prior patrilineal system whereby a focal ancestor provided the criterion for inclusion in the group. It is just as likely that some sort of bilateral structure preceded the present kindred structure. The parallel inheritance of names, land, and possessions supports the latter rather than the former hypothesis.

R. T. Zuidema (1977a) has formulated a model for the system of kinship of Inca nobility in which the principle of four degrees of relationship operated. A distinction was made between near and distant relatives, but a distant relative for Inca nobility was a third cousin who was reckoned as a fourth-degree relative. Sibling terms were extended to first, second, and third cousins, with "near" and "distant" differentiating marriageable from nonmarriageable relatives for commoners. The Inca ruler married his full sister, his "nearest" relative, and commoners their "distant" relatives.

In modern Chuschi, the distinction between "near," nonmarriageable, and "distant," marriageable, relatives is one degree closer than that observed during the Incaic period. There is one other modern case of permitted second cousin marriage, described by E. Mayer (1977) for the community of Tangor in the department of Pasco. Tangorinos distinguish near relatives as "of the same blood" and call them *kasta*; marriageable relatives are designated *ayllu*. Two other modern communities have been reported by Webster (1977) and Bolton (1977) to observe the Incaic model described above. The divergence of Chuschi, and perhaps Tangor, might be explained by the adoption of Spanish surnames and the Catholic restriction against marrying someone of the same name.

5.3   The Importance of a Name

In 5.2, it was argued that the structure of the kindred in Chuschi deviates from the structure of the Incaic and modern kindreds of the Andes by virtue of its reduced genealogical distance and consequent different distinction of near and distant relatives. Chuschi's kindred is of first cousin range;

the Incaic kindred was of second cousin range with marriageability determined at the genealogical distance of third cousin, not second cousin as in the case in Chuschi and Tangor. It was suggested that this difference might be explained by the adoption of Spanish naming customs and the prohibition of marriage between persons sharing paternal surnames of both parents. The only stated marriage rule in Chuschi is that one cannot marry anyone with the same paternal or maternal surname. A child has the paternal surnames of his or her father and mother. The diagram of the *ayllu-karu ayllu* demonstrates the importance of naming practices today, even though an examination of the earliest marriage records in the village archive beginning with 1661 reveals that other customs were operative at that time.

An analysis of the first twenty-five years of records to determine naming practices for the period discovered only thirteen out of seventy-four surnames common today in Chuschi were used at that time. Certain names appear to have been associated exclusively with males and others with females. The records from Chuschi and neighboring Quispillaqta, representing a total of a hundred and fifty marriages, were tabulated. Each record contains the bride's and groom's parents' names, their residence, often their *ayllu* and tribal affiliation, and their age and marital status at the time of the marriage. Witnesses and compadres were recorded also. A comparison of transmission of names was made on the total sample of a hundred and fifty marriages to determine what pattern was followed. The majority of men and women carried only one surname, as is the preference today. Only eight men and seven women had double surnames, and the pattern does not appear to be entirely Spanish. For example, in Chuschi there were only four surnames shared by men and women, and three appeared in compound form:

Males	Females
Quispe-*Guamán*	*Guamán*-Cargua
Chiclla-Taipe	Nabin-*Chiclla*
Paco-*Taipe*	*Taipe*-Chumpi

All of these names also occurred in the records as independent names; Cargua and Chumpi never appeared as males' names, nor Quispe and Paco as females' names. (Today, Pacotaipe and Quispe are common surnames of males and females in both villages.)

In the neighboring village, Quispillaqta, four instances of compound names were registered: two for males, Guitierez Pardo and Guamán Pienafil; and two for females, Asto Chumpi and Curi Cargua. The above-mentioned women's surnames appeared often in the marriage records as females'

surnames only, not as males'. Spanish surnames reported above for Quispillaqta males are part of a total of nine Spanish surnames found, seven for
men and two for women. Only one surname in Quispillaqta, Sullca, which
means "younger," was common to men and women alike. Furthermore, o
of a hundred and four distinct surnames (discounting repeated compound
names) for the sample of three hundred individuals, only one surname—
Tomailla—was recorded for men and women of both villages. Interestingly
this was the name of a cacique in a document dated 1621.

Of the hundred and four surnames, sixty-six were from a hundred and
three marriages with the males residing in Chuschi, and thirty-eight surnam.
were from forty-seven marriages with the males residing in Quispillaqta.

A breakdown of the Chuschi marriage records into two groups, 1661-
1675 and 1676-1685, found that new surnames appeared in the latter time
period, eight for males and twelve for females. Compound names for wom
were recorded in the latter period that previously had occurred as single
surnames: Asto-Sisa, Asto-Poco, Asto-Chumpi, Sisa-Cargua, and Sullca-
Chumpi. Of these, only Sullca was registered as a man's name in the marriage records, but Asto appears in other documents as part of a chief's
name, such as Astocabana. Also, Asto was the name of an area in the
province of Angaraes, and Astocabana appears as a place name. *Sisa* means
flower, and *chumpi* signifies a woven belt or the color brown; both of thes
were recorded numerously. Descriptive and place names also were commo
among males' names; for example, *quispe* is crystal, and *paco* today means
alpaca, though César Guardia Mayorga (1967) lists *paku* (a free variant) as
an earring that noble Indians used during the Inca reign to enlarge their
pierced ears in order to wear the large earplugs that denoted nobility.
Either rendering could indicate social status, conversely herders or nobility.
Another of the most common women's surnames for the late 1600s was
Poco, either singly or as a compound name. *Puqu* means to mature or
ripen, *puku* to blow on.

A comparison with modern marriage records for Chuschi between the
years 1936-1970 exemplifies a greatly reduced number of surnames for this
forty-year period; 74 distinct names for 552 individuals were recorded, in
contrast to 66 names for 206 persons in the twenty-five years between
1661-1685. Furthermore, of the 74 modern surnames, exactly 50 percent
were Spanish rather than Quechua. Obviously, some patterns of transmission of names were observed in the late 1600s other than that discussed
in 5.2 whereby an individual receives the paternal surnames of his or her
father and mother. In the diagram of the *ayllu-karu ayllu*, ego's paternal
surname is "A," and "G" is his mother's father's name. He marries a
woman whose names are "EC," and their children carry the surnames "AE,

the latter using their paternal "A" in everyday interaction. The only persons prohibited in marriage are those with the same set of surnames "AE," for they are considered close relatives. We have seen that this pattern was not followed in the period 1661-1685. Very few double surnames are present in the records, and, of these, several appear to be exclusively used by males and others by females. Out of the 150 marriages recorded for this period, the following tabulation was constructed for 83 males and 82 females, where information was complete, to determine if their surnames were the same as their fathers' or mothers' or different from both. Only one surname was recorded for all parties, not two as is the bureaucratic practice today. Table 3 demonstrates a non-random pattern of transmission of names.

TABLE 3
TRANSMISSION OF NAMES IN CHUSCHI AND
QUISPILLAQTA (1661-1685)

	Same as Fathers'	Same as Mothers'	Different from Both Parents'	Total
Males	60	0	23	83
Females	3	37	42	82

Chi squared   94.1

Parallel transmission was obviously one of the rules of naming in Chuschi and Quispillaqta. This custom is mentioned in the *Tercer Concilio Limense* of 1583 (Vargas Ugarte 1951: 327), and other researchers have reported it also, Albó (1977) for the Aymara community of Mocomoco in 1750 and Núñez del Prado (1969) for the Quechua community of Q'ero in the seventeenth and eighteenth centuries. Núñez del Prado (1969) also notes that "new names" were adopted as well. R. T. Zuidema (1977a), using H. Trimborn's translation of Avila's *Dioses y hombres,* argues for a cross-transmission rule of mother's brother to sister's son and father's sister to brother's daughter. Zuidema further contends that surnames were not used in pre-Hispanic Peru, but rather that, in addition to parallel and cross transmission, names were kept within a community and members could choose freely from the corpus. Furthermore, a person had different names throughout his lifetime, but we have only a scant idea about naming practices. The data presented from Chuschi and Quispillaqta suggest the following:

1. Parallel transmission of names was practiced
2. There was a corpus of names for men and another for women
3. Over 50 percent of the women carried a name different from both parents, compared to 28 percent for men
4. Whatever governed the non-parallel transmission of names, name inheritance across sex lines was not practiced
5. ˉA greater proliferation of names was present in the seventeenth century— 66 distinct names for 206 individuals for a 25-year period—as compared to 74 modern surnames for 552 persons for the period between 1936 and 1970
6. In a 10-year period (1676-1685), new names appeared at a higher rate for women (55 percent) than for men (36 percent)
7. Many of the early names appear to be descriptive of social status or relative age or to denote place of origin
8. Few names were common to both villages: of the 104 distinct names tabulated, only one was common to both sexes of both villages, and 10 were shared by females, 3 by males

The above data not only point to naming customs different from today's practices, they also point to distinctive naming practices for men and women. This fact, coupled with the observation offered in 5.2 that men have a longer generational view than women, demands a historical analysis of birth, death, and marriage records for the total time period between 1661 and today from a parallel point of view. That is, the models of evolution that would be constructed must be from the perspective of both sexes, for it seems that the sexes experienced different developments of naming practices and marriage cycles. Whatever evolutionary perspective future analysis reveals, it is clear that the structure at contact times was bilateral, but perhaps not identical for the sexes.

5.4   Affines: The Expression of Symmetric and Asymmetric Relationships

Affines in the structure of Chuschino kinship embody both symmetric and asymmetric principles. Interaction between two groups joined by marriage is symmetric or equalized and nonhierarchical; the individual who has married into a group stands in an asymmetric and subordinate position to that group. Both of these concepts will be discussed.

5.4.1   Awra: *A Symmetric Relationship*

Affines are not incorporated into *ayllu* or *karu ayllu* membership; they are a kinship category that expresses "structural equivalence" (Goodenough 1970: 96) through the usage of reciprocal terms. *Ayllu* members, excluding ego and his or her spouse, address one another as *awra*. When asked to gloss the term in Spanish, informants responded that *awra* are like compadres or spiritual relatives. Interestingly, both categories are ritually redefined as nonmarriageable, and in their words *awra* and compadres become like our blood kin; "we cannot marry one another, nor can we commit *lisuras*" (impudent behavior or joking). The greatest respect must be shown once the ritual tie has been performed. For the *awra*, this ritual is called the *perdonakuy*, or pardon, one of the rituals comprising a wedding. The *perdonakuy* is described in 5.6. If the marrying couple has eligible generation mates, they do not take part in the *perdonakuy* ceremony, in the hope that a subsequent union will take place and strengthen the bond between the two *ayllus*. *Awra* indicates a symmetric relationship between two consanguineal groups joined by marriage. The term is used when the speaker is referring to the members of the *group* who stand in a reciprocal relationship to his consanguineal group, the *ayllu*. *Awra* is therefore a symmetric concept relating to collectivities.

The term itself is a puzzlement. No reference to the term was found in Quechua dictionaries or Andean studies. However, Salvador Palomino (personal communication) has provided a description of perhaps the same concept in the neighboring village of Sarhua, where double ears of corn are called *awrama (aurama)*. The word also signifies the act of drinking in pairs from double vessels or two vessels. The couple who share the drinking vessels are called *yanantin*. In an excellent paper on affinal reciprocity during house-building rituals, E. Mayer (1977) discusses the term *yanantin* in conjunction with the concepts *masi* and *tinkuy*. *Yanantin* signifies equal entities in a mirror relationship; husband and wife are conceptualized as *yanantin*. Mayer gives the example of right and left hands. *Masi* refers to individuals or things that stand in an equal and analogous relationship to something else. Mayer gives the example of a pair of siblings of the same sex. One often hears the term used in reference to persons from the same village, *llaqtamasi*, or same *ayllu*, *ayllumasi*, or any other co-relationship. The term *tinkuy* is interesting in that its polysemy includes the encountering or meeting of persons, the place where rivers join, and (Mayer 1977) "the harmonious meeting of opposite forces." I believe the same concept is embodied in the term *awra*, which perhaps has been borrowed from the Spanish *aunar*, to unite, combine, join together.

5.4.2   Masa *and* Llumchu: *Subordinate Individuals or "Foreigners"*

In contrast to the symmetric relationships of *awra* or members of two *ayllus* joined by marriage, the bride and groom are socially and ritually subordinated to the *ayllu* members of their spouse's *ayllu.* A male is called *masay* by his wife's *ayllu* members. He enacts the role of an outsider in all rituals, usually as a clown, woman, or servant to his father-in-law or brother-in-law. Every ritual has two *masas,* who serve the sponsor of the ritual. The woman who has married into an *ayllu* resides with her husband in his paternal home for a period of years before separate residence is established. During this time, she is subordinate to her mother-in-law and sisters-in-law, who call her *llumchuy.* Her labor is essential to the preparation of food and chicha for rituals and festivities, but her ritual role as an outsider is not as dramatic as that of *masa.* Two *masas* who are ritually attendant to the sponsor of a ritual are *masamasi* to one another; affinal women helping to prepare the food and corn beer are likewise *llumchumasi* to each other. They share subordinate roles in the activities of their spouses' *ayllus.*

5.5   Compadres

In reviewing the literature on compadrazgo (ceremonial co-parenthood), I found no mention of one form of ceremonial sponsorship that is common in Chuschi. It is called "compadres de ramo," which is the most important compadrazgo relationship between adults.

When I collected genealogies, informants were asked to enumerate their compadres. Consistently, informants would name this type of compadre first, the compadres de ramo, then list the lesser compadres, such as those who sponsor a religious confirmation, a special mass for a child's health, a baptism, or a wedding.

Among comuneros, the relationships between compadres de ramo endure a lifetime and are essential to adult interaction. Compadres de ramo are acquired during one of the rituals of a wedding, the *ramo apay* (literally, "to bring the branch or new growth"), discussed in 5.6.8. The ceremony is one in which men and women, bearing gifts for the newlyweds, volunteer to become compadres de ramo. The number of volunteers indicates the status of the couple. The relationship is a parallel one, compadre to the groom and comadre to the bride, with as many as six to ten volunteering their services. It is customary for married couples to serve in this capacity, but this is not a hard and fast rule, as is that against having compadres who are *ayllu, karu ayllu,* or *awra* (5.2 and 5.4). The fact that compadres de ramo offer their services is diametrically opposed to the usual manner of contracting compadrazgo relationships in which the parents of a child (or owner of an object—almost anything can be baptized) seek out godparents and request their patronage.

The *ramo apay* symbolically creates male and female offspring for the new couple when the compadres de ramo baptize bouquets of flowers representing the ramos, or new branchings of the kin groups. What is interesting is that both sexes are symbolically created, which is consistent with the argument that the kindred is sibling-centered (5.2). The link between brother and sister is the core of the new kindred and all future marriage alliances. This essential link is symbolically created in the *ramo apay* and perpetuated by the compadres de ramo, who ideally serve as compadres of baptism when the couple have children. Having found no parallels to this type of compadrazgo in the literature (Mintz and Wolf 1950, Foster 1953, Ravicz 1967, Gillin 1947, Stein 1961, and Doughty 1968), I suggest that it is an Andean form of sponsorship that perhaps functioned in the past for the parallel transmission of male and female names (5.3).

In Chuschi, the one overriding rule in choosing a compadre or comadre, as mentioned above, is that the person cannot be a member of one's *ayllu, karu ayllu,* or *awra.* Like the *awra* discussed in 5.4.1, compadres share reciprocal terms and are ritually defined. This same rule of acquiring compadres who are not related has been found in Saraguro, Ecuador (Belote and Belote 1977), and in Cusipata in the department of Cuzco, Peru (Malengreau 1972). However, in Callejón de Huaylas in northern Peru it is common to prefer the groom's grandparent or older brothers or sisters for wedding godparents and the father's parents as baptismal godparents (Vásquez and Holmberg 1966: 294-295, Stein 1961: 131-132, 278). In Matahuasi in the department of Junín, Long (1977) found that baptismal godparents were preferably siblings or cousins. And in Compi, in the department of La Paz, Bolivia, distant relatives were chosen as compadres (Buechler and Buechler 1971).

It appears that members of peasant communities like Chuschi who choose compadrazgo relationships with nonrelatives are widening their network of mutual aid. Perhaps this also correlates with the amazing elaboration and expansion of compadrazgo found throughout peasant Latin America. Stein (1961: 129-136) provides an excellent description of compadrazgo, which he argues has its roots in Catholic religious sponsorship of a child other than the child's parents. He states that such ceremonial sponsorship is diagnostic of Latin American folk culture. Foster (1953: 8) points out that there are more than twenty occasions for naming ceremonial sponsors in Latin American peasant societies. Gillin (1947: 104) and Doughty (1968: 115) have both classified fourteen types of compadres for the mestizo communities of Moche and Huaylas, ranging from baptism to such first rites as hair cutting, nail cutting, and ear piercing. The usual Catholic observances of confirmation and marriage were also reported. Even such events as sponsorship of fiestas and brewing jars were marked by compadrazgo relationships. However, in both communities baptismal and marriage sponsorships were the most important. Gillin reported one case of a man with sixty-seven compadres and only fifteen godchildren, clearly demonstrating the extension of compadrazgo to solidify relationships between adults.

Compadrazgo relationships among Chuschino comuneros are horizontal, to use the term of Mintz and Wolf (1950). That is to say, compadrazgo relationships are contracted between persons of the same social class. One comunero explained that an *apu* (rich) compadre is for the rich, and a *wakcha* (poor) man seeks a *wakcha* compadre. *Qalas* (mestizos) prefer other *qalas* or "foreigners" as compadres. The pattern is for comuneros to choose fellow villagers, and *qalas* to prefer one another or outsiders, as compadres.

However, other students of Andean peasant communities have noted that vertical compadrazgo relationships (Mintz and Wolf 1950: 342), wherein the godparent plays a patron role to his or her client godchild, are on the increase (Lambert 1977). It would stand to reason that, as members of peasant communities make the decision to become part of the national culture and economy, that is, to transform their closed societies into open ones (2.4.2), they would use compadrazgo relationships as vehicles for access to resources and upward mobility outside of their communities.

Godparents (*padrinos*) to child relationships are universally of authority and respect in the Andes. Baptismal godparents in Chuschi are responsible for their charges until they marry. A godfather castigates or whips a boy if he misbehaves or is lax in his duties; a godmother guides, teaches, and castigates her goddaughter. The marriage godparents have the heavy burden of guiding and supervising the newly married couple. If a husband neglects or beats his wife, it is his godfather who visits him at four in the morning with the whip. Likewise, the behavior of the bride is under the domain and authority of her godmother.

The demands of compadrazgo are extreme in this subsistence farming community. It is not unusual for any one person to have as many as five to ten compadres to whom one is obligated for reciprocal labor and aid in the form of gifts of goods, cash, and attendance at one's compadres' ritual obligations. I did not become a social person in Chuschi until I acquired compadres, and my most severe criticism came from a group of women who upbraided me for not attending a compadre's Herranza, the marking of his cattle and payment to the Wamani (6.3). One is expected to appear with several bottles of trago to demonstrate affection and esteem. Unwittingly, one of the strongest social contracts in the village, the obligations of spiritual co-parents toward one another, had been broken.

5.6   The Ideal Ritual Steps toward Marriage

I have observed eight indigenous rituals considered to be integral steps in the process by which a Chuschino changes his or her status as a nonparticipating child to a full married adult member of the society. In addition, there are two ceremonies that are Hispanic in origin; one is the civil marriage demanded by law, the other is the religious ceremony demanded by the church. The former takes place sometime during the three- to five-day marriage celebration; the latter can take place at that time, or years later. The practice of waiting several years before finalizing the union in the church has diminished under the watchful eye of the local priest, who has waged a constant battle to eradicate the practice. He said that during his first year in the parish of Chuschi in 1961, he held a mass wedding ceremony in which twenty couples were married. He added that he only charged 20 *soles* apiece (about a dollar at the time) rather than the customary 80 *soles*—a bargain. The practice of waiting several years to marry in the church has almost disappeared in the village, but the custom has re-emerged in Lima, where the admonishments of the church are more remote. It is customary for a young male migrant to return to the village and complete the first steps in the marriage process, but then for the couple to wait at least a year before completing the civil ceremony in Chuschi. (See plate 8.)

The rituals dramatize all of the elements that concern the Chuschinos at this most critical time. Each ritual is accompanied by rounds of obligatory reciprocal drinking in which an individual toasts another with the words "We drink together" and pours a drink for the recipient, who then searches for a drinking partner to toast. There is a rule against drinking alone, and the result is continual drinking until everyone is drunk or the alcohol runs out. Preferred beverages are chicha and the now common cane alcohol also used for lamps, but cut with water for communal drinking. The following description of ideal rituals reflects concern for:

1. Sexual prowess (5.6.1)
2. The marriage contract between the two *ayllus*, and designation of inheritance (5.6.2 and 5.6.3)
3. The separation of the girl from her paternal home (5.6.4)
4. The equality of male and female and of their respective *ayllus* (5.6.5)

5. Fecundity and prosperity (5.6.6, 5.6.7, 5.6.8, and 5.6.10)
6. The ritual redefinition of relationships between the two *ayllus* (5.6.9)

5.6.1 Vida Michiy—*"To Pasture Life" with the "Game" of Courtship*

Fiestas are the principal times of courting in Chuschi. Young people
exchange clothing "so their parents won't recognize them," and they meet
in groups to dance and sing during the celebrations, counting on the inebria-
tion of the adults to aid their deception. The girls sing in high-pitched
falsetto voices, with their *llikllas* (shawls) over their faces and their hats
over their eyes, to the accompaniment of *chinlilis,* small guitar-like instruments. After drinking, dancing, and singing in the plaza and streets, groups
ascend to the puna for the *pukllay,* or "game," consisting of singing, dancing,
and riddle contests between males and females. If the young men tire before
the girls do, they are insulted and chided by the women, who say they are
old men, lazy, or crippled. The game continues through the night, and when
everyone is drunk they have sexual intercourse indiscriminately. The high,
savage *sallqa* or puna is considered the appropriate place for such sexual
activity, which cannot occur in the civilized village. Young unmarried
people also celebrate *vida michiy* at the cemetery, another "uncivilized"
locality outside the boundaries of the village.

Individuals arrange similar meetings in the following manner: a young man
snatches an article of clothing or an ornament from a girl, and if she does
not make an effort to retrieve it, then she has agreed to a sexual encounter.
Such meetings can result in "giving each other their word," involving an
exchange of rings or other ornaments and swearing intent of marriage while
making the sign of the cross with the right hand. Breaking an engagement
is done by simply "returning your word"—that is, by returning the items
exchanged and making the sign of the cross with the left hand. If a couple
does not break the relationship, the boy will request that his parents ask
the girl's parents for her—in Chuschi this act is referred to as "making their
mouths water," *yaykupakuy.*

5.6.2 Yaykupakuy: *"The Formal Approach"*

At four o'clock in the morning, the family of a prospective bride is
visited by a delegation representing the hopeful groom-to-be; he is not present but leaves this negotiation to his father and mother and his baptismal
godparents. This ritual is called *warmi urquy,* "to remove the woman." The
delegation approaches the girl's parents with enough trago to insure intoxica-
tion, coca, and cigarettes. After a few hours of reciprocal drinking, smoking,

and chewing coca, the girl's parents' "mouths are watering" and the question of marriage is broached. If there are no violent protests, a contract is made whereby both sets of parents announce what they will contribute to the marriage—land, animals, or other possessions are promised at this time but given at the parents' discretion. With the current exodus of young males to Lima (see chapter 8), it is common for the parents of a boy to seek an advantageous marriage for their son and reach an agreement with the girl's parents without prior courting. However, forced marriages are frowned upon and called "crude" or "uncooked," *chawachan*. If the requests for a girl are refused, the rejected family suffers dishonor and ridicule, and the couple has the option of running away, with the hope of settling elsewhere, or of residing in the household of the boy and becoming incorporated again into the girl's kindred. Such action is looked upon as stealing and causes animosity between the couple's kindreds. By running away, the couple faces the possibility of being disinherited by the disapproving parents. Parents do not actualize the promised marital inheritance for some period of time after the couple has taken up residence in the groom's paternal home. The period of service to his parents can last for years.

5.6.3   The Exchange of Rosaries

When an acceptable contract has been reached, the boy and girl are summoned, and godparents for the wedding are chosen, observing the rule that they cannot be *ayllu, karu ayllu,* or *awra* to either party. The godfather officiates at a ceremony performed in the girl's house in front of a crucifix with the parents present. The couple is asked if they intend to marry, and, upon answering affirmatively, they exchange rosaries; the wedding is now imminent.

5.6.4   The Pani: *Separating the Girl from Her Home*

After the marriage contract has been settled, the girl is separated from her paternal home in the ritual known as the *pani*, which literally means "sister," male speaking. At four o'clock in the morning, the boy's sisters and female first cousins, his brothers and male first cousins, two *masas*, and his parents arrive at the girl's house, where they are fêted with a special meal consisting of a mixture of potatoes, *ullucos,* and *ocas,* all root crops. The waiting bride is dressed in her finest, bedecked with a garland of bright-colored ribbons and a gold coin that hangs in the middle of her forehead. A rope is tied around her waist by the *panis*, who lead her along the streets of the village to the household of the groom. In procession with the bride, the *panis* sing and the *masas* shout triumphantly as the girl is greeted by the boy's *ayllu* members and the godparents chosen for the wedding. The civil ceremony and registry of the marriage can take place before or after the *pani*. Likewise, the Catholic rite can be performed at any time during the series of indigenous rituals, or the couple can wait even a period of years if they can avoid the vigilant eyes of the priest.

Sergio Catacora (1968: 71-72) has observed that in the neighboring village of Huarcaya the parents of the groom return from the ceremonies by a different route, signifying the establishment of a new line in the *ayllu*. Also, he reports that the boy's *wawqes*, "brothers," bring flowers and branches to be used later in the "gathering of silver" (5.6.5) and the "bringing of the branch," *ramo apay* (5.6.8), which signifies the birth of progeny and a new kindred. Catacora interprets the fact that the groom's brothers provide the flowers as an indication of agnatic emphasis. I would like to draw attention also to another aspect of the *pani:* the generation mates of the couple are the active participants in the village, not the parents. However, the *pani* ceremony appears to emphasize a group of sisters as the wife-giver and/or wife-taker, depicted by Lévi-Strauss (1969) as the minimal unit of exchange. Or we might also say that the groom's sisters, his *panintin,* are husband-givers/wife-takers and a bride's brothers, her *turintin,* are wife-givers/husband-takers in this Andean society concerned with symmetry.

5.6.5 Qollque Qonopa: *"The Gathering of Silver"*

The groom's house is the scene of the remainder of the ritual steps toward marriage. *Qollqe qonopa* is literally "the gathering of silver or money." The coins gathered are believed to give off a powerful vapor, called *wapsi,* that also emanates from mysterious buried treasures called *waris*. When massed on the collection plates, they are treated as if they were *waris*. The *masas* pour the coins onto the table to count them, and the couple is admonished never to spend the coins, in order to insure prosperity.

A *masa* of the groom and a *masa* of the bride (or of their parents) place two special baskets called *tunkus* onto a poncho-covered table that has been placed in the center of the roofed, three-sided portal area. Flowers are brought by the groom's "brothers," and the *masas* evenly distribute them into the two baskets. I have seen water lilies or red flowers used. A third small round basket containing red flowers along with a miniature spindle whorl and a ball of red wool are placed on the table. All baskets are manufactured of *totora,* a reed that grows along river beds. After the ritual table has been laid, the groom with his godfather at his side and the bride with her godmother are seated. For the remainder of the rituals, the godfather serves as master of ceremonies.

As members of the two *ayllus* and their compadres and affines enter, kneel, and cross themselves in front of a crucifix placed above the table, the *masas* cajole, plead, and mockingly threaten them with a whip until they contribute money in equal amounts to the young couple's plates of "silver. Each *masa* approaches the members of the *ayllu* into which he has married The first to make donations are the godparents—an equal amount to each plate—and each donation is accompanied by drinking. Periodically the money is counted and the amounts announced with ebullient shouts. If the amounts are uneven, the *masa* of the person with the lesser quantity agitate for higher donations, jokingly calling that person's relatives stingy and selfish. At the end of the day, after the wedding congregation has been fêted by the boy's family, the money is again counted. The *llumchu,* the women who have married into the *ayllu*, are expected to help prepare the ritual meal. The godparents are served a whole chicken, guinea pigs, or some other delicacy in gratitude for sponsoring the wedding. Great quantities of alcohol are consumed. As the last act of the day the *masas* count the money with great fanfare and even up the amounts "so that the couple start out equal." The money is then entrusted to the godparents, and the *puñukuy* is performed.

5.6.6   The Puñukuy: The Consummation

Puñuy is the verb to sleep; *-ku* is a reflexive verbal suffix. Therefore, *puñukuy* means "to sleep together." The couple is taken inside the boy's paternal house, their clothes are removed by their godparents, and they are put to bed on a pallet of thorns of cactus. They are given one last drink, and the door is locked from the outside. All return to their respective homes, thoroughly drunk and satisfied that the marriage is publicly consummated. The boy's parents bed down on the ground in the enclosed portal area, which is the customary sleeping place. Grains and personal possessions are stored inside, but all life activities occur in the patio, the cooking hut, or the portal area in front of the house, except for the consummation.

5.6.7   Takyachiy Puyñu: To Insure Prosperity, Fecundity, Longevity, and Equilibrium

The ritual unification of bride and groom in equilibrium with one another throughout life is symbolized by the *takyachiy puyñu,* which literally signifies "the water bottle that sustains equilibrium." Two such containers are ritually prepared and given to the bride and groom, who place them in the rafters of their house, where they remain.

The morning after the *puñukuy*, everyone gathers again at the house of the groom's parents. After the bride and groom are freed and their clothes returned, they resume their places of honor at the ritual table. The infliction of ribald sexual joking heaped upon the couple is led by the *masas*. They receive the money from the godparents, ceremoniously count both quantities, and replace it on the two plates, soliciting more contributions from all arrivals with antics, insults, and brandishings of their whips, to the enjoyment of all. A round of drinking "to cure the head" begins the day's activities. Breakfast of bread and hot coffee is served, and then serious drinking begins with members of each *ayllu* toasting one another. Everyone brings alcohol, but larger quantities are expected from compadres and affines of the parents. Soup is served around noon.

The *masas* instruct all present to remove their shoes, threatening anyone who refuses, and even forcibly removing the shoes of those who ignore them or are too drunk to do so for themselves. Women place ears of dried corn onto a man's poncho in front of the table in two distinct piles. The *masas* distribute six ears of corn to each person; the *masa* representing the boy's *ayllu* passes out ears of corn contributed by the boy's uterine kin and the bride's *masa* does the same with the ears donated by her uterine relatives—three ears of corn from the uterine members of each *ayllu*. The bride stuffs the six ears of corn she has been given into her blouse, which gives her a bumpy pregnant look. Symbolically pregnant with the supreme fertility symbol in the Andes, she gives birth to a boy and a girl child (5.6.8) during the next ritual step, *ramo apay*.

Everyone assembled removes kernels from the two extremities of the ears and throws these back onto the poncho. Then the central parts of the ears are disgrained and kept in one's lap until the *masas* signal the godparents to begin filling the two baskets containing the flowers brought by the groom's *wawqes* ("brothers"). The *masas* stand over the baskets and threateningly brandish their whips as each person kneels, kisses the ground, and carefully deposits half of the kernels into each basket. If the assembled guests spill kernels of corn onto the poncho or do not distribute the corn equally, the *masas* lay the whip on their backs as if punishing them, while shouting admonishments.

The baskets are called *tunku*, a term peculiar to the province of Cangallo (Parker 1969: 206). The bride's basket is low and round, with a large mouth; the groom's is tall and cylindrical, with a more constricted mouth. This brings to mind obvious sexual symbolism denoting male and female genitals. Both baskets have been holding the male element, flowers picked by the groom's *wawqes,* and now the female element, corn, is added to the receptacles. This symbolic act is analogous to the union of the male and female elements of both kindreds, a clear expression of bilaterality. Water lilies are preferred over other flowers. Water from the *ñawin taytacha* (6.2) is the force or energy that impregnates Earth Mother. It appears that flowers, especially water lilies, symbolize the same masculine energy that is united with the female element. Within this context it is interesting that the male element, the flowers, is present first and the female element, corn, is added to the flowers. Perhaps this is an expression of agnatic primacy, which is also reflected in the structure of the *ayllu*.

Uterine emphasis is manifest in the next phase of the ritual. After the disgrained corn has been deposited in the two baskets, the *masas* tie their ponchos around their necks and all throw their corn cobs into the ponchos. Some people toss in large stones, and the *masas* stagger exaggeratedly, to the pleasure of everyone. Then the "leavings" are placed on the poncho with any discarded kernels. Two miniature pottery bottles called *puyñus* are stationed on the poncho. The bride's mother plucks white hair from an old woman's head and drops the hairs into each bottle. Ancestral reckoning and longevity are expressed as feminine concepts. Then the bride's mother places a tiny cross, plaited from a high altitude grass, and gold coins into the bottles. Each person comes forward, kneels, kisses the ground, and with cupped hands carefully scoops a few kernels from each basket into the bottles. Lilies are then placed in the bottles, which are carefully lowered into the baskets.

The *masas* carry away the baskets containing the pottery bottles and the flowers. The two bottles (*puyñus*) are placed in the rafters of the house to give the household prosperity, fecundity, longevity, and equilibrium. I was told that the bottles remain in the house even after the couple's death. The kernels in the two baskets are used for the couple's first planting. On returning, the *masas* count the money for the last time. At one wedding, the contributions totaled 50 *soles* (a little over a dollar) each for the bride and groom. Each *masa* keeps a few coins for himself and, after spending over an hour counting the money with great shouts and antics, they turn the money over to the bride, who stuffs it into her blouse. Her godmother delivers a speech stating that the couple should never spend this money, for it will bring them prosperity if they guard it and poverty if they spend it.

5.6.8   The Ramo Apay: *"To Bring the Branch"*

One of the most important steps toward marriage is the *ramo apay*, which symbolically creates the nucleus of a new kindred by figuratively bringing forth the "new branching" or "new growth" in the form of two symbolic offspring, a male and a female. The terms *ramo,* Spanish for branch, and *apay,* the Quechua infinitive to bring, are better understood if we substitute the Quechua word for branch, which is *mallki,* meaning branch, new growth or sapling, and ancestor. It is a symbol of regeneration and continuity (see 9.4). The act of symbolically creating social and genetic continuity in the form of male and female offspring of the newlyweds is the duty of compadres de ramo, the most important type of compadres in Chuschi (5.2).

Those who wish to become compadres de ramo to the new couple arrive with bottles of cane alcohol, bread, and sometimes fruit; these will later provide a ritual meal. The *masas* bring flowers and swaddling clothes for the "new infants." (S. Catacora [1968: 78] says that the flowers are those that were provided by the groom's "brothers" at the *pani* [5.6.4], but I have not verified this.) The groom cups his hands and receives the flowers from the *masas.* He then hands them to his bride, who swaddles them into two bundles and gives a "male infant" to its new godfather and a "female infant" to its new godmother. The compadres de ramo leave the congregation and baptize the bouquets of flowers, giving them names. I have seen compadres de ramo return to the festivities with facsimiles of baptismal certificates. The names given the "newborn" are used for the couple's children, and the compadres de ramo are the actual baptismal godparents.

Informants describe how funerals are sometimes enacted, as if the "newborn" had died. The swaddled flowers are carried, accompanied by the singing and dancing participants, to a shaft tomb and buried in the tradition of an infant's burial.

When the compadres de ramo return with their new godchildren, the godfather gives the "boy child" to the groom, and the "girl child" is given to the bride by the godmother. The "new infants" are passed among the two *ayllus,* and the members deliver soliloquies concerning their relationships to the new additions. The fathers of the couple tell the boy "babies" how they will teach them to plant and herd. The "girls" are told by their grandmothers that they must learn to spin, cook, and work in the fields. Finally, the boy "infant" is given to the groom's mother and the girl "infant" to the bride's mother, who carry them in their *llikllas* (carrying-cloths) in the traditional manner of carrying infants. The bride and groom drink with their new compadres, and a special ritual meal is shared, consisting of the bread brought by the compadres de ramo soaked in the cane alcohol they provided. Plates are prepared and sprinkled with rose petals and passed among the guests. This meal is called *caldo de gallina,* referring to the customary whole chicken served to godparents. However, this offering is a reversal of the usual custom; the compadres de ramo provide the meal for the entire assembly. When this important ritual step is completed, the newlyweds are considered adults capable of assuming appropriate social responsibilities.

5.6.9   The Perdonakuy: Defining New Relationships

The *perdonakuy*, or "pardon," is one of the essential rituals of the series, for it redefines the relationships between the members of the two *ayllus* as *awra,* nonmarriageable affines, and also ritually redefines compadrazgo relationships. All who participate in the perdón must show great respect for one another and observe the rules of reciprocal aid (see chapter 7). As mentioned in 5.4.1, if a couple has marriageable siblings or first cousins, these do not participate in the ritual, in the hope that another alliance will take place and further solidify the relationships between the two *ayllus.*

A crucifix is placed on the table, and a poncho or *lliklla* on the floor for people to kneel on. The ritual begins with the godfather kneeling and the groom's *masa* kneeling to his right. They embrace the cross in a double embrace, with the right arm raised and then the left. Facing one another, they repeat a ritual apology for any wrong they might have commited against one another, kiss each other's right hand, and reembrace in the fashion described above. The marriage godfather goes through this ritual with the groom, his new compadres, and his *ayllu* members, as well as with the bride, her comadres, and her *ayllu* members. Likewise, the bride and groom enact the same "pardon" with their new compadres and each other's *ayllu* members. Each member of the bride's and groom's *ayllu* repeats the same ritual with the others, thereby defining their relationships as respectful *awra* or, in their words, "like compadres." Also, through this ritual, compadrazgo relationships and terminology are extended throughout the two *ayllus.* Rounds of reciprocal drinking seal the pact between the two *ayllus,* and thus the marriage is concluded.

5.6.10   The Dote

Days or even weeks after the *perdón,* the girl's family, led by two of their *masas,* files in procession through the streets singing while the *masas* carry on their backs gifts to the bride, such as pots and pans, a new spindle whorl, and new clothing. These are delivered to the girl's new residence in the house of her father-in-law. She has now severed her ties with her home. If she has problems with the *ayllu* of her husband, she and her children can return to her paternal home. It is the responsibility of the marriage godparents to prevent such a breakup.

5.6.11   An Aberrant Case

During our first field session in 1967, just two days before we were scheduled to leave the village, my husband and I were asked to become god-parents sponsoring the wedding of a local fifteen-year-old girl and a "foreign" man twenty-two years old. The girl had met the young man in Ayacucho while she had been working in one of the market stalls of a relative. They returned to the village after several months of cohabitation. The girl's parents, *apu* (rich) comuneros, are well respected in the village, but since the groom was not of the village they reasoned that "foreign" godparents would be appropriate. Therefore the groom-to-be approached us and asked if we would sponsor their wedding. We consented, explaining that we were scheduled to leave. After long consultations, the girl's *ayllu* members de-cided that we could sponsor the civil and religious ceremonies in one day and after that as many of the essential rituals as possible before we departed. We were instructed to choose proxy godparents who would supervise the remaining ceremonies that were considered essential and would "control" and guide the new couple in our absence.

After the civil and religious ceremonies, attended only by ourselves, the *masas,* and the couple (which is customary), we returned to the girl's paternal home, since the groom had no relatives in the village. The *puñukuy,* the public consummation, was dispensed with since the couple had been living together and the girl was pregnant. *Qollqi qoñupa,* the gathering of silver, was performed, with two *masas* of the bride's officiating. We were fêted with the traditional meal of a whole chicken.

It was decided that the *ramo apay,* the baptizing of the infants (flowers), would be performed the next morning. Again, the instance was aberrant; the boy's "brothers" and his other *ayllu* members were not present. Also, they had to contend with godparents who were naive anthropologists, whereas the godfather is usually the ritual expert and master of ceremonies. The next morning we assembled to be served the traditional breakfast. We had guarded the "silver" during the night and returned the two bundles to the *masas,* who continued to solicit contributions. A young man and woman came forward and volunteered themselves as compadres de ramo. They were not married to each other. The man was employed in one of the local stores, a "foreigner" who had married into the village. The new comadre to the bride was married and native to Chuschi.

Toward late afternoon we explained that we had to leave, and surrogate godparents were chosen. Contrary to rule, a "distant" aunt and uncle of the bride volunteered, explaining that they were not the real godparents and therefore it was all right. They decided to perform the *takyachiy puyñu* to insure the couple's prosperity and fecundity, as well as the *perdonakuy* to redefine the young man's relationship to his wife's *ayllu* members as well as to the new compadres. It disturbed the congregation that we could not be incorporated into this net of relationships on which reciprocity depends. On our return in 1969, the bride's parents greeted us with the address compadre-comadre, but we were reminded that we had not gone through the *perdonakuy* and therefore were not really compadres. This example serves to demonstrate not only the flexibility of the ritual system but also the decision-making process of comuneros when faced with a situation that does not fit the ideal.

5.7 The Ritual Birth and Death of the *Ayllu*

Ramo apay (5.6.8) is the ritual symbolic birth of a new sibling-centered kindred as *ayllu*. Both sexes are symbolically conceived, baptized, and integrated into the *ayllus* of the bride and groom. The ritual steps toward marriage carry one strong covenant for the new partnership: *be productive,* both with progeny and products. The *takyachiy puyñu* (5.6.7) is a mandate of productivity using corn as the central symbol for agricultural and human fecundity. With the baptism of the flowers, the fecundity of the couple is ritually realized and a new *ayllu* is born. As the fictitious infants are passed among the two *ayllus,* each member defines his or her relationship to the child. This act expresses the sexual parallelism that pervades Chuschino social order: the boy "child" is passed among the men and the girl "child" among the women of the two *ayllus*, ending with the two grandmothers, who are structurally important in that one can marry a person with the same surnames as one's grandmothers (see figure 4 in 5.2). In that regard, grandmothers can be thought of as the most distant link in the *ayllu* chain, whereas siblings of grandmothers are the closest *karu ayllu* relatives.

The ritual baptism defines the group that is potentially available to the yet unborn children for nurture, instruction, and mutual aid. Grandparents and godparents play important roles in the early life of children, and the grandparents verbalize their obligations during the *ramo apay*. When the male child reaches the age of seven or eight, he assumes his first ritual obligation, and his *ayllu* and *karu ayllu* are called upon for reciprocal aid.

During a comunero's lifetime, the reciprocal network grows as affines and compadres are added at marriage and as the individual contracts more compadrazgo obligations. Furthermore, as the comunero advances up the ladder of the prestige hierarchy, civil and ritual obligations demand full utilization of the reciprocal network. Then, on his retirement from civil-religious duties, the comunero's participation begins to revolve around younger members of the *ayllu*. As siblings die, their *ayllu* as an interaction group dies, for the *ayllu* is sibling-centered and only full siblings share the same *ayllu* members. The *ayllu* self-consciously restructures itself at the one-year anniversary celebration after an individual's death, after a mass called the *watan misa.*

The *watan misa* is the last of a series of expurgations to insure that the deceased does not visit his or her malevolence on the bilateral kindred, affines, and compadres left behind. After the *watan misa* is performed, the only obligation the *ayllu* members have toward the deceased is to prepare a special meal for the dead on All Souls' Day on November 1 and to visit the graves of dead relatives. Failure to do so could incur the wrath of these dangerous spirits, resulting in sickness, death of animals, crop failure, or some other disaster.

A description of a *watan misa* I attended in 1967 will demonstrate how the *ayllu, awra,* and compadres restructured themselves hierarchically to focus on the survivors and institute a new "head of the *ayllu.*" The night before the major celebration was scheduled, a mass was said in memory of the deceased and a wake was observed in his house. The dead man's clothing, complete with jacket, shirt, pants, hat, sandals, and poncho, was arranged on a table in the roofed portal area of the house in imitation of a prone body with a whip in the right hand. The clothing was oriented so that the head of the supposed cadaver faced south, the opposite orientation observed during four wakes immediately after death. A silver cross was placed at the head, candles and a holy water bucket at the feet; a black wall drape with skull and crossbones was hung on the wall behind the head. All of the above funeral paraphernalia had been rented from the church. About twenty people gathered, and as they entered they knelt before the table and crossed themselves. Each participant brought alcohol, coca, or cigarettes, all dutifully recorded.

The deceased was survived by his widow, two married sons, three married daughters, and twenty-five grandchildren. The youngest son was seated at the head of the effigy with his elder brother next to him, and the deceased's male generation mates, affines, and compadres, along with more distant relatives, sat at the feet. The widow was seated on the ground on the opposite side of the funeral table from her youngest son, her daughters next to her. Two of the daughters' husbands served the youngest son as *masas* (his brothers-in-law). During the night-long vigil, the *masas* had to see that everyone stayed awake and was served adequate chicha, coca, cigarettes, and trago. At about three in the moning, the *llumchus* aided the youngest son's wife in preparation for the festive meal for the next day. As the night wore on, important events in the deceased's life were recounted. As the stories were related, the widow would wail a high-pitched mourning song. She was the only person wailing.

At seven o'clock in the morning another mass was celebrated. The comuneros express the idea of "buying a mass," and there are several classes of memorial masses, which vary in price. I never saw the Catholic priest atten a funeral or a wake. His services and ritual paraphernalia are "rented" or "bought." After the mass, which was attended only by a handful of people a male cousin of the youngest son knelt and scooped the dead man's clothing from the table. The mortuary trappings were returned to the church, but the whip was left on the table. A much different atmosphere prevailed, with joking, drinking, and loud talking. People began to arrive, and again on entering they knelt, but this time before a wooden cross on the wall. By ten o'clock almost forty people had assembled for the remova of the black garments worn during the year of mourning. The ritual change of clothing represented the restructuring of the hierarchy of the *ayllu* members. Furthermore, the deceased was ritually removed forever from the interaction groups and a new focal member was installed, the youngest surviving son, who had, with his wife, remained at the side of his parents for fourteen years. His eldest brother had emigrated to Ayacucho, and his younger brother, who had married and moved away from the parental hom had died several years before. Therefore, he was the favored son. In recom pense for contributing the labor of his nuclear family to his father's and mother's interest, he received the lion's share of the inheritance from his father. His mother became subservient to him, and his wife was elevated to mistress of the cooking hut and house.

The ritual began with the youngest surviving son, his wife at his side, kneeling at the foot of the table. His two *masas* removed his black poncho and black hat, then his black shirt and jacket. They put a new colored shirt on their brother-in-law, and with loud exclamations of admiration they slowly lowered a new brown poncho over his head. As one *masa* prevented the poncho from falling into place, the other yanked at the man's black homespun pants. He cursed them and clung to the waist of the pants with one hand while trying to free his head from the poncho with the other. One of the *masas* grabbed at his crotch and exclaimed, "He doesn't have one!" These antics brought appreciative roars of laughter from the crowd. The poncho fell into place and the man changed pants under its cover, slapping at the now exaggeratedly solicitous hands of his *masas*. His face bright red, he cursed his *masas*, who feigned contrition. After he had his pants in place, the *masas* placed his new hat on his head with great seriousness and then yanked it over his eyes. The clowning was admired, and there were comments about what good *masas* they were. After the newly installed "head of the *ayllu*" rose, the *masas* helped his wife remove her black *liklla*. She put on a new, brightly colored skirt over her black skirt and a new, brilliantly colored *liklla* was placed on her shoulders. The *masas* did not joke with any of the women: the sexual jesting that is directed toward the men is not tolerated with the women except for that which occurs between a man and his wife's sisters or first cousins. He jokingly calls these women "my wife." Remember that these women remain marriageable, and sororate and levirate are practiced.

After completing the change of clothing for the "new head" and his wife, the elder brother and his wife were attended, but with less clowning. Then the widow knelt alone and was respectfully helped by her sons-in-law. The eldest sister and her husband were next, followed by the *masas'* wives, who knelt together. The children of the new head of the *ayllu* knelt together and changed their clothing in the same manner as the adults. Finally, this ritual act of renewal concluded with the *masas* kneeling together and comically changing each other's clothing.

As each member and his or her spouse removed their black garments, these were piled onto the table. One of the *masas* picked up the whip and the other pulled a bit of thatch from the roof and set it afire. He spread the burning grass over the clothing and then snuffed out the fire with his hands. When he had finished, the other *masa* proceeded to beat the clothing with the leather whip, chanting "In the name of the Father, the Son, and the Holy Ghost." The new head exclaimed, "Now death will not visit our family again!" People retrieved their belongings, and the fiesta took on a relaxed, gay atmosphere, with people admiring each other's new clothes. Rounds of reciprocal drinking resumed.

One of the *masas* clowningly attempted to butcher one of the sheep tied in the patio. When the women shouted at him, he ran into the cooking area and repeatedly tried to snatch the llama meat that was stacked waiting to be cooked. The fifteen to twenty women surrounding the large caldrons brandished their spoons at him and told him to serve the guests chicha as a good *masa* should.

Toward dusk, the new head's *llumchu* (brother's wife) served him two wash basins of corn soup, one with an enormous hunk of meat balanced across the rim of the basin. He ate what he wanted and his wife provided a bucket for the remainder. Each male guest was served according to his generosity in contributing alcohol, coca, and cigarettes. Large contributions were repaid with two bowls of soup and one serving of meat; small, with only one bowl of soup and no meat. The person designated to keep the list of contributions stationed himself by the cooking pots and loudly read the contributors' names and the quantities donated, while the women served each portion accordingly. Women and children were served last. Women's contributions were acknowledged by the same guidelines.

At one point during the serving, the new head of the *ayllu* rose with his *masa's* staff of office in his right hand and proclaimed that with the staff of office everyone had to obey him. The staff had been stationed upright against the wall to give the new head authority.

Drinking continued into the small hours of the morning until everyone collapsed drunk. During the time after the formal meal, the separation between the sexes broke down, and dancing to a radio began when everyone was adequately inebriated. Before leaving after midnight with the festivities still in full swing, I saw the new head and one of his *masas* struggling over the dead man's poncho. The *masa's* wife berated her brother for not giving her an adequate share of their father's clothing. Next morning the guests awoke to more drinking "to cure the head" and a small meal served without ceremony. Around noon, the assembled returned to their homes to sleep off their twenty-four-hour celebration.

The *watan misa* celebration expelled the spirit of the dead from his own house for the last time. The belief is that during the year of mourning, the dead can return to familiar places. After the ritual change of clothing that symbolizes the renewal and restructuring of the kindred, the living focus their reciprocal aid and attention on a newly installed head of the *ayllu*— in the case cited, the deceased's youngest surviving son, who had remained at his father's side for fourteen years.

5.8   Endogamy, Exogamy, and Incest

5.8.1   Endogamy versus Exogamy

Comuneros prefer to marry other comuneros from the village and of the same social status. In contrast, the vecinos or *qalas* strive to widen their alliances outside of the village through marriage and compadrazgo. Therefore, we have an ideal pattern of village endogamy for comuneros and village exogamy for *qalas*. Furthermore, the exogamic preferences of *qalas* are not only for marriage to nonvillagers but also for marriage alliances with persons from the district capital or from remote places. If exogamy is not practiced, marriage alliances are contracted between *qala* families within the village. These people tend to marry later than comuneros; the records show that twenty-five or older is the common age for marriage for *qala* men and women in contrast to the typical fifteen to twenty age range for comuneros.

A comparison of the marriage records for 1661-1685 with those of 1950, 1955, 1965, and 1966 demonstrates that the village of Chuschi is more endogamous today. See table 4. Originally the years 1950, 1955, 1960, and 1965 were chosen for comparative purposes. However, 1960 was the year

TABLE 4
ENDOGAMY AND EXOGAMY IN CHUSCHI

	1661-1685		1950-1966								1950-1966	
	#of		1950		1955		1965		1966		Total	
	cases	%	#	%	#	%	#	%	#	%	#	%
Endogamy	19	44	12	67	9	56	30	83	12	86	63	75
Exogamy	24	56	6	33	7	44	6	17	2	14	21	25
TOTAL	43	100	18	100	16	100	36	100	14	100	84	100

the village priest "rounded up" all couples living in unions not sanctioned by the church; thirty-eight endogamous marriages were recorded for that year and only one exogamous union, in which a woman from Chuschi married a man from nearby Cancha-Cancha. Of the percentages for exogamous unions in the recent sample, 1955 has the highest percentage of village exogamy—44 percent. Four of these unions are with persons from the annex of Uchuyri and one is with a woman from Quispillaqta, whereas only two are with persons outside of the district. Table 5 compares the residences of spouses of Chuschinos for

TABLE 5
RESIDENCE OF NON-CHUSCHINO SPOUSE BY SEX (1950-1966)

	Males	Females	Total
Uchuyri	1	5	6
Quispillaqta	4	3	7
*Huanca-Sancos	0	1	1
*Lucanas	1	0	1
*San Pedro de Cachi	0	1	1
*Huanta	0	1	1
*Ayacucho	0	3	3
*Nazca	1	0	1
TOTAL	7	14	21

*Outside of the district.

the recent sample of 1950, 1955, 1965, and 1966. Marriages with persons residing in nearby Uchuyri or Quispillaqta constitute 62 percent of all exogamous marriages for the four chosen years. Also, among Chuschinos, males contracted 67 percent of the exogamous unions and females only 33 percent. The thirteen marriages with persons from Uchuyri and Quispillaqta are of comuneros, whereas the three women from Ayacucho and the woman from San Pedro de Cachi married *qalas* residing in Chuschi.

Table 6 gives comparable data for the period 1661-1685. During the fifteen years between 1661 and 1685, 56 percent of Chuschino marriages were village exogamous. More foreign males married females from Chuschi;

TABLE 6
RESIDENCE OF NON-CHUSCHINO SPOUSE BY SEX (1661-1685)

	Males	Females	Total
Quispillaqta	8	3	11
Cancha-Cancha	1	2	3
Auquilla	0	1	1
Choque Huarcaya	0	1	1
Sarhua	0	1	1
*Totos	1	0	1
*Guamanga (Ayacucho)	2	0	2
*Santa Rinjo	0	1	1
*Chalhuanca	0	1	1
*Yucca	1	0	1
*Cuzco	1	0	1
TOTAL	14	10	24

*Outside of the *curato*.

Chuschino women contracted 58 percent of the exogamous unions and men 42 percent. There were more alliances between Chuschinos and Quispillaqteños during this time: 42 percent of all the exogamous unions. In contrast, only 33 percent of exogamous unions were with Quispillaqteños during the years 1950, 1955, 1965, and 1966. Perhaps the battle over grazing land boundaries between the two villages in 1951 accounts for the decline. For example, there were no marriages recorded between the two villages in 1960, the year following the battle in which three men died. However, the dramatic decline of village exogamy from 56 percent for the period between 1661-1685 to 25 percent for the selected years between

1950-1966 demands explanation. The Spaniards eliminated the bureaucratic structure of the Inca empire, which reached down to the local level
through census, labor taxation, and a state religion. The preponderance of
exogamous unions in 1661-1685 reflects the degree to which Chuschi still
maintained alliances with their tribal affiliates, the Aymaraes and the
Angaraes, as well as within the established colonial entity, the seven villages of the *curato* (2.5). During the following centuries, the village has
closed in upon itself to ensure cultural and social survival. This isolationist
attitude is mirrored in the modern concepts of comunero (member) versus
qala (foreigner), in spatial organization (2.8), and in the reduction of the
prestige systems. The lack of participation in the national polity or the
national economy has intensified this closed corporate view of the world,
which defines a Chuschino as a participating comunero, not as a Peruvian.
The effects of migrants on these concepts and attitudes are discussed in
chapter 8.

5.8.2   Incest

   Incest is defined by comuneros of Chuschi as sexual relations with one's
ayllu members, compadres, or those affines with whom the *perdonakuy*
(5.6.9) has been performed. They believe that such forbidden acts take place
on the puna, the savage *sallqa*. *Sallqaruna,* people who live and herd on the
puna permanently, are said to engage in incestuous affairs. Those who do
so are called *condenados,* the condemned ones. There are degrees of incest,
with sexual acts between members of a nuclear family as the most contempt-
ible and those between minor compadres as less serious. However, incest
between compadres de ramo or of baptism is deemed injurious to the
moral and social fabric of the village.
   Persons engaged in incestuous relations are condemned by God to a life
of suffering and are compelled to wander at night in the bodily form of
domestic animals such as dogs, pigs, or donkeys, wearing articles of clothing
or with bells around their necks. If touched while in this form, the condemned ones are transformed back into human shape, and thereby reveal
their identities.
   Villagers tell a story about a man and his adolescent daughter who were
punished as *condenados.* For several consecutive days strange cackling sounds
echoed from the *sallqa.* The *varayoq* were sent to investigate the sounds,
which were rumored to have a supernatural source. On arriving on the high
sallqa, the *varayoq* found a man and his daughter playfully pulling off each
other's clothing. As they chased one another, they laughed and threw the
clothes. Their laughter echoed down to the village 2,000 meters below as

the piercing cackling sounds heard by the villagers. The *varayoq* apprehended the man and daughter, now nude, tied their arms behind their backs, and marched them naked and barefoot into the village. They were stationed in the plaza for all to see and revile. For one night and two days they were on public display, during which time villagers gathered to ridicule them, pelting them with produce and garbage. The alcalde *varayoq* whipped them. When released, they fled from the village and have not been seen since.

6. Three Essential Rituals

6.1 The Importance of Ritual

In 1.3, ritual was defined as a series of formalized actions that are obligatory and standardized. These actions form a pattern of symbols that dramatize shared values and beliefs regarding the natural and social world. A symbol was defined as a motivated entity, such as a word, an action, an image, or an object, that has a complex of meanings shared by a collectivity. And an icon was defined as a representation that stands for an object by virtue of likeness or analogy. Victor Turner (1967: 20) has stated that it is necessary to study ritual symbols in a time series in relation to other "events"; for, in his words, "symbols are essentially involved in social process" (ibid.). I have found that the only method of discovering the meaning of symbols is to ascertain the relationships of symbols to one another within a given context. Meanings unfold as the temporal drama of the ritual unfolds. The construction that results communicates and reaffirms basic concepts to the participants. Also in 1.3 a concept was defined as a self-regulating whole containing attributes (or symbols) existing in polar relationships to one another. It is helpful to think of bundles of symbols constituting concepts, and in ritual contexts these concepts are communicated through the events of the drama ritualized. The end result is a series of symbolic combinations and associations that unambiguously impart specific concepts.

Investigators of symbolic and ritual activities agree that ritual symbols have multiple meanings or referents. Furthermore, rituals everywhere function to remind the individuals who make up a society of the underlying order that is supposed to guide their social activities (Leach 1965: 16). The process of "reminding" or of reinforcing certain values, concepts, and beliefs is often accomplished through the use of dominant symbols that reappear in different ritual contexts. A superb example of a dominant Andean symbol that has multiple referents but that reappears as a dominant symbol in various rituals is the cross. We have seen the cross as the symbol of death (or the ancestors) in the celebration of the *watan misa* (5.7) and as the icon for the powerful Wamani (2.8) During the *takyachiy puyñu* (5.6.7), the cross is used to symbolize fertility and abundance. Likewise, the cross appears in all rituals and serves to remind participants of the sacredness and seriousness of the events under way. Finally, the constellation of the Southern Cross symbolizes the synthetic union of male and female elements (see chapter 9).

The meanings that emerge from ritual activities are constructed symbol by symbol and connection by connection until fully developed into shared concepts, and these concepts are communicated unambiguously through the process of construction. Just as the cross is understood as the symbol for death and the ancestors in one ritual context, so it carries the meaning of fertility and abundance in others (see chapter 9).

Three rituals illustrate the process of symbolic construction: (1) the Yarqa Aspiy, the cleaning of the irrigation canals in September that signals the beginning of the rainy season and subsequently planting; (2) the harvest ritual on May 3, Santa Cruz, which also ushers in the dry season; and (3) the Herranza, the fertility rite involving branding cattle and sheep accompanied by payments to the Wamanis, in August and February, when Earth Mother is "open." These three rituals were chosen because they survived the reduction of rituals effected by popular vote in 1970, when comuneros decided to abolish the *hatun varayoq* prestige system and not to publicly observe Easter, Lent, or Christmas. The observances of the Yarqa Aspiy and Santa Cruz fall to the prestige system of each barrio; the Herranza for the church's cofradía herds is the responsibility of the *sallqa* prestige system. The first two will be described from my observations during 1967 and 1970. I have not observed the Herranza performed by the *sallqa varayoq*, but I have observed private ceremonies held by individual families. I am indebted to my husband, W. H. Isbell, for the major collection of data on the Herranza; I will also refer to the published study by Ulpiano Quispe (1969) of the Herranza in Choque Huarcaya and Huancasancos. He investigated both familial and cofradía Herranzas. Due to my lack of information on the cofradía Herranza, the data are not comparable to the data on the public celebration of the Yarqa Aspiy and Santa Cruz. However, the same complex of concepts is expressed in familial Herranzas.

6.2   The Yarqa Aspiy, September 1970

This all-important rite, observed in September at the time of the equinox is preceded by three days of communal labor supervised by two barrio alcaldes *varayoq*. The first day is occupied by a total canvass of the barrios to inform all households that they must supply one male for one day's labor for the actual cleaning of the dual irrigation system. Failure to attend one of the three communal work days results in a ten *soles* fine. The two alcaldes are responsible for supervising the work and collecting fines.

On the first day, the *vara* members of each barrio ascended to their respective *ñawin taytacha*, the puna springs, in the *sallqa* and began the actual cleaning of the dual irrigation system with the men of each barrio. They continued the cleaning until the entire length of the major canals, as well as the smaller feeder canals, had been cleared of debris, sedimentation, and weeds. The three days of cleaning took place in a very sober atmosphere, with no drinking allowed. However, coca and cigarettes were provided by the municipal government. These were distributed to the two alcaldes by an official appointed for the occasion, the inspector of water. He represents the municipal government during the cleaning, and the moiety alcaldes are directly responsible to him. Map 6 is a sketch of the dual irrigation system. Upper Barrio's irrigation canals (*yarqas*) are fed by Lake Matuma, situated north of the village at an altitude of 4,000 meters; Lower Barrio's canals originate at the puna spring, Ñawin Sullcaray, northeast, also at about 4,000 meters. Each source is considered the residence of powerful Wamanis, and ritual payments are made at Lake Matuma and Ñawin Sullcaray during the Yarqa Aspiy. *Ñawi* signifies eye, *ñawin*, the best, principal, or initial. It is an abstract notion. The springs are called *ñawin taytacha*. *Taytacha* means god; therefore the term signifies "god eye" or "god initial." The hierarchy of the resident Wamanis is described in 6.4.1.

The irrigation canals are generally utilized only twice a year, before and immediately after planting. For the rest of the growing season, there is usually adequate rainfall. Should a drought occur, the irrigation canals provide the necessary water. Another interesting aspect of the Yarqa Aspiy is that a much smaller work force could keep the canals free of rocks and debris. Yet both barrios demand full representation of one male from every household for the actual cleaning. The cleaning appears to be more essential in its ceremonial context than in its economic one; nevertheless, irrigation does insure early planting.

On the first day of the ritual, the *vara* members of each moiety assembled, dressed in new clothing, with women's carrying-cloths *(llikllas)* tied to their backs to symbolize their burden of office. The carrying-cloths were given to the regidores by the alcaldes, and the regidores in turn provided the garments for the lowest officials, the alguaciles, the young, single boys newly initiated into the *vara* system. For the *varayoq* of each barrio, the Yarqa

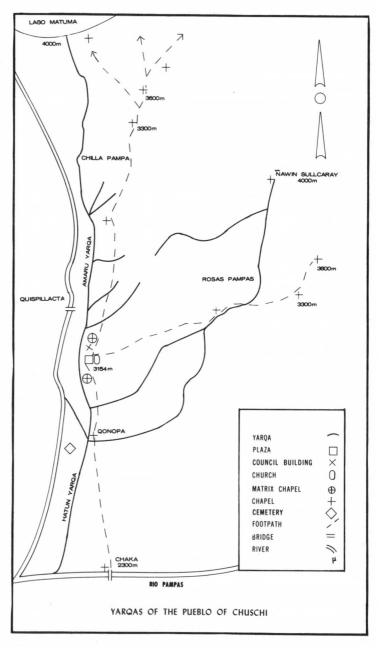

MAP 6

Aspiy is the most important responsibility of the year, and successful completion of their duties gives them higher status. The exchange of garments symbolizes the increase of status and prestige.

The *vara* members of each barrio climbed to the *sallqa*, following the newly cleaned canals. They took with them coca, trago, and chicha to leave as offerings for the Wamanis of the *ñawin taytacha,* and of course great quantities for themselves. The *varayoq* of Upper Barrio assembled at Lake Matuma and those of Lower Barrio at Ñawin Sullcaray. They descended toward the village by the major trails of their respective barrios, stopping at every chapel, where the *varayoq* made offerings of coca and chicha. Their descent was a festive occasion with music from paired wooden reed instruments called *chirisuya.* Musicians always play in pairs, and for this festivity they were contracted by the regidores. At each chapel marking boundaries between zones or subzones (see map 5 in 2.3), the processions stopped and repeated the offerings of chicha and coca. Great quantities of chicha were consumed at each of these stops. The chicha is carried and served by the *masas* and the womenfolk of the *varayoq* (see chapter 7). Outside the village boundary, in two corn fields in the *qichwa* zones of each barrio, designated Chilla Pampa and Rosas Pampa (see map 6), the *varayoq* members were met by a group of women bringing a special potato dish called picante de papa. It is the same meal that the bride's family serves the groom's when his sisters arrive to lead the girl to her new affinal home, during the *pani* ceremony. Interestingly, the meal consists of root crops and is served to the *varas* as they leave the lower *sallqa* and enter the corn-producing *qichwa.* Also, the meal can be interpreted as the ritual meal served by the bride's uterine kin to the groom's family. In this case, the bride is Earth Mother, Mama Pacha, and the groom is the Wamani who resides in Lake Matuma for Upper Barrio and the Wamani residing in Ñawin Sullcaray for Lower Barrio. Mama Pacha has, in this ritual instance, two grooms—one from each moiety. (See plate 9.)

During the meal, the alcaldes selected men to act out the following dramatization on the last day of the celebration: the *naqaq,* the dreaded supernatural being that extracts one's body fat, castrates men, and eats small children; the *chunchus,* the Chuschinos' characterization of lowland tropical Indians; and the *hamites,* the long-distance herb traders from Lake Titicaca. The roles of the priest and his idiot sacristan were played by men from Lower Barrio, for they believe that the church "belongs" to that barrio. An army officer was depicted by a man from Upper Barrio, for the bureaucratic government is situated there. These characters are traditional actors in the final day of the Yarqa Aspiy, the greatest communal

Plate 9. Yarqa Aspiy. A payment of chicha to Mama Pacha (Earth Mother) at one of the sacred localities delimiting the productive zones.

celebration of the year. The characterizations burlesque the outside world as the village conceives of it. The priest dramatizes religious domination, and his idiot sacristan is the comunero who has been duped into servitude to the church. The army officer brandishes a whip and threatens everyone in his portrayal of political domination. The lowland Indians and herbalists from Lake Titicaca are the comuneros' depiction of indigenous outsiders with whom they have had contact in the past. Herbalists from Lake Titicaca reached Chuschi in the near past, but I am sure that most of the comuneros have never seen a lowland Indian.

The dual processions continued their entry into the civilized village. Both groups stopped at the chapels delineating the village's outer boundaries to distribute coca and chicha to the gathering crowds. Then they proceeded to their respective matrix chapels within their barrios and again distributed coca and chicha. After pausing at their chapels, the processions continued to the village plaza, where the groups paraded around the plaza in opposite directions, the *varas* marching in reverse hierarchical order, followed by their womenfolk, who were singing the following song:

> Matuma (Sullcaray) patamantan pusakamuni
> Chuyay warmita pawsa lliklla
> Wachakichayoqta, wachakichayoqta.

> I have been led from high Matuma (Sullcaray)
> A clean (pure) woman, *pawsa lliklla*
> Owner of a beautiful shawl, owner of a beautiful shawl.

Lliklla is the name of the multicolored alpaca shawl worn by women; it also serves as a carrying-cloth. *Pawsa* refers to a particular design that is considered the most beautiful, a double scroll— ∾ —the universal symbol of fertility. Therefore, *pawsa lliklla* is a shawl with this design. *Kimsa pawsa* is the name given to the ceremonial bundle of ritual paraphernalia used in the ritual propitiation of the Wamani. The term also refers to a gathering of Wamanis (Quispe 1969: 22).

The women are purified and ready for conception; Earth Mother, Mama Pacha, is open, cleansed, and awaiting the final act of union with the masculine energy, the moving force of water from the puna-dwelling Wamanis. We might even think of the irrigation water as the semen of the Wamanis. Certainly it is apparent that the Yarqa Aspiy is more important to the comuneros of Chuschi as a conception ritual for Mama Pacha than as a functional act to repair and clean their irrigation canals. The final act of conception, the union of the male and female elements, occurred on the last day of the Yarqa Aspiy.

The last day of the Yarqa Aspiy was the most elaborate celebration of the year. The villagers gathered in the streets dressed in their finest and often newest clothing with their hats decorated with *angoripa*, an upper *sallqa* plant that is used to symbolize ancestors. The *vara* members entertained their respective barrio residents in front of their matrix chapels with abundant amounts of chicha provided by the two alcaldes and antics from the costumed *naqaq, chunchus, hamites,* army officers, priest, and sacristan. The *naqaq* threatened castration; the *chunchus* attacked with bows and arrows; the *hamites* paraded their wares; the army officers attacked with their whips and swaggered in high top boots and sunglasses; and the priest performed mock marriages and baptisms and sprinkled everyone with "holy water" (which was actually ten-day-old urine). These antics represent the end of one time sequence and the beginning of a new one in the annual cycle. The Yarqa Aspiy is the rite of renewal, conception, and gestation.

After the residents of each barrio drank with their respective alcaldes, they descended to the chapel in Lower Barrio marking the boundary of the village and the *qichwa.* This chapel is called *qonopa.* The villagers say this term signifies the locality where everyone gathers to drink. And indeed the entire village gathered at the *qonopa* and drank until the sun went down. The last official act of the ritual takes place the following week, when the young single boys, the alguaciles, of each barrio return all of the crosses, brought into the village decorated with produce during Santa Cruz, to their respective places marking zonal boundaries (see 6.3). The crosses are said to guard the fields, in gestation during the rainy season.

The *qonopa* chapel delineates the boundary between the civilized zone of the village and the corn-producing *qichwa.* It is also located at a point between the convergence of the irrigation canals near the cemetery. The irrigation canal that drains all of the canals of the village into the Pampas River is called *hatun yarqa,* great canal. This point of convergence is ritually important, for it is the site of the *pichqa,* the rite of washing a deceased's clothing, traditionally five *(pichqa)* days after his death. The residents of Upper Barrio perform the same rite for their deceased at a place below Chilla Pampa where the canals converge to form *amaru yarqa,* which runs the length of the village boundaries. The word *amaru* has several distinct meanings: it is a general term for snake, it means the rooting of a pig and the violent movement of water or earth, and it refers to a bull. *Amaru yarqa* becomes *hatun yarqa* at the *qonopa,* the site of the great communal celebration commemorating the impregnation of Earth Mother. Now the fields can be planted. With the rains in November, Earth Mother begins the long period of gestation until the harvest festival in May, Santa

Cruz, the Feast of the Crosses, when the crosses accompany the produce into the civilized center.

6.3   Santa Cruz: The Harvest Festival

Santa Cruz occurs the first three days of May, and there are two major activities that occupy the villagers: one is the harvest festival, when all of the crosses are decorated with produce from the zone of their locality and brought into the village, and the second is the installation of new *taksa varayoq* for each barrio. The following description is based on my observations of Santa Cruz during 1967.

In addition to the participation of the *taksa varayoq,* there are thirteen mayordomos, or sponsors, one for every chapel cross belonging to the two barrios. Comuneros stated that in order to assume the office of mayordomo of one of the thirteen crosses, a man must own land and be of age. I interpret "being of age" as being married, in that according to informants one becomes of age upon marriage and not before. The mayordomos also pay the village priest a small fee (usually ten *soles*) for the privilege of sponsoring one of the crosses.

Santa Cruz is initiated with all-night vigils at the chapels marking the boundary between the lower *sallqa* and upper *qichwa* zones of Upper and Lower Barrios. In Upper Barrio, after meeting in the alcalde's house to receive a portion of coca and trago for each member, as well as kerosene for the lanterns carried by the alguaciles, the *varayoq* proceeded to the chapel on the boundary between the lower *sallqa* and upper *qichwa,* with the alguaciles and regidores leading and providing light for the others. The alcalde brought up the rear. They entered the chapel in this order, but the alguaciles and regidores waited until the alcalde entered and took his seat in the center of the chapel. The regidores sat at his left and right, "like his arms," and the alguaciles remained standing after placing the lanterns in the wall niches. The alcalde of Upper Barrio had died during the year, and his eldest son was officiating in his stead. He was a young single man not yet twenty years of age, but all the respect accorded the alcalde was shown him.

Three *sallqa* crosses were brought by their mayordomos. One large, nine-foot cross that usually graces the top of one of the highest passes and a smaller trail cross were brought down to the chapel by the alguaciles. Two fathers of alguaciles were performing the duties of their sons, and the other four were young single boys.

Formal drinking began with each of the mayordomos stepping forward and raising his cup to the alcalde, who in turn drank with the regidores, who then turned and drank with one of the alguaciles. The latter drank with the wives of the mayordomos, who squatted on the floor. Coca was distributed by the mayordomos. This ritualized hierarchical drinking and coca-chewing continued until dawn, accompanied by blasts from pairs of *waqrapukus*, trumpets fashioned from coiled cattle horns. These musicians were hired by the mayordomos.

The procedures among the *varayoq* of Lower Barrio were identical, with the exception of the number of crosses united at the boundary chapel between the upper *sallqa* and lower *qichwa* on the trail to Calcabamba (see map 5). Calcabamba is above Chuschi geographically, but there are areas of the region where corn can be grown as well as root crops. The herding area, Sullcaray, is beyond and above Calcabamba in altitude. The *varayoq* members of Lower Barrio met with one mayordomo at the *sallqa* chapel on the path of Calcabamba, where they were in vigil all night observing the entering, seating, and drinking order described for the officials of Lower Barrio. Early the next morning, the *sallqa* cross from Sullcaray and the cross from the chapel of Calcabamba were brought by their mayordomos to the chapel where the *varayoq* were waiting. The alguaciles climbed to the tops of two passes to bring the large *calvarios,* as the nine- to twelve-foot crosses are called. They also returned with one small cross that protects one of the lower foot trails.

During the night, both Upper and Lower Barrio *varayoq* observed a ritual that is a display of authority the alcaldes manifest to their subordinates. It is called the *albadukay,* which is not a Quechua word but one from an unknown Spanish term—perhaps *obedecer,* to obey. The alcaldes knelt in front of a table and grasped the whip that had been placed there. Each regidor knelt to the alcalde's right and kissed the silver cross on the staff held by the alcalde. Then the alguaciles one by one followed suit. Finally the outgoing mayordomos present knelt in the same manner followed by the mayordomos for the coming year. The mayordomos for the chapels not represented on the first night's vigil observed the same ritual with the alcalde at their chapel during the formal visitation that takes place on the next night's watch. During this ritual of authority and subordination, the alcalde may castigate his underlings for not performing their duties appropriately during their year of office. He has the authority to whip them in the presence of the gathering. As each participant knelt with the alcalde, they each begged forgiveness for any wrong commited during their tenure of service together. The ritual closed with each man embracing the alcalde in a formal embrace. After the *albadukay,* a relaxed informal atmosphere prevailed, with increased drinking and coca chewing as well as joking and laughing, until the morning meal was served by the wife and the *llumchus* of the mayordomo. In Upper Barrio, I was told that the mayordomo should have furnished a traditional *pachamanca,* a ritual meal of corn, meat, and potatoes and other root crops cooked in the ground. However, only boiled potatoes and *ocas,* another tuber, were offered. In Lower Barrio, the mayordomo served the traditional *pachamanca.*

After the morning meal on May 2, when all of the crosses were present, the mayordomos provided produce from the *sallqa* zones, such as potatoes, cheese, *ocas, ullocos,* and *mashuas,* and the alguaciles tied the produce together to fashion necklaces for the crosses. The alguaciles also decorated the chapels with *angoripa.* They called the branches *mallki,* which is a general term for sapling or young tree ready for transplanting. The verb *mallkiy* means to transplant. However, the noun *mallki* is a general term for ancestor as well as sapling. As with the symbolism associated with water discussed in 6.2, we see that *mallki* is utilized in a semantically bipolar fashion to signify renewal as well as continuation through the generations.

The mayordomos drunkenly took up their crosses, the alguaciles took turns carrying the large path crosses, and the entourage began its descent into the village. As the crosses were removed from the chapel at the border between the root-crop-producing lower *sallqa* and the corn-producing *qichwa,* garlands of corn and flowers were added to the crosses. People waited along the paths and added necklaces of newly harvested produce to the crosses. The crosses were deposited at the chapel marking the outer boundary of the village, and the groups adjourned to the alcaldes' houses to drink a few more "*copitas,*" little cups of trago and chicha provided by the alcaldes. Drinking continued in both alcaldes' houses until midafternoon, when the participants literally stumbled home for a few hours of sleep before the vespers procession around six o'clock in the evening.

As the church bells tolled vespers, each mayordomo carried his cross into the church (see plate 10). Women brought their household crosses decorated with garlands of flowers and produce. Two additional crosses appeared—the cross from the Church's cofradía herds carried by the *sallqa* alcalde along with the *hatun* alcalde and the cross kept in his house during his year of office. (The offices of the *hatun varayoq* were not abolished until 1970.) The caretaker of the bridge *(chaka)* brought the cross that guards the suspension bridge over the Pampas River. The crosses were carried through the streets draped with white cloth covering the face of Christ, accompanied by the music from flutes, drums, and *waqrapukus.* All of the crosses were deposited on the altar of the church, the household crosses in the center, the crosses of Upper Barrio with the *sallqa* and *hatun* alcaldes' crosses on the left as one faces the altar, and those of Lower Barrio and the *chaka,* suspension bridge, on the right. The *varayoq* did not enter the church;

Plate 10. Santa Cruz. The *varayoqkuna*, holding their staffs of office, bring the produce-decorated

they waited outside with their high staffs until mass was over. The barrio crosses were taken to the two matrix chapels; the *hatun* and *sallqa* alcaldes took their crosses to their houses, as did the caretaker of the bridge.

The vigil of May 2 was dedicated to the two matrix chapels, and their mayordomos were expected to treat the visitors who came to revere all of the chapel crosses deposited there. Upper Barrio's mayordomo served coca, cigarettes, trago, and chicha, making sure that someone was there all night to receive visitors. The mayordomo of the matrix chapel of Lower Barrio had died during the year after sponsoring the same cross for six previous years, and his family chose not to fulfill his ritual obligations. They remained in the *sallqa* during the three-day celebration. As the procession from Lower Barrio entered the chapel, the alcalde demanded that someone find the mayordomo, meaning that someone from the immediate family should be found to assume the duties. However, his alguaciles and regidores returned stating that no one was in the house and that the chapel was without a mayordomo. The gathered throng left the chapel grumbling that the family was stingy, mean, and not good comuneros, for they had failed in their responsibilities. The loudest complainer was the young man from Upper Barrio who was fulfilling the duties of his father, the dead alcalde. He kept saying that Upper Barrio was fortunate to have such responsible people as himself and his family who saw to it that custom was upheld. I was told that every chapel must be visited and drunk to by all the *varayoq*, including the *sallqa* and *hatun* alcaldes as well as the devotees wishing to observe the customary all-night visitation.

The major activity of May 3 was the installation of new *taksa varayoq*. It was said that eligible men came forward to take up the eighteen staffs with good faith voluntarily—*con buena voluntad*. However, on the morning of the third when the priest read the list of *taksa varayoq* prepared by the municipal officials, only two men came forward and knelt, kissed their staffs, and received the blessing of the priest. The man who had been named alcalde for Lower Barrio was forcibly brought before the table where the waiting staffs and priest were positioned in front of the door of the church. He was accompanied by his wife, and they both were struggling with the *hatun* regidores, who were restraining the woman as they dragged the man forward. In front of the ritual table a general fracas ensued, with the priest receiving a heavy blow to the side of the face, to which he retaliated with a hearty whack on the top of the reluctant man's head. The obstinant man's poncho was forcibly removed, and three men pushed him to his knees, holding his arms behind his back. The priest pushed his face to the staff, obliging him to kiss the cross on the staff. Then he was released as the crowd clapped, cheered, and joked.

Together he and his wife delivered an angry oration, calling the priest and
the *hatun varayoq* men, as well as the municipal officials, several vulgar
names. The gist of their protest was that he had just completed *taksa* regidor and that they were now too poor to fulfill another year of service to
the community. Their surplus of produce was expended, and their relatives
would not help them. The answer of the gathered villagers was that he had
enough and now he had to accept, for he had kissed the staff and it was his.
Indeed, the man fulfilled his duties satisfactorily and did not shirk his
obligations. Another man was similarly impressed into service, totaling only
four out of eighteen positions to be filled. They had until the end of the
month to find men for the remaining positions. The usual remedy—jailing a
reluctant man for a few days until he changed his mind and accepted the
staff of office, or the threat thereof—worked: at the end of the month, all
of the offices were occupied. In 1970, after the abolition of the *hatun
varayoq* structure, eight of the possible eighteen came forward willingly
and accepted their staffs of office for the barrio authorities. There was
no undue pressure, and the positions were filled within two weeks after
Santa Cruz. One informant voluntarily accepted the staff of regidor and
said, "Everything is up to us now. We must serve without complaint." He
felt that expenses would be less, but my research during 1970 showed that
the expenditures of one of the alcaldes were comparable to those of other
years (see chapter 7).

After the installation ceremony, mass was observed, with the *hatun*
officials attending and taking up their positions at the front of the altar.
The *taksa varayoq* members waited outside until mass ended. They are not
associated with the church, and it is not obligatory that they attend festive
masses. This obligation was one of the duties of the *hatun varayoq*. After
mass, the priest collected several of the garlands of produce decorating the
crosses for his own consumption. A procession counterclockwise around
the plaza took place after the mass, with the priest flanked on the left
and right by the barrio crosses carried by the mayordomos, followed by
women with their individual house crosses. Leading the procession were
the outgoing regidores, carrying the staffs of office. After the procession,
which was accompanied by flutes, drums, and *waqrapukus,* the barrio crosses
were returned to the two matrix chapels, where they remained until the
Yarqa Aspiy (6.2). During the Yarqa Aspiy, the incoming alguaciles
return the crosses to their respective chapels to guard and protect the
planted fields. The large *calvarios* and path crosses are returned in the
month of May by the incoming alguaciles. This act initiates the young
boys into the *varayoq* structure. The presence of the chapel crosses within
the boundaries of the village signals the arrival of the harvest into the

village. In June, the herds are brought down from the high *sallqa* to graze on the harvested fields and to fertilize the fields for the next planting after the Yarqa Aspiy. Before the ritual cleaning of the irrigation canals in September, the powerful mountain deities, the Wamanis, are propitiated in August with the Herranza.

6.4   The Herranza: Ritual Payments to the Powerful Wamanis

6.4.1   The Wamanis

The Wamanis control life-giving water and are appeased during the Yarqa Aspiy, the ritual cleaning of the irrigation canals (6.2). However, the most elaborate offerings are prepared during the Herranza, the branding of cattle in August and marking of sheep in February. We have been told that the Herranza is still performed for alpacas and llamas, but we have witnessed only the ritual branding of cattle in August. Small stone effigies of cattle, sheep, and horses called *illas* are manufactured today to be used in the Herranza, and prehistoric miniature figurines of llamas and alpacas have been identified by Chuschinos as *illas* also. *Illas* are said to be the animals belonging to the Wamanis, who are believed to be the owners of all animals and material possessions.

In 2.8 it was mentioned that the Wamanis operate within a hierarchical organization likened to the bureaucratic governmental structures of the national, departmental, and local governments. Some informants maintain that the Wamanis carry staffs of office of gold and silver and have positions as alcaldes, regidores, and alguaciles. However, Wamanis do not progress up through the hierarchy; rather, their status is fixed according to the height of their residing place, either a lake or a mountain peak. Others say that the Wamanis are like doctors, lawyers, and políticos. A peak outside of the department capital is called El Médico, and the resident Wamani is believed to have special curing powers. There are three superior Wamanis in the region: (1) a snow-covered mountain near Ayacucho, Rasuwillka; (2) a peak east of Lucanas in the southern portion of the department; and (3) a mountain in the south toward Cuzco. These three mountains and Wamanis are compared to the modern capitals of Ayacucho, Ica, and Lima. They are said to delegate duties and responsibilities to subordinate mountain deities below them. (See plate 11.)

The subordinate Wamanis of the Pampas River region include the mountain peak Comañawi, the most powerful of the region, and his underlings around the various districts and population centers. For the district of Chuschi, the local commanding Wamani lives in the high puna lake,

Yanaqocha, near communal lands of the village of Chicllarazo. He is said to be the owner of all of the church's cattle and sheep, and an annual payment is made to him for the protection and fecundity of the herds. The ritual is sponsored by the local church. The Wamani of Yanaqocha receives orders from those above him and meets periodically with his subordinates to relay the chain of command. Under this maximum Wamani of the district of Chuschi there are two minor deities who are revered by individual families in the village of Chuschi; one resides in the puna lake, Tapaqocha, and the other in the mountain peak, Ontoqarqa. Each family "owns" a particular place of payment called a *caja*, a depository or safe. U. Quispe (1969: 35) states that among the villagers of nearby Huarcaya the youngest son inherits his father's place of payment. As mentioned in 6.1, my concentration was not on the Herranza nor on activities in the *sallqa*, and my data are not complete. Nor did I investigate the inheritance or ritual payment localities; however, each household has a ceremonial bundle of ritual paraphernalia necessary for the Herranza, inherited by the person who inherits the house. It is probable, in my opinion, that the place of payment to the particular Wamani is also associated with a house, and the offspring who inherits the house acquires not only the ceremonial paraphernalia but the place of payment or *caja* as well. It is possible, therefore, that the Wamanis are deities generally inherited and shared by the agnatic line of a kindred. In 5.7, a description was given of the ritual restructuring of the *ayllu* at the one-year anniversary of the death of the head of the kindred. The youngest living son was instituted as the new head of the kindred, and the duties and privileges inherited included the ceremonial Herranza paraphernalia. Unfortunately, I neglected to ask about the ritual place of payment, the *caja*. Also, we do not know if all of the agnatic members of a kindred make their ritual payments at the same place to the same Wamani. If this is the case, the kindred has an agnatic lineal focus functioning in the *sallqa* associated with herding.

The potency of the Wamanis is evident in the stories told about encounters with them. They are both benevolent and malevolent, and a person never knows their moods or inclinations. The following stories will illustrate their capriciousness.

A Huarcaino fell asleep at Pichqa Pukyu (the five springs considered the residence of the five principal Wamanis of Huarcaya). He had coca in his mouth, a cigarette, and a portion of *tuqra* (the lime prepared from *quinua* chewed with coca) in his hand. Upon waking, he heard the *Cerros* Wamanis calling one another. One said, "You should have taken his heart to punish him." The other replied, "No, I couldn't. His mouth stinks, he has fire, and he is chewing rock." Upon hearing all of this, th man grabbed his testicles, thinking that he had lost them, but nothing had happened. He jumped up and ran from the place. (U. Quispe 196 39)

The Wamanis can also be benevolent. A story told to my husband and myself by a resident of Quispillaqta:

One night I was sleeping in my hut beside my corral in the puna. As I slept, I dreamed I got up and checked the animals in the corral. Accidentally, I entered the spring, which is the house of the Wamani. The house was of pure glass, and the Wamani was there. A woman brought a gold plate and a piece of wool. Then the Wamani called me by name and showed me the gold plate. He gave me the piece of wool to keep and told me to go. I awoke in my hut and feared that something had happened—perhaps someone was stealing my animals. I went out to look, but it was so dark that I could see nothing—only that there were still animals in the corral. I went back and went to sleep again. In the morning, I went to see my animals and found among them four tiny lambs. They were gifts from the Wamani, and I call them *illa* (the name of the Wamanis' animals). They have been wonderful producers, and m flock has grown. As payment, I make offerings to the mountain: fruit, wine, cigarettes, coca, candles, and perfume.

The above gifts are the prescribed gifts preferred by the Wamanis, as re-affirmed in a tale related to us by a resident of Chuschi:

As a boy, I attended an Herranza for sheep in the puna of Quispillaqta. At the end of the ceremony, the offering was prepared for the Wamani. However, certain fruits that were not easily available were omitted from the offering basket. The hole or tunnel (the *caja*) at the edge of the spring was dug out—the spring is the resting place of the Wamani—and the owner of the herd placed the basket with offerings into the ground. While the man's arm was in the hole, the Wamani grabbed him by the wrist and would not let go. I began to pull, and so did the others, and finally we got him free. As we returned to the corrals, a voice cried out from the spring. After we entered the herder's hut beside the corral, the man became violently sick, vomiting straw and earth—he had not eaten either. The man almost died; his life was barely saved by a *curandero* (curer). If a man owns animals and does not pay the Wamani, he will die.

The most propitious time to make payments to the awesome Wamanis is in February and August, when Earth Mother is open and receptive. Ritual offerings are also prepared in late June, usually beginning on June 24, currently the celebration of San Juan, the patron saint of cattle. The *sallqa varayoq* descend as a group into the village at this time and enact savage and uncivilized acts of incest and impiety. An informant in the village of Sarhua told Salvador Palomino (1970: 120) that "in these days of our little mother and little father (during August and February), the earth opens and the gods are hungry, therefore they receive our gifts readily. But they can also eat the hearts of men who dare to walk alone in the mountains at these times. The rocks talk, the *illas* walk, the *ichu* (puna grass) converts itself into rope, the trees move, and the ravines call out."

The ritual payments are carefully prescribed, and failure to follow the formula can bring death to the herds and family members. Not having seen the actual payment made, since the presence of a foreign woman at the *caja* or depository was not allowed, I will rely on the description by my husband, W. H. Isbell, who has witnessed one such offering, verbal accounts of informants, and the excellent study by U. Quispe (1969). The payment to the Wamani is the last act of the Herranza, which has three parts: (1) the vespers preparations made the night before, (2) the actual branding of the animals and the "marriage" of a heifer and a young bull, and (3) the payment to the Wamani.

6.4.2   Vespers: Preparation of a Potent Concoction

On the evening before the branding and payment are to take place, the sponsor (or sponsors) of the ritual and members of his family leave the village and climb to their *sallqa* corral and hut. We participated in an Herranza for cattle during August. A young compadre of ours was acting in behalf of his father, who had died six months before, and his mother took the role of the principal female. His ten-year-old brother assisted him. His wife, who should have attended, remained in the village with their two infant sons but joined the gathering the next morning. We took with us a large quantity of trago, coca, a branding iron, and the ceremonial bundle. On arriving at the *sallqa* house, the family began the vespers with a round of ceremonial drinking and songs. The sponsor opened the ceremonial cloth bundle and spread out the various contents, which included another tightly tied cloth bundle holding a special powder called *llampu* in which there were several small stone figures—a cow and sheep of recent manufacture and a bird probably of pre-Columbian origin. Another tied cloth contained a special red *llampu* called *puka* (red) *llampu* in a sea shell. The ceremonial paraphernalia also included two chunks of minerals referred to as "crude gold" and "crude silver," another red mineral, a small knife, a bottle of trago, and one of chicha called *ñawin,* the best or finest. Montaña and tropical forest products were also included, notably coca seeds and several sacks, two of which contained different seeds, one called *willka*—the term for descendant—and the other called *wayluru.* The former are dark brown, flat, tear-shaped, bean-like seeds, and the latter are red and black bean-like seeds. *Willka* (also called *vilca* in other areas of Peru) was used in divination rites during Inca times, and R. E. Schultes (1972: 29) has identified the seed as the *Anadenanthera colubrina* used in the manufacture of hallucinogenic snuff. Altschul (1967) has reported on the uses of *vilca.* *Wayluru* has been identified by Quispe (1969: 22) as *Cytharexylon herrerae.*

Llampu is a special concoction that serves as one of the essential element of the offering. It is a prophylactic against contamination, capture, and illnesses caused by the Wamanis, as well as a purification agent for ritual preparation. A comunero never expends his supply of *llampu*; the ritual bundle is kept in the eaves of the house from year to year and a new preparation is elaborated only when needed. Our compadre had an ample supply that had belonged to his father, but we persuaded him to prepare the *llampu* anew for us. He brought into the hut a flat rock and cobble, explaining that the cooking grindstone could not be used. Then he selected ears of corn; the number is unimportant, but there must always be pairs of everything. Each ear must have all of the grains present and only white, large-grained corn can be used. Before beginning, our compadre offered a drink to the Wamani. He poured trago into a sea shell, stepped out of the house, removed his hat, and poured the liquor on the ground. Then everyone present drank from the same shell. He explained that if he did not offer the Wamani a drink, the Wamani would make him sick to his stomach as he ground the *llampu.* He took a drink of trago and chewed a bit of coca with *tuqra.*

First, the grains were carefully removed from two ears of corn, while he explained that if any of the grains escape the grindstone, animals will be lost or will die. His mother wrapped a blanket around the edge of the grindstone to prevent grains from skittering off onto the dark floor. As the grains of corn were coarsely ground, his mother played the small ceremonial drum used by women, the *tinya.* He added two *wayluru* and then two *willka* seeds, and his mother intoned the following song:

> *Wayluru* and little *willka*
> They say that you are very manly
> *Wayluru* and little *willka*
> They say that you are very handsome

Wayluru and little *willka*

Wayluru and little *willka*
They call you handsome
Wayluru and little *willka*
They call you the very manly
Wayluru and little *willka*

The third addition was four pairs of coca seeds, and the fourth was one pair
of white carnation flowers. Then two minerals were added, the first red and
the second white, called red *llampu* and white *llampu*. The last ingredients
to be added to the concoction were "crude gold" and "crude silver," both
called *chakin*. Tiny pieces were chipped off the larger chunks and dropped
onto the grindstone. Our compadre checked all the ingredients and ground
vigorously for a while. Then he stopped for a ritualized rest, during which
he drank trago from a cup made from a cattle horn. Everyone present
followed him in a round of drinking from the horn cup. He continued
grinding and commented that the *llampu* was not red enough, so he added
more *puka llampu* (the red mineral) and ground some more.

When the *llampu* preparation was finished, our compadre poured trago
into a shell and sprinkled *llampu* over the liquid, then a small quantity of
achita (Chenopodium pallidicaule). He prepared an identical mixture in a
horn cup and drank from both. We followed him by drinking the double
concoctions in turn. He explained to us that the double shots would protect
us from the Wamani. Anyone who arrived late had to drink the same double
potion as a prophylaxis. He concluded the grinding ritual by scooping the
llampu from the grinding stone with a shell and adding it to the old. The
atmosphere relaxed, and drinking and singing continued through the night.

6.4.3   The Branding and "Marriage"

Just as dawn was breaking, our compadre and his little brother quietly
left the hut so as not to awaken us. He did not want the gringos along on
his dangerous mission. Our compadre carefully tied his ceremonial bundle
to his back in a woman's shawl, a *lliklla*, in a manner denoting subordinate
status. They walked about two miles to a nearby lake to make the *llallipay*
payment—it means the "gaining advantage" payment—to the Wamani. My
husband, W. H. Isbell, followed and watched from a distance. He reports
that the bottle of *ñawin* trago was removed from the bundle and a drink
was poured into a gourd. Some of the liquor was thrown into the lake and
the remainder was poured onto the *caja*, the offering place. A second cup

of trago was offered to the Wamani. The earth was carefully scraped away
with a sickle and the stones covering the *caja* most cautiously removed. The
stones are called the "lock and key" to the "safe." One sea shell of *llampu*
was poured into the hole, next *ñawin* chicha. If the *llampu* swirls clockwise
animals will die or be lost; counterclockwise swirls foretell fecundity and
good fortune. Our compadre and his brother judiciously replaced the
stones, and each drank one shot of trago to escape capture or illness. On
the return to the hut, coca was chewed for further protection. The young
man stopped outside of the corral, and his brother excavated a small hole
near a natural outcropping of rocks. He poured one shell full of *llampu*
into the hole, then it was covered and another shot of liquor was consumed

On entering the hut, our compadre remembered that they had forgotten
bread, one of the favorite gifts of the Wamanis. He sent his younger brother
down into the village to buy the bread, a two-hour walk. The discovery
caused concern among the gathering, for the Herranza must be completed
in one day once it is begun, and our compadre had awakened the Wamani's
avarice with the "gaining advantage" payment.

Other people began to arrive—the all-important *masa,* who was our
compadre's father's sister's husband, a minor compadre and comadre of our
compadre, the patron of the ritual, and a man who was contracted as a
branding expert and his assistant. Each arrival drank the double *llampu*
and trago mixture from the shell and horn cups. Our comadre arrived, and
the ritual retinue faced a problem. If her father-in-law were alive she would
serve as *llumchu,* but she would not attend her husband in this capacity
even though he was acting in behalf of his dead father. Reluctantly, our
compadre's mother cooked and served the morning meal, which should have
been the responsibility of her daughter-in-law. However, since her son was
living in the house of *his* mother-in-law, the usual subordinate position of
the daughter-in-law was forfeited, thus causing an anomalous situation.
Ideally, a patron of an Herranza should have two *masas* and two *llumchus*
in attendance as well as a branding specialist, someone to assist him, and
waqrapuku players.

The younger brother returned from the village and proceeded to manufacture necklaces called *wallqas* of bread and fruit to be worn by the major
participants and draped on the cattle. Our compadre's other compadre
gathered *cirse* reeds, and the *masa* fashioned a new cross to replace the
cross over the entryway to the hut. The cross was made of three bunches
of reeds bound together at the bottom with a stick about two feet from
the base serving as the crosspiece to bind the bunches of reeds together.
The finished cross was three feet high and about two feet across. When the
masa finished with the cross, he and the branding specialist (not a relative)

decorated the branding iron with a piece of dry cow dung on the branding piece and a lump of fat on top of that. Two pink and two blue ribbons were bound around the dung and the fat; a necklace or *wallqa* of fruit and bread, along with a bottle of trago, was tied to the iron with a pink ribbon. The finished product was quite attractive.

The ritual entourage paraded to the corral with the *masa* leading the way and carrying an armload of reeds; the branding specialist followed with the branding iron; and our compadre and his mother brought up the rear. He carried the reed cross and had the ceremonial bundle tied to his back. His mother carried her small ceremonial drum. The rest of us followed the principal participants to the rock outcrop where the *llampu* had been buried. An offering of coca *quintu,* whole leaves without blemish, was left on the rocks.

Now the ritual table was laid, but first another round of prophylactic drinking—one drink of trago and one of chicha, each served by our compadre, the patron of the ritual. He extended a poncho in front of the cross and branding iron, both of which had been propped against the wall of the corral. The seeds were placed in front of the poncho by the *masa.* The ceremonial bundle was opened and placed beside the cross. A basketry loop about six inches in diameter and three inches deep along with a lasso had been added to the ceremonial paraphernalia. The larger cloth of red *llampu* was untied and the figurines, the *illas,* were carefully set upright in the *llampu.* Another cloth contained a sea shell filled with lighter-colored *llampu,* several fossil shells, and some red wool. Our compadre sprinkled three lines of *llampu* on the poncho, then coca leaves were carefully scattered along the lines. The small knife was dipped in *llampu* and placed near the center line. The chunks of "crude gold" and "crude silver" were stationed on the other lines. Now the ceremonial table was complete. The *masa* and the branding specialists knelt before the table, crossed themselves, and mumbled a prayer to the Wamani, and then the patron and his mother knelt and repeated the performance. (See plate 12.)

Meanwhile, the *masa* and the branding specialist readied the iron, carefully removing the decorative offerings and tying them to a bunch of reeds. Coca and several rounds of trago and chicha were consumed "to prepare ourselves." The *masa* knelt and gathered up the reeds and placed them at the entrance to the corral. Four animals were driven into the corral, three mature cows and one bull calf. The patron sprinkled *llampu* from a shell into the air, making a counterclockwise circuit around the corral. Another round of double drinks and more coca followed. The women seated themselves in hierarchical order beside the cross, our compadre's mother next to the cross, her sister-in-law, her daughter-in-law, and then her son's comadre. The lesser compadre and comadre decorated everyone's hats with white blossoms. We were now

Plate 12   The Herranza: A ritual table

ritually prepared, strengthened, and purified.

If there are immature animals that have not been sanctified before, a male and a female are chosen for a "marriage" ceremony. The Herranza of this compadre did not include the marriage, for there was only one bull and no available young female animal that had not calfed. Later, I attended a joint Herranza of another compadre and his father-in-law in which eighteen animals were ritually treated and a "marriage" performed. A young bull and a female calf were brought before the ritual table, and four *masas* prepared a bed for them of *cirse* reeds. The assistants to the branding specialist roped the animals, throwing them to the ground in a ventral to ventral embrace. Reeds were placed on their legs, and the wife of the patron sprinkled three lines of *llampu* on the sides of each animal. "Crude silver" and "crude gold" were rubbed on their hooves. One of the *masas* placed a blanket over the animals, and bread, coca, and toasted grains were placed on the blanket. The *masas* and *llumchus* knelt and passed reeds across the animals to the two patrons and their wives. Then the patrons cut the ears and tails of the two animals and the blood was caught in a shell. The *llumchus* tied the ritual necklaces of produce, the *wallqas,* to the horns of the animals and draped the same around the necks of the male owners. The *masas* placed the necklaces around the necks of the two principal females. Ribbons were fastened in the ears of the animals by the *llumchus.* The *masas* placed the flesh from the ears and tails on the table. They distributed reeds to all present, and we made two crosses of them by holding the reeds between our fingers to form three strands. With these, we danced around the animals and as they were released we threw the reeds at them. A ritual meal was served of bread, toasted grains, and the double drinks of trago and chicha mixed with the blood of the animals. Coca was distributed afterward as we rested.

U. Quispe (1969: 92) reports that in the Herranza of several neighboring communities the ceremony of "putting the cattle to bed" is enacted, and animal copulation is simulated by the principal males and their wives.

The Herranza under discussion excluded the "marriage and consummation" ceremony, proceeding with the actual branding. Our compadre's mother sprinkled three lines of *llampu* on each animal, and her sons tied the necklaces on the horns and fastened ribbons in the animals' ears. The branding specialist applied the brand to each animal and the *masa* poured chicha on the wounds. The calf was more elaborately treated, following all of the ritual steps described for the marriage, excluding the "marital embrace." An act evidently believed to give the young bull potency was substituted. The patron rubbed the animal's groin with the "crude silver" and "crude gold." The calf was not branded. After the animals had been ritually prepared, the patron and his *masa* distributed the *cirse* reeds. We made the two crosses and drove the animals out of the corral through a break in the wall that had been pushed out by the *masa.* The patron waited behind the wall, and as each animal jumped through the break he sprinkled it with *llampu.* As the animals exited we threw the *cirse* crosses at them. Drinking, singing, and coca chewing continued through the night.

6.4.4   The Payment to the Wamani

As mentioned in 6.4, I have not witnessed the final act of the Herranza, the payment or *pagapu* to the Wamani. The following description is a summary of the events of a *pagapu* in Choque Huarcaya reported by U. Quispe (1969: 35-: Chuschino informants concur with the description, except that women in Huarcaya accompany the men to the *caja* of the Wamani, whereas in Chuschi they do not approach this most dangerous place. This may be an indication of stronger sexual differentiation and agnatic emphasis in Chuschi. Clarification will require further investigation. Also, a few other differences are worth mentioning. The contents of the ceremonial bundle in Huarcaya evidently lack the effigies of the Wamanis' animals, the small stone *illas.* And the *llampu* is kept in gourds, not in cloth bundles. Otherwise, the contents are identical. From Quispe's data (1969), it is evident that the composition of the payment can vary, but there are invariable ingredients as well. The bits of ear and tail, called *señales,* are always included, along with carnations, whole unblemished coca leaves, coca seeds, *willka* seeds, *wayluru* seeds, fruit, and *llampu.* These ingredients are placed in a *cirse* basket, called the *tunku.* It is the same shape and manufacture as the *tunku* basket belonging to the bride during the *qollque qonopa,* "the gathering of silver" (5.6.5), of the marriage ceremonies. Two small clay bottles (*puyñus*) are filled with trago and chicha. Sometimes "crude gold," "crude silver," cigarettes, and wine are added to the offering, along with indigenous grains such as *quinua* and *achita* and various beans of both indigenous and Spanish origins. Rice is sometimes offered as well. None of the offerings described included potatoes or corn, the two major food product Corn is ground in the *llampu.* However, I have never seen potatoes ritually used.

The *pagapu* is made at dawn the morning after the branding ceremony. The retinue proceeds to the special *caja* belonging to the patron of the ritual. Of course, they have purified and protected themselves by drinking trago and chicha and chewing coca. They carry *cirse* crosses, and the patron carries the ceremonial bundle on his back, symbolizing his burden. The patron, or some other male, excavates the *caja* of the Wamani after "rinsing" his hands in *llampu* and offering the Wamani liquor. The two clay bottles buried on the last occasion are removed and ceremonially served by the *masa* in two containers (in Chuschi, a shell and a horn cup). The patron throws *llampu* into the air and sprinkles or pours *ñawin* trago and chicha into the hole before lowering the basket and refilled clay bottles. Chuschinos say that candles must be fastened to the basket also. The *caja* is covered with earth, and the large stone "lock" and smaller stone "key" are replaced. The congregation kneels and prays to the Wamani as the *waqrapuku* trumpets are played. If anyone falls during the payment ceremony, it is believed that the Wamani can take the fallen victim's heart. To prevent this, either *llampu*, or *ñawin* trago, or *ñawin* chicha, or the buried liquors, and coca must be consumed. After the ritual, the retinue drunkenly makes its way back to the corral and hut to sleep and eat before disbanding. If the Herranza has been carefully prepared and executed, the herds will increase and be protected by the Wamani. Animals are a measure of a person's wealth and prestige that the Wamani can provide or withhold capriciously at will.

6.5 Major Themes and Concepts—Major Lines of Defense

The overriding concern expressed in the three rituals is productivity and fecundity. The process of copulation and impregnation is ritually enacted during the Yarqa Aspiy, with Earth Mother as the purified bride and the two Wamanis residing in the sources of irrigation water, Ñawin Sullcaray and Lake Matuma, as her grooms. The entire village celebrates the final consummation at the *qonopa,* the site of the convergence of the canals at the boundary between the village and the *qichwa* zone. The major canal running through the center of the village is called *amaru,* which signifies such animals as a snake, a pig, and a bull. S. Palomino (1970: 124) maintains that the concept of *amaru* is the violent movement of earth or water. We can see how such movement can be conceptualized as the necessary energy for fertilization. Within the context of the three rituals under discussion, that force is the descending water of the irrigation canals. Zuidema (1972: 40) argues that the *amaru* (as snake) is not only associated with water but also with the ancestors and the underworld. He states that in Cuzco the irrigation system of the Incas converged beneath the Temple of the Sun, where the mummies of the nobility were kept. In a similar fashion in Chuschi, the *qonopa,* the site of the impregnation of Earth Mother, is located not only at the convergence of the canals but adjacent to the village cemetery. The ritual of regeneration and renewal, the Yarqa Aspiy, is finalized within sight of the resting place of the dead, the village cemetery. The cycle of renewal necessitates death; all regeneration requires both death and birth. Likewise, the annual cycle is divided into two halves: the rainy season, beginning in October and lasting through April, and the dry season, beginning in May and ending in September. The rainy season is associated with sickness, death, and scarcity, while the dry season brings to the Chuschino mind memories of abundance and renewal. Yarqa Aspiy cannot be performed until the rains begin. The fertility rite marks the beginning of the scarce epoch when Earth Mother is in gestation. She "gives birth" to the harvest in May during Santa Cruz, and the cycle begins over again.

All powerful Wamanis, as the owners of all animals and material possessions and as the sources of irrigation water, are propitiated twice a year, during the dry season in August and again during the wet season in February. Both of these months are said to be dangerous or *loco*, crazy. The earth "opens" at these times; therefore, offerings are readily accepted by the mountain deities. These two months are called the time of our "mother and father," which tempts one to propose ancestor worship of lineal ancestors as the function of the Herranza. However, when the Herranza and accompanying offerings to the Wamanis are viewed as a part of a ritual complex that expresses major Chuschino concerns and concepts, the Herranza is another fertility rite as well as an effort to appease the capricious male deities from whom the essential male element, water (semen), is necessary for fertilization.

Quispe (1969: 103) proposes the structure of Earth Mother opposed to the sky, symbolized by the Wamanis and mediated by water, the *amaru*. I believe that the three rituals demonstrate the concept of fertility as the union of female (Earth Mother) and male (Wamani) elements to produce abundance. The force that unites the two is the moving irrigation water (the *amaru*). The resultant harvest (Earth Mother's issue) and abundance are symbolized by the cross. In the Herranza, the cross symbolizes the union of male and female, which is expected to result in fecundity. The dominant fears expressed by Chuschinos are of castration by the Wamani and the *naqaq*, death or sterility of herds, and crop failures.

On the social plane, the three rituals embody the concepts of closed, bounded social space dichotomized as civilized (the village) and savage (the *sallqa*). Agricultural zones mediate between the two. The closed corporate nature of Chuschino society is depicted and reinforced through the characterizations of foreign domination in the portrayals of the priest, the military officers, and the *naqaq*. Spatially, foreigners occupy the center of Chuschi, the plaza, while comuneros live in the surrounding two barrios. This bounded, closed corporate universe embodies the most ancient of oppositions constructed by man: "We versus they." In Chuschi, this opposition finds expression as comunero (insider-member) versus *qala* (outsider-nonmember). These three rituals remind the Chuschinos that their society is socially and spatially closed and bounded. Furthermore, their survival in the past has been facilitated by their definition of the entire outside world as the threatening "other" opposed to "us," the members. P. Maranda (1972) maintains that structures function as mechanisms to annul history and prevent entropy. The three rituals discussed above are expressions of Chuschinos' efforts to abate entropy and insure continuance of order, as they conceive of it, by insuring fecundity and reproductivity. Therefore, it is clear why these rituals were retained whereas the observances of Christian rituals such as Easter, Christmas, and Lent were abandoned. The latter have not been incorporated into their major themes of productivity, fertility, and vertical exploitation, upon which their economics depend. They have been successful thus far in preventing the events of history from causing entropy in their ordered universe. Today, they face increasing pressures. Recent events that impinge on the comuneros' major concepts and the possible dialectic between their experiences and concepts are discussed in 8.4. Nevertheless, Chuschinos continue to defend themselves from the encroachments of the foreign outside world by perpetuating their concepts through the necessity of obligatory and standardized activities—rituals—that maintain the underlying order of their society and cosmology. Andean people have thus far defended themselves well—a great deal of symbolic continuity has been maintained.

The major line of successful defense is the Andean pattern of control over diversified production in vertical ecological zones (2.8). The zones are demarcated by the location of chapels housing crosses that are the responsibility of the civil-religious hierarchies. The celebrations of Yarqa Aspiy and Santa Cruz codify the critical information for successful agricultural exploitation of the vertical Andean environment into emotionally charged synthetic rituals. These rituals are considered essential to cosmic, spatial, economic, and social order. The maintenance of all three of these economic rituals—Yarqa Aspiy, Santa Cruz, and the Herranza—depends on the mechanisms of private and public reciprocity, the subject of the next chapter.

7. Private and Public Reciprocity

7.1 Types of Reciprocity

According to comuneros, there are four kinds of reciprocal exchange. Two involve agreements between individuals and two between the community as a whole and some institution such as the church or the state. I shall designate these two types of reciprocity as "private" and "public."

Private reciprocity entails what is called *ayni* and *minka*, and public involves *mita* and *faena*. According to the Chuschino definition, *minka* is when an individual calls for aid, usually in the form of labor of some kind, and those who respond to his call are "lending *ayni*," for which they expect repayment in comparable labor or service. The same network is called upon when a ritual obligation demands many hands and much trago and chicha for successful completion. Examples of private reciprocity will be given in 7.2. Public reciprocity will be discussed in 7.3. *Faenas* are public work days called by the municipal government. *Mita* means "turn" and implies taking turns at serving another. We will begin with private reciprocity, the backbone of Chuschino society.

7.2 Private Reciprocity

An illustration of how *ayni* and *minka* function is given in an example of the strategy used by a man who was an *hijo político* (3.8), that is, was the illegitimate son of a married person. In his words, he was born of a woman not his father's wife and had not received an inheritance or the promise of one from his father. He had become the *hijo de juramento* of an *apu*, rich man. This is a form of adoption wherein a simple ritual is performed in front of witnesses and a cross, resulting in special fictive or adoptive relationships that are rather fragile. In order to strengthen the relationship to his adopted father, he assumed the role of the dutiful son. When his adopted father sponsored a *minka* to build one of his genealogical sons a house, the adopted son was one of the eighteen men who attended four days of labor in response to the call for a *minka*. He told me that he intended to build a new house next year and had attended three house-building *minkas* in order to assure adequate *ayni* in return. Those people for whom he had worked must repay him when he calls a *minka*. The type of labor is not always equivalent, that is, one does not have to repay house-building with house-building, but can substitute planting or other labor. A strict accounting is kept of debts and credits. The comunero who is ostracized from participating in the mutual aid network cannot survive without recourse to cash for hired labor, and most comuneros do not participate in the cash economy of the nation. The example of the *wakcha* woman who had been socially ostracized, discussed in 3.6, demonstrates the plight of such a person.

In many cases, it is very doubtful whether the *ayni-minka* exchange system is economically the most advantageous form of labor. The influential *apu* comunero discussed above, who utilized *minka-ayni* to build his son's house adjacent to his own, claimed he had spent over 3,000.00 *soles* on the *minka* (about 70.00 dollars). He could have hired skilled laborers for less, but reciprocal aid is essential to the social fabric of Chuschi. Participation is one of the criteria for comunero membership as well as the principal mechanism by which one acquires status and demonstrates wealth. The sponsor of a *minka* must provide three meals for all participants as well as coca, trago, and cigarettes for four rests during the day. House constructions and roofings occur during August and September and have a festive air. (See plate 13.) For an excellent description of the rituals accompanying a house construction, see Mayer (1977).

For the fulfillment of ritual obligation, one calls upon the same network of consanguineal, affinal, and spiritual kin to help with the heavy burden of one's office. For all of the rituals described in chapters 5 and 6, a wide network was utilized for successful execution of each of the rituals. Two or three weeks before the ritual preparations are begun, corn is buried to ferment for the chicha; grains are prepared for the caldrons of soup; and the *carguyoq*, "one with a responsibility," assigns special tasks to members of his network. He will ask certain affines to act as servers of chicha and trago; he will pick two of his *masas* to enact the required subordinate roles; the *llumchus* will work at preparing chicha and food; and a compadre will be requested to stay sober and keep a list of all the contributions of the *kuyaq*, "those who love him." The *kuyaq* are all those who have contributed goods or labor to a person holding a ritual responsibility. After the public observances are over, the recipient of *kuyaq* aid holds a special private celebration to repay them

Plate 13. Private Reciprocity: Communal House-Roofing.

with food and drink in proportion to their generosity. I attended this special celebration in the house of the alcalde of Lower Barrio after the public celebration of the Yarqa Aspiy in 1970. An analysis of the contributions of the *kuya* reveals not only the structure of the aid network but the structure of the bilateral kindred as well.

In an interview, I asked the alcalde who had helped him with the fiesta, and our conversation is transcribed below.

QUECHUA	ENGLISH
Q: Pikunataq ayudan chay fiesta pasananpaq?	Who helps you complete this fiesta?
A: Munay gustokullawanmiki ruwakuniku.	With our own love we do it.
Q: Peru, kan familiankuna yanapaq?	But don't your relatives help you
A: Peru, chayqariki aylluykuqa yanapayllam yanapawanku maski imatapas.	But that is just it, we, the *ayllu*, we help ourselves in whatever wa possible.
Q: Imakunawan?	With what?
A: Kuyaq nispa botellawan iskay botellawanpas.	It is he who loves us, expressing (his love) with one or perhaps tw bottles.
Q: Mana familia kaqkuna . . . ?	And those who are not your family . . . ?
A: Compadrekuna y karu familiakuna chaykunallam. Taytamaman-chikpam obligatorio chayta yanapanakuy.	Our compadres and distant famil members, that's all. It is an oblig tion of our parents to help us.
Mamayku este trago [pointing to the chicha]. Chay suegranpa mamanpam debernin.	From our mothers comes this dri [pointing to the chicha]. It's the duty of the mothers-in-law and t women [or mothers].

Thirty-five people were present in the alcalde's house, of whom seven were not *ayllu, karu ayllu,* or compadres to him. Six represented subordinate *varay* who are obliged either to make a personal appearance in the house of the alcalde or to send someone with a bottle of trago as a symbol of their esteem. The other non-related person was a cook from the nearby village of Quispillaq contracted by the alcalde to prepare the special meal for his *kuyaq.* It is

worth remembering that all eighteen members of the village's two *vara* systems
were simultaneously celebrating the *kuyaq* festivities. However, of greatest
magnitude were the observances of the two barrio alcaldes. They had borne
the heaviest expenses in goods and energy and had amassed the greatest *kuyaq*
contributions. The alcalde of Lower Barrio had expended the following:

Three and a half *arrobas* (87 pounds) of trago	@	120.00 *soles* each	=	420.00
20 packages of cigarettes	@	3.00 *soles* each	=	60.00
3 pounds of coca	@	10.00 *soles* each	=	30.00
		Total expended in cash:		510.00

In addition, he had slaughtered three llamas for the communal meals and to
feed his *kuyaq*. The women of his *ayllu* and the "mothers-in-law" of his *ayllu*
provided approximately 120 liters of chicha (30 *urpos*) for the festivities. One
"distant aunt" represented these women by fulfilling the ritual role of *dispensera*. His *kuyaq* contributed a total of 25 bottles of trago and forty *soles* in
cash. All of these contributions were carefully recorded by a compadre, who
was instructed to stay sober during the festivities in order to keep an account
of all donations. He was literate and therefore kept a written record, but in
the past such accounts were committed to memory. At the feast of the *kuyaq,*
he read aloud each contribution, and the donor was served according to his
generosity. The person who had given one bottle of trago was served soup,
but the man who had contributed cash or four or five bottles of trago was
served a large portion of meat as well. (See plate 14.)

Figure 5 displays the gifts of ego's *ayllu, karu ayllu,* and his affines—his
wife's *ayllu.* The donations of his three compadres are not shown; they consisted of four bottles of trago from one and one bottle each from the other
two compadres. Nine bottles of trago and two *soles* were donated by non-
kuyaq persons. These people were predominantly *varayoq* or their representatives, who appeared at the "convidio" with a bottle of trago as a demon-
stration of their esteem for the highest official. Such formal visitation is
expected of all subordinate *varayoq.*

The compadre who compiled the *kuyaq* list told me that people had performed as expected. The alcalde was pleased with his *kuyaq* and felt that his
last year of public office was successful due to the completion of the Yarqa
Aspiy. He could now retire from civil-ritual obligations, and would be considered by his fellow comuneros as *apu*, or rich. This term is applied to
comuneros who have material wealth and a large network of kin that can be
relied on (3.5). A man with material wealth but without the necessary kin to

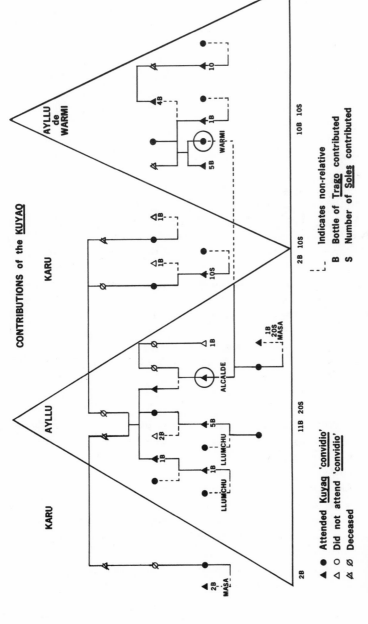

FIGURE 5

execute his civil and ritual obligations is *wakcha,* poor or orphaned (3.6).

An examination of the chart of contributions reveals that certain features of the structure of the *kuyaq* kin group are reflected in the contributions made to the alcalde. On a general level, trago and money are expected from men, labor and chicha from women. As the alcalde explained, "Chicha is the obligation of our women or mothers and our mothers-in-law." Contributions are expected from ego's male generation mates of his *ayllu* and *karu ayllu* (his classificatory "near" and "far" brothers). Men who have married women of ego's *ayllu* and *karu ayllu* are also expected to contribute. Moreover, the heaviest obligations rest with ego's *masa,* a male who has married ego's daught or his female *ayllu* generation mate ("sister"). The *masa's* obligations are in large part ritual.

A *masa* symbolically dramatizes the role of a male who has married a wom of the *ayllu*. He is not addressed by name during a ritual; he must assume female duties such as serving chicha and he must perform the antics of a clown. In all, his behavior is a caricature of an outsider to the *ayllu* who has a position inferior to that of its members.

In our example, the alcalde's daughter's husband contributed heavily— twenty *soles* in cash and one bottle of trago—even though he could not attend the three-day celebration and assume his ritual duties due to the demands of wage employment. The alcalde found an appropriate substitute among the other affines. A male who had married a *karu pani,* a "distant sister," of the alcalde was chosen to assume the ritual duties of *masa*. On the diagram, the female counterparts to *masas*, the *llumchus*, are women who have married into the *ayllu* of the alcalde. This position is analogous to that of *masa* in that it signifies an outsider to the *ayllu* who has married a male member. The ritual duties of this position include service to one's husband's mother and her female *ayllu* generation mates. The position does not have the symbolic asym metric characteristics of the male outsider, the *masa*. Perhaps this is due to the fact that the *llumchu,* or a female who has married into an *ayllu,* resides in the house of her father-in-law and must serve her mother-in-law for a period of years before the couple is allowed to establish a residence of their own. The *masa* acts out the role of an outsider who has not been incorporate into the group.

The alcalde himself stands in a *masa* relationship to his wife's father (in this case, her step-father) and to her full brother and step-brother. However, as the alcalde's *kuyaq*, these men contributed substantially to his ritual obliga- tion. When they have a similar obligation to perform, theoretically they can call upon the alcalde to fulfill his ritual duties as their *masa*. However, with his exalted status as the highest indigenous official of Lower Barrio, he would be spared such a subordinate position and a younger, less prestigious "outside to the *ayllu*" would be chosen.

The *ayllu* of the alcalde and the *ayllu* of his wife interact with one another in the symmetric relationship that is in opposition to the asymmetric relationship of *masa* and *ayllu*. All of the members of each *ayllu*, excluding ego and his wife, are *awra* to one another (5.4). The expectations that ego has toward the various persons occupying the categories of *ayllu*, *karu ayllu*, *awra*, and compadre reflect structural features of the kin network. Examination of the chart of *kuyaq* contributions reveals that different behavior is expected from males than from females. Donations of trago and cash come from the following males: (1) ego's *ayllu* generation mates, his "brothers," to whom ego stands in an equivalent relationship; (2) ego's wife's generation mates, her "brothers," to whom ego stands in a *masa* relationship; (3) ego's *masas*, the symbolic outsiders to his *ayllu;* and (4) ego's compadres de ramo, his spiritual kin (not shown on chart), who sponsored his real or potential children.

Women are expected to provide labor and chicha. Those who marry one of ego's male generation mates or one of his sons are *llumchu* to ego and are expected to aid the women of ego's *ayllu* in the preparation of ritual food.

Finally, the category of *dispensera* (dispenser of corn beer) is occupied by a female *karu tía*, or "distant relative." It is interesting to note that the descendants of this person are potentially marriageable to ego. It is possible that the position of dispenser symbolizes also the provider of women to one's *ayllu*, or female wife-givers.

Each of these categories of kinship displays distinct agreed-on rights, duties, and expectations. The organizing principles of differentiating by sex and equivalence of generation mates are dramatized in reciprocal exchange. Also, the concept of "my group" *(ayllu)* as opposed to "the outsider who has married into my group" is portrayed by the subordinate roles of *masa* and *llumchu*. The symmetric relationship of two *ayllus* joined by marriage is reflected in the generosity of ego's affines. Terminologically, this structural equivalence is reflected in the reciprocal *awra* term that is applied to those affines who have been ritually redefined as "like consanguines." They are opposed to those affines who occupy the subordinate category of "outsider"— the *masa* and *llumchu*.

The category of compadre is interesting because we see only one type of compadre participating—the compadre de ramo. This relationship is also structurally equivalent and terminologically reciprocal. More important, however, the ramo ritual is essential for the symbolic formation of a new kindred.

The kindred structure is reinforced and perpetuated by the acts of reciprocity. The network of exchanges reaffirms the boundaries as well as the expectations of the *ayllu*, the *awra*, and compadrazgo relationships. The "game of reciprocity" is the focal point around which these ego-centered groups function. The *kuyaq* reciprocal network not only reaffirms the kinship structure, it also perpetuates the prestige system of the *varayoq*, which is the expression of social hierarchy among comuneros of the village. If the *kuyaq* network of the eighteen *varayoq* malfunctioned, the elaborate prestige system would decline.

In order to adequately perform the rituals that express social and cosmo-logical order and insure fertility and abundance, the *vara* members of the two barrios as well as the mayordomos depend on the aid and generosity of each individual *kuyaq* network. In exchange for these ritual services, the *vara* members, the mayordomos, and their *kuyaq* receive prestige and esteem from the village. We might say that this is an instance of public reciprocity, whereby the institution of the *varas,* as guardians of important sacred places and ritual officiants, functions as a reciprocal relationship to the entire village. The new agricultural cycle cannot begin until order as defined in the ecological parti-tioning of the comuneros' territory is established. In addition, the fertility of Earth Mother (and of women) is assured by the appropriate enactment of the Yarqa Aspiy. The fruitful results are dramatized during Santa Cruz and the series of marriage ceremonies. Even the agnatic-centered Herranza depends on private kin-based reciprocal aid for successful execution.

7.3 Public Reciprocity

The two forms of public reciprocity defined by Chuschinos are communal work days, *faenas,* and serving in turn, *mita.* Communal labor, *faena,* is used by government bureaucracies to build roads, schools, clinics, and bridges and to carry out other public works projects such as the installation of potable water, even though communal labor was abolished in 1810 (Fuenzalida 1970: 71). In Chuschi, *faenas* provided the labor for the road connecting the village and the neighboring village of Cancha-Cancha in 1961. In 1966 the road was brought from the boundary of the village to the plaza with communal labor. During 1963-1964, the village provided the labor and public works the material for a bridge across the Taksa Mayo, the small river separating Chuschi and Quispillaqta. A water reservoir for potable water was constructed in 1969. And finally, in 1970, I witnessed the beginning of work on a road to connect Chuschi with the new link to the coast, Los Libertadores. Each comunero household is required to provide one male laborer for a prescribed number of work days. The alcaldes of each barrio are responsible for attendance. They supervise a canvass to notify all barrio residents and impose and collect fines from delin-quents. The municipal government provides coca, trago, and cigarettes for two half-hour breaks. Coca is weighed and apportioned to each male along with one portion of trago and one cigarette for each break. Each comunero household provided six days of labor toward the installation of the potable water canal. The comuneros explained that the *qalas* (mestizos) did not work at all, yet they benefit from the water. One *qala* family hauled sand by horseback to prevent complaints. In 1969, seven *qala* men, most of them schoolteachers, worked one day on the new road. Comuneros commented that it was the first time *qalas* had participated in *faena* labor.

Aged informants claim that *mita,* rotation labor, is declining. The only instance in which *mita* is used today is by the church. I observed obligatory labor by turn to repair the church and lay a new tile floor in 1967. The *hatun* alcalde, as a servant to the church, was responsible for providing laborers. With the abolition of the *hatun varayoq* structure, this form of labor is probably in danger of disappearing, as other forms of *mita* have in the past. Within the memory of informants, *mita* was used by prominent *qala* families, the priest, and the military to provide themselves with household servants and field laborers. The comuneros have rebelled against such personal servitude, but *mita* is still "prestado" (loaned) to the church. The church reciprocates with coca, trago, and chicha. Public agencies are viewed as standing in an exchange relationship with the community; labor is exchanged for the esteemed coca, cigarettes, trago, and chicha. Workers disband when an agency does not reciprocate with these expected items.

Both public and private reciprocity have played an essential role in Chuschino migrants' successful adaptation to Lima's *pueblos jovenes,* the squatter settlements. It appears that private kin-based and public institutional reciprocity are not only basic Andean patterns but are also exchange structures that have facilitated adaptation to the urban environment. Now let us examine the mechanisms by which adaptation is occurring.

8. Migrants' Construction of an Urban Identity

8.1 The Scope of Migration in Peru

Chuschinos have participated in the tremendous onslaught of highland peasants who have descended upon Lima in search of employment. In 2.2 I discussed the push and pull of Peruvian migration. The capital of Lima, where 72 percent of the nation's industry is located, has borne the heaviest portion of the migratory burden. Over 25 percent of the country's 13.5 million lives in or around the city. Lima's population has more than doubled during the period between 1940 and 1972, corresponding to the post-World War II industrial development. Other cities are experiencing rapid growth as well. According to the 1972 census, 53 percent of Peru's population lives in the urban centers of Lima, Trujillo, Arequipa, Cuzco, Puno-Juliaca, and Huancayo (Alcántara and Vásquez 1974: 15). Carlos Delgado estimates that during 1967 alone 75,000 persons migrated to Lima (1971: 125). If the current rate of mass exodus from the highlands continues, by 1980 Lima will have a population of 5,800,000 (ibid.).

Chuschino migrants join the hopeful mass of highland peasants who make up close to 40 percent of Lima's 3.5 million. However, their hopes are too often unfulfilled and they find themselves among the economically inactive. During the ten years between 1961 and 1971 there were 200 economically inactive persons in Peru for every 100 persons working (Alcántara and Vásquez 1974: 26). Lima's recent migrants often find themselves in the unemployed category and facing a rapid inflation rate (estimated as over 150 percent for the last ten-year period).

The migrant must call on a wide network of kin and co-villagers for survival in the competitive urban environment. Furthermore, the threat of failure motivates migrants to maintain strong ethnic and economic ties with their places of origin. Paul Doughty (1970: 32) has aptly stated: "That situation facing the individual migrant in Peru is complex, and one must be startled not by the fact that there is apparent social chaos and anomie at times, but that so many individuals and families are indeed able to retain their integrative structure or to reorganize their lives in meaningful ways." Doughty offers an analysis of the clubs or regional associations as an integrative mechanism facilitating adaptation to the urban environment. Likewise, Mangin (1967) has emphasized the positive aspects of the ability of the squatter settlers to cope with potentially adverse urban situations.

An analysis of the manner in which migrants from Chuschi have manipulate the traditional symbols of their place of origin provides an illustration of the process by which migrants restructure their shared identity to accommodate their urban experiences and render them meaningful. The migrant might be called the "bricoleur" (Lévi-Strauss 1966) of traditional concepts and symbols he takes the elements at hand and rearranges them for his own purposes; he is an innovator and constructor of symbolic structures. Nevertheless, he is constrained by the structural elements available to him. The interplay between the migrants' collective experiences and the transformation of key traditional concepts gives rise to the formation and construction of structures. This chapter applies structuralist methodology to the urban phenomena of migration.

Pierre Maranda (1972: 338) has stated that, in order to communicate, people must share common mythic conceptions, which are a society's effort to preserve its identity over time in spite of the entropic effects of history. As the random and chaotic events of history impinge on a society, the members construct a "mythical conception" of those events. This case study provides an example not only of how an Andean society made the chaotic events of migration and illegal invasion orderly but also of how it utilized the experiences to restructure shared identity and shared mythic conceptions.

8.2   A Brief History of Migration

In the late 1930s the first villager to journey to Lima was a young monolingual Quechua speaker, with no formal education, who had been conscripted into the army. He returned to Chuschi and convinced a male first cousin to join him in Lima. The two found lodging in one of the inner city's block slums and established a small commercial business in the major market. The first migrant never married. He returned to the village in his advanced years and died there. Several of the subsequent migrants were widowed women who preferred to set up small enterprises in the major market of Lima or establish a house as ambulatory vendors rather than remain in the village and try to remarry. Vending has remained a major occupation of women to the present day. None of the migrants from this particular village have been employed as household servants. They consider such positions beneath their status; perhaps this is understandable in light of the absence of hacienda domination or of influence on the village of origin. Chuschi has been an independent administrative center since Inca times, and during the colonial era it was the seat of administration for a *repartimiento,* but no haciendas developed in the area. Villagers jealously guard the communal pasture lands, and they view themselves as an independent closed corporate community and not as part of the national culture.

This independence and lack of hacienda history helps explain the migrants' preference for self-employment in small independent businesses. In 1970 such enterprises included a small wrought-iron furniture shop, a taxi service from the squatter settlement to the major market, several small stores in the settlement, and, as mentioned above, market vending as a major occupation of women. Migrants from Chuschi have begun to penetrate the textile and shoe factories and other wage employment requiring completion of primary school. This correlates with the increased education of the first migrants. Concomitantly, factory employment has fostered union membership and political awareness.

By 1941 there were perhaps fifteen to twenty Chuschino migrants residing in Lima in various inner city *tugurios* (densely populated block slums). In that year they organized the Progressive Society of Santa Rosa of Lima, with Santa Rosa as their patron saint. The declared purpose of the society was to promote and safeguard the welfare of the village. In the same year they presented the petition and documentation necessary to obtain the legal status of indigenous community for the village. With that action the society was recognized as the legal representative of Chuschi and has continued to handle legal matters, supervise elections, audit books, and inspect records in the village. The society also raises funds for the village schools, buying such items as sports equipment, uniforms, and band instruments.

In 1946 the members of the society participated in the squatter invasion of San Cosme, now one of the largest *pueblos jovenes* or "young communities" in Lima, located on the central highway about five kilometers from the central city. Matos Mar (1966: 19) estimates that in 1955 the population density of San Cosme had reached 857 inhabitants per hectare (over 85,000 per square kilometer). The population in San Cosme continued to expand, and the original migrants from Chuschi sponsored newcomers from their village of origin, offering temporary housing to those who wanted employment during the period between November and April, the interval between planting and harvest. With the concentration of the migrants in San Cosme, two types of migration emerged:

1. Cyclical migration, whereby migrants depend upon relatives and compadres for housing and aid in finding temporary employment during the period between November and April
2. Permanent migration, whereby migrants decide to become permanent residents of Lima when their economic situation becomes stable enough. They retain control of their lands and provide cash for seed, often returning to the village to supervise the harvest. A relative agrees to plant the migrants' fields for one half of the harvest.

The literature on migration in Peru has not differentiated the dynamics of migration; however, Héctor Martínez (1968: 10) offers a useful typology of migration. It appears that for Chuschi cyclical migration responds to the employment potential in Lima, but I have no records or observations to demonstrate how migration fluctuates with economic development or declines. It would be most illuminating to study the process by which temporary migrants become permanent migrants and contrast this process to that which typifies perpetual temporary migration. The migration process is a continuum that we know only fleetingly. Mangin (1959, 1960, 1967, 1970) has described cityward migration, but to my knowledge no one has described temporary migration in Peru or the return migration and the resultant effects on the rural villages.

Chuschi has suffered a decline in population during the past decade. The census of 1940 lists a population of 1,310, but in 1961 the population had dropped to 1,099. A survey completed in 1967 by the Ministerio de Trabajo (Bolívar de Colchado 1967: 16) tabulated the outward migration between January and August of that year. They found that forty villagers migrated to Lima, ten to Ayacucho, the department capital, and ten to a coca plantation in the department of Jauja. They did not determine whether these migrants were seeking temporary employment or intended to remain permanently at their destinations. It is common for villagers to migrate to Lima and to the department capital to seek temporary wage employment during the period between planting and harvest. Migration to the coca plantation in Jauja is always contractual for the coca harvest. During the dry season a Chuschino can catch a weekly bus to Lima, a two-day trip, and arrive within walking distance of the squatter settlement where his fellow villagers are now nucleated. He can communicate back and forth between the rural and urban places without speaking Spanish or adopting western dress or crossing the Plaza de Armas in the center of Lima. He can work for relatives in the major market or find employment near the new nucleated squatter settlement called 7 de Octubre, where the majority of permanent migrants live. The settlement bears this name due to the fact that the original invasion took place on October 7, 1963, on the eve of President Belaúnde's birthday.

8.3   The Invasion of 7 de Octubre

On October 7, 1963, twelve migrant Chuschino families residing in San Cosme participated in a "spill-over" invasion across the central highway into an unpopulated area owned by a housing cooperative comprising six hundred market venders. One of Lima's leading papers, *La Prensa*, reported that 2,000 people took part in the October 7 invasion. The police and the Guardia Civil successfully expelled all but 200 of the invaders on the day of the 8th. The twelve Chuschino families were among the entrenched 200. They reported that they defended their position by fortifying the upper entrance of a double-mouthed cave, the only access to the top. A system of signal lights was used to warn the hilltop defenders of advancing troops. The police and Guardia suffered eleven wounded and the invaders many more—the exact number was never reported. On October 9, 1,000 squatters returned to the site, and the authorities did not contest their claim to the area. The squatters elected a seven-member junta whose names were not revealed to the press—they were designated by numbers only. The first activities of the squatters were to de-lineate plots with stones, to construct mat shelters, and to make paths up the steep hillside. The events of this invasion parallel those described by Mangin (1970). The invaders of 7 de Octubre followed closely the formula for a suc-cessful takeover except that the area they chose to invade was private rather than public property. The market venders' cooperative has attempted to reclaim its land legally, but nothing has been resolved.

During the first months of occupancy the seven-member junta instituted a defense system whereby each household was responsible for one day of guard duty at the entrances to the settlement; failure to comply resulted in a fine imposed and collected by the junta. This effort was not totally effective in keeping out latecomers to the area, and informants say that the first few months saw many new squatters pouring into the area. The first rule of squatter invasion is continuous occupancy. If a mat shelter was left unat-tended, informants report that it would be immediately occupied. One of the original invaders left his plot for only two weeks in order to participate in the village harvest; he returned to find his plot occupied by persons he called "foreigners," a family not from his village.

The first months of occupation in 7 de Octubre not only saw the creation of a quasi-military-political organization but also evidenced territorial division, strife, and fraud as well. Six distinct localized zones developed. The Chuschino migrants' territory was literally in the middle, in the third zone. Those in the first and second zones complained to the junta that their plots were smaller than those of zones four through six. They attempted to take over areas adjacent to their zones, causing open battles to occur. Informants relate that they were compelled to carry straw shields to and from work to protect themselves from the barrage of stones as they passed through the first and second zones. A mat shelter could not be left unoccupied even for a period of a few hours for fear of takeover by those of the first and second zones. Anxiety over possession of individual plots heightened, and the squatters were ready prey when one of the members of the junta fraudulently sold titles to the land. Complaints were brought against him; he was tried and currently serves a prison sentence for fraud. In spite of the territorial strife an fighting, the settlement united in order to construct a primary school. They were successful only after battling government forces and suffering casualties in the fracas.

At the time of this research (1969-1970), the migrant population from Chuschi totaled approximately 275 persons residing in 55 households in 7 de Octubre and 45 persons residing in 9 households in San Cosme. A household typically includes someone from the village, usually a relative, who is in Lima temporarily. These persons generally have minimal facility in Spanish and rely upon their relatives for aid in seeking temporary employment. They often work for their relatives in the market as street venders or as construction laborers. They are the cyclical migrants discussed in 8.2.

The ties of kinship and compadrazgo are essential to adaptation to urban life, and the bilateral personal kindred of the village is flexible to the demands of the city. Out of a sample of 59 unions of persons residing in 7 de Octubre and San Cosme, only 18 were with persons other than co-villagers. Of these 18 "foreign" unions, 5 were with persons in the same district or province, and the remaining 13 were with other migrants of highland origin. The preferred pattern is to marry someone from Chuschi after a period of residence together. One informant had not known her husband prior to her arranged marriage at the age of fifteen to a young man who had established himself in Lima with wage employment. He returned to the village after the two families had successfully negotiated the marriage and brought his fifteen-year-old bride-to-be to Lima. They lived together for a year in what is traditionally called "a year together" *(watanakuy)*, after which they returned to the village to be married in the church and by civil law. The custom of "a year together" has been almost eradicated in the village by the priest, but it has reemerged in Lima, where church influence is remote. Migrants explain their preference by saying that fellow villagers are "our people" and also by the practical considera tion that land and animals can be consolidated with a propitious marriage.

Compadres are overwhelmingly chosen from villagers or from co-villagers living in 7 de Octubre or San Cosme. Essentially the same forms of compadrazgo are practiced in the squatter settlement as in the village (chapter 5). Changes in both marriage preferences and compadrazgo selection will probably occur with the next generation, who see themselves as Limeños rather than villagers. They will prefer to intensify their urban identity at the expense of their rural ties. One wonders whether the typical forms of reciprocity will be abandoned. Chapter 7 differentiated two types of village reciprocity— public work days for community projects, and private reciprocity, which is kin-based and directed toward individuals or families. The latter is repaid in kind, and the former guarantees membership in the society. In Lima both public and private reciprocity are utilized, and mutual aid has been a key factor in the success of the migrants' adaptation to their self-constructed community. House construction is usually carried out over a period of years, during which both wage and mutual aid are utilized. Turner (1970) estimates that the self-construction characteristic of Lima squatters extends over a twenty-year period. The priorities followed by Chuschino squatters parallel those outlined by Turner; they constructed temporary mat shelters first and then built one-story cinder block shells without roofs, flooring, plumbing, or electricity. Adequate living space is the first consideration; a second story is added on as the migrant family is able to pay for the materials. Most often mutual aid is utilized for part of the construction labor, but wage labor is used for special skills such as brick laying. Communal labor is essential for the later priorities— sewers and electricity. In 7 de Octubre electricity is often illegally obtained by hooking up to lines from a commercial urbanization project below the settlement. Public reciprocity is being utilized to construct the social and ceremonial center of Chuschino urban life—the club house. (See plate 15.)

The club house was begun under the auspices of the Progressive Society of Santa Rosa of Lima in 1966. They held dances, sports events, and lotteries to finance the materials, and public work days were called on Sundays with the society providing beer for all workers. The club house has been built around the lower entrance of the double-mouthed cave that was crucial to the defense of the migrants' claimed territory against government troops during the invasion. The building is a three-sided structure, with the cave serving as the back wall, and the upper entrance has been closed off. As of yet, the building has not been roofed, so the cave itself is the place of congregation where public occasions are held, often accompanied by the retelling of the invasion story. The club house is the physical self-constructed icon of migrant unity and identity. The recounting of the invasion story is the manifestation of the creation of a modern urban origin myth or "mythic conception." The choice of the cave as the site for the club house is not coincidental, but rather demonstrates the influence of Andean concepts. One of the Inca origin myths describes the emergence of the founders of the Inca nobility out of the mouth of

Plate 15. 7 de Octubre Invasion Settlement. Chuschino club (white building) in the mouth of a cave.

a cave (Rowe 1963: 316). In Lima we see an Andean theme applied to the urban experiences of invasion, squatting, and construction of an urban community. Their new urban origin is symbolized by the construction of the community club house at the mouth of the cave.

8.4 The Transformation of Andean Concepts

We have seen that within traditional village contexts, the basic concept of "my group" versus the outside world has the following configuration (2.8, 4.3.3):

+	−
INSIDE	OUTSIDE
MEMBER	NONMEMBER
COMUNERO	*QALA*
CIVILIZED	SAVAGE

The question we will now address is, How was the structure of this concept transformed by the migrants? The most obvious transformation occurred in conjunction with the notions of social space. Chuschinos conceive of themselves as members living inside the boundaries of the civilized village as opposed to the entire foreign world, which has penetrated the center of their sociopolitical space and has come to dominate the political and spiritual spheres of village life.

In Lima this dual structure is not an appropriate interpretation of the migrants' social space. The members of "my group of squatters" are localized around the club house, whereas the element most threatening to their social space is the presence of other squatters around them who covet their territory.

The migrants' experiences have been such that they do not see the world as foreign and threatening and have redefined the term in accordance with their experiences. They are upwardly mobile and desire integration into the national culture. Most often this is expressed in terms of the possibilities for their children to become professionals or bureaucrats. Their notion of social space is still concentric and dual, but the organization has been rearranged. The "bricoleur" migrant has taken the traditional elements of the structural organization of space and rearranged it thus:

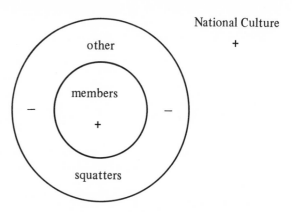

The values have been reversed, and there has been a transformation from the concept of the closed, corporate, bounded "we" versus the foreign threatening "they" to a conceptualization of the unified members nucleated together around the club house as the physical symbol of membership versus the threatening squatters adjacent to their territory. The outside world is viewed positively as a potentiality for membership and national urban identity. The transformation can be presented diagrammatically:

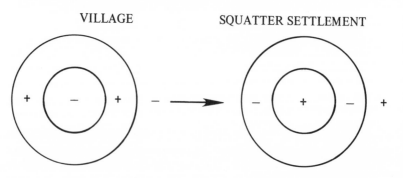

8.5   New Rituals and a New Opposition

Turning to the role of the minor saint, El Señor de los Temblores (The Lord of Earthquakes), we see that this small male saint represents an *outside* subordinate political unit. The early migrants carried this small effigy to Lima to symbolize their colonizer subordinate status. A religious organization was formed for the cult of this minor saint; its membership is responsible for this small male saint's return once a year to visit his "father," the major saint, housed *inside* the village church. This new pilgrimage is reminiscent of the traditional one taken by the seven minor saints representing the seven villages subordinate to Chuschi, the religio-political center (2.10).

In 1941 a group of migrants formed the Progressive Society of Santa Rosa of Lima with the female major saint, Santa Rosa, as the patron. Santa Rosa became the principal cult object, signifying that for the immigrants who invaded and settled in 7 de Octubre, a new opposition had been formed:

+	−
Santa Rosa	El Señor de Los Temblores
Major	Minor
Represents Urban Lima	Subordinate to Village
Female	Male

With the construction of this opposition, urban Lima became identified as no longer threatening or savage, but rather representing to the migrants a possible category for membership and identification. This is not to say that the urban place is not without threatening or "savage" elements. It is possible that the government troops and Guardia occupy this position vis-à-vis the migrants, but during the celebration of Santa Rosa in August, 1970, the caricatures of political, religious, and supernatural dominators—that is, the priest, the military office, and the *naqaq* (6.2)—were conspicuously absent. The flyer announcing the celebration had listed their appearance, but the only traditional portrayals were positive ones: a boy and a girl in traditional dress depicted the sponsors of the bullfight enacted on the streets of the invasion settlement with a papier-mâché bull, accompanied by the blasts of two cattle horn trumpeters imported from the village for the occasion and the migrants' brass band. A procession sponsored by the mayordomo of the fiesta, carrying the effigy of Santa Rosa to the club house, resembled the processions in the village except that the mayordomo was in this instance the head of a sports club claiming two hundred members with the same surname. Twenty-three young men residing in Lima shared the expense of the celebration, and their kinsmen in the village sent the traditional musicians, corn, potatoes, and llama meat. The traditional network of kinsmen was employed for the success of the fiesta; moreover, we see that in the urban setting the generational emphasis of reciprocity among age mates has taken the form of a sports club.

The absence of the icons of oppression and domination that are an integral part of village rituals delineates the migrants' changing view of the outside world. They appear to be molding the positive traditional symbols of identity, and the obvious question is whether new portrayals depicting negative forces will emerge. It is unlikely that migrants will focus on the outside world as dominating, threatening, or savage, but they might caricature their fellow squatters in some way to remind themselves of a nearby threat. Currently, the migrants appear to be ritually focusing on success and prosperity as well as on the time-honored concept of prestige. Sponsorship of the celebration of Santa Rosa of Lima has become one of the means by which migrants gain prestige and status in the eyes of their fellow migrants. Several families informed me that they were saving to sponsor the festivities, usually three to five years hence, and it is clear that an urban prestige hierarchy is under construction.

Sponsorship of another ritual serves as a mechanism for gaining status and prestige. However, it is a ritual foreign to Chuschi and has become exclusively the prerogative of the *nouveau riche* migrants, those who have become financially successful and prominent. The ritual is called the *corte monte,* or tree cutting. It is commonly observed in some parts of the Andes during carnival, but in Lima the celebration can take place anytime. According to informants, the ritual was borrowed from other migrants in 1967.

In the invasion settlement, two sponsors for the *corte monte* are required, one male and one female. They must be affluent: the man must purchase a grown tree and transport it to the invasion settlement, and the woman must buy gifts, such as small bottles of wine and alcohol, small bags of coins, plastic household items, and candy, gum, and cookies—all purchased items. None of the items are made by the sponsors themselves; the ritual requires a great deal of cash.

Once the tree has been decorated and planted in the middle of the street, the festive cutting down of the tree takes place. Only those wishing to sponsor next year's celebration participate in the ritual dancing around the tree. As the group dances around the tree, each dancer takes the ax and cuts into the trunk. The last couple to wield the ax when the tree finally falls must sponsor next year's celebration.

The nonparticipants watch and wait for the tree to fall to scramble for the gifts. They are the less successful, who have not accumulated the wealth (in cash) to expend on such a display.

During the 1970 *corte monte* that I observed, the participants wore the costumes of the hacendado class. The men were dressed in cotton ponchos, sunglasses, large straw hats, and bright-colored neck scarves.

In an earlier publication (Isbell 1974a: 253) I argued that the affluent migrants were emulating the prosperity and success of the hacendado class, and that, moreover, the traditional concept of displaying generosity was being used in the urban environment to gain prestige. The form of generosity utilized in the *corte monte,* however, requires cash and therefore differentiates those who have succeeded in the capitalistic economy of Lima. In addition, sponsorship of the ritual demands individual wealth that cannot be supplied by the mutual aid of one's kin network. In contrast, the 1970 Santa Rosa sponsors were members of a collective—a sports club. The traditional collectivity of kin-based mutual aid has been transformed into the urban manifestation of a sports club. But the *corte monte* sponsorship demands individual wealth, an expression of capitalistic values.

In the postscript (10.4), we will discover that in 1974 the same group of affluent migrants further elaborated traditional symbolic expressions of generosity to construct literally an "upper class." In other words, my analysis of the successful migrants' emulation of the prosperity of the hacendado class was only partially correct. They consciously used rituals to construct a class structure and place social distance between themselves and their co-villagers. Therefore, we see the dynamic creation of social classes in the urban environment among a group of migrants who also manipulate ethnic identity and solidarity for other purposes.

In the role of cultural brokers, the migrants successfully manipulated the basic opposition of "we," the comuneros, versus the exploitative elements of the outside world. Below, the events of 1970-1971 are discussed, and in 10.3 the subsequent changes effected by the migrants between 1970 and 1975 are detailed.

8.6   The Impact of the Urban Transformations on the Village

Turning to the question of the impact of the transformed concept of "we" versus "they" on the villagers' traditional ideas, I have stated that migrants have played an important role as legal representatives and "cultural brokers" for the village. Their position has been extra-legal in that they often sought solutions to village problems outside of the sanction of the law. For example, the Progressive Society of Santa Rosa tried for several years to remove the director of the schools from office. They charged him with neglecting his public office to attend to his private businesses, a store and a truck service. The director belonged to one of the *qala* families of the community. He is a descendant of the first schoolteacher who came to the village four generations ago. He was also charged with plying comuneros with alcohol and cheating them out of their land. Finally, in a public denouncement in 1970, the migrants charged that the director was "an enemy of the revolution." Charges and counter-charges proliferated over a ten-year period, culminating in success for the migrants in 1971. During the period of 1970 to 1971 they were jailed on several occasions for their activities against the director and the church. The church was their second focus of attack.

The members of the Progressive Society formulated a plan to confiscate the church's holdings in land, cattle, and sheep and to convert these into a cooperative in the name of the community. Again, after several stormy attempts resulted in repeated arrests, the migrants were able to instigate a court action whereby a village cooperative would be formed from the church herds and lands, comprising 250 head of cattle, 1,500 head of sheep, and thirteen large corn plots located in the most desirable agricultural region below the village in the *qichwa* zone. Each one of the thirteen corn plots equals the total amount of agricultural land owned by the average comunero family (about one to two hectares).

In 1971 the Agrarian Reform Office supported the migrants' efforts by coming repeatedly to their defense and releasing them from jail. The dispute with the church was placed under the jurisdiction of the 1970 Agrarian Reform Law; the priest was transferred to another locality, and the matter is currently before the courts. This incident is an example of the agrarian reform officials following behind and supporting grass-roots efforts generated at the local level. Two neighboring villages have had similar histories of efforts instigated by migrants to transform church possessions into cooperatives.

The migrants were not only opposed vigorously by the church, they also had to deal with the apathy of the villagers. Over the years, the villagers opposed the migrants' efforts because, as they said, "You come from Lima and stir up trouble and then you return to Lima and leave us with the trouble." Due to the pressure of the 1970 Agrarian Reform Law, several migrants have returned to the village to retain usufruct rights to their land, and their return has legitimized their efforts for progressive reform. It is highly probable that the majority of migrants from this village hold agricultural plots, and the migrants who have returned to the village to comply with the residence requirements of the law are doing so to maintain legally defined comunero status (4.2.1 and 4.2.2). Two migrants have been elected to the newly created posts of president of the administrative committee and president of the vigilance committee. Both are active members of the Progressive Society of Santa Rosa in Lima and have been active in the movements to form cooperatives from the church's holdings and to remove the director of the schools. Their efforts and position are no longer extra-legal; they have reintegrated themselves into the fabric of the community.

In structural terms, the returned migrants are now occupying the position in the center of the village formerly occupied by the foreign, dominating *qalas*. The returned migrants have learned to deal with bureaucracies through their invasion experience; labor union membership has provided them political sophistication and organizational skills; but they identify themselves as "sons of comuneros," and they value the cooperative and reciprocal bases of the village social structure. They are true mediators between the urban and rural ideologies, and now their position as legal representatives and interpreters of the law has been legitimized.

I predict that the rate of change in this village will increase, for the migrants have the opportunity to enforce the revolutionary laws to form co-ops and incorporate the village into the national culture. Moreover, the process of incorporation will begin with a transformation of the conceptual structure of social space in the following manner:

Traditional Structure   Migrants' Structure

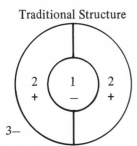

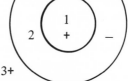

1. Foreign dominators   1. Nucleated migrants
2. Moieties   2. Other squatters
3. Outside world   3. National culture

New Structure in the Village, 1971

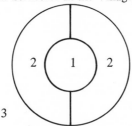

1. Migrants in position of power as governmental officials
2. Moieties
3. National culture

The migrants now occupy the positions of authority in the district and village. They are installed in the governmental offices on the plaza; they are also attempting to socialize the church's material wealth, which will lessen its influence as a foreign dominator. The migrants have dual identities—they see themselves as members of the national culture as well as members of the community. Thus they are the mediators between the urban ideology of the national culture and the traditional ideology of the village. Their success in mediation depends in part on historical events beyond their control. The transformation of this closed corporate community also depends on the degree of opposition from the traditional moieties and the members of the prestige hierarchy. The network of reciprocity discussed in chapter 7 maintains what Wolf (1966: 7) has called a "ceremonial fund," which provides the economic basis for the symbolic and ritual expression of understandable social relations among comuneros—the inclusive "we" opposed to the entire foreign world. The basic opposition of "we"-"they" will become transformed by the legitimate, authoritative presence of the returned migrants, who now occupy the category defined as threatening, "peeled," savage, and from the outside. They are attempting to mediate socially and structurally.

In structural terms, their position is currently ambiguous, and therefore I have not assigned positive or negative values to the proposed new structures. The degree of resistance to or acceptance of them as the vehicles of reform will determine in part the values of the new opposition. The logical possibilities include: (1) the traditional moieties stand opposed to the migrants and the outside world; (2) the migrants and the traditional moieties unite in opposition to some element of the national culture, such as governmental bureaucrats, the national police, or the church; and (3) the villagers lose their closed corporate attitudes and perceive the possibility of integration into the national culture; they would still define the outside "they" as neighboring villages with which they continue to battle over land boundaries.

The conditions under which any one of the above becomes the dominant pattern in the village will depend on historical events and accidents. I can outline some of the conditions that would impinge on the conceptual structures under consideration. Possibility 1 would result from strong opposition from the traditional sector of the village. This is likely to occur immediately when the migrants attempt to implement the Agrarian Reform Law. If they attempt to alienate the comuneros from their privately-held agricultural plots, then I predict strong opposition and the return to the traditional village structure, with intensifications of the conceptualizations of the comuneros standing opposed to an outside world that has become more threatening. Possibility 2 could be precipitated by a union of the migrants and the traditional comuneros against a common foe. If this occurred, the migrants' chances of introducing urban ideas and concepts would be increased: they would identify as members of the established traditional "we." This situation is already a potential with the current court case concerning the formation of a village cooperative out of the church's land and animals. Possibility 3 also depends on the success of the migrants in introducing new ideas and concepts. If the proposed cooperative is successful and benefits the village economically, the door will be open for integration into the national culture through participation in the national market. The three possibilities outlined could occur serially, with one structure dominating for a period of time and then giving way to another. It is clear that the traditional closed corporate structure of the village, which has withstood previous onslaughts, is currently under the strongest of pressures. It is very likely that the closed corporate organization that is maintained by the dichotomy of "we" versus the entire outside world will in time disappear. We have seen that an urban prestige system is forming. The time dimension and the process depend on the interaction between the ambiguous structure of the migrants' present social position and the experiences of the villagers. The basic Andean opposition of "we" versus "they" that has served as an interpretive device by which villagers have rendered their social world intelligible will become transformed. In other words, to use the phraseology of Robert Murphy (1971), the outcome will depend on the dialectic between ideas and activity. In applying structural methodology to such a dialectic in the case under consideration, I have found two dialectical processes occurring simultaneously. One is between the ideologies of the villagers and the ideologies of the returned migrants; the other is the dialectic between ideology and the vicissitudes of history. Using structuralism as a heuristic device to order the seemingly chaotic events of migration, invasion, and return to the traditional home of origin, I have tried to gain new insights into the dynamics of these events and their interaction with ideology. By focusing on the dialectic between ideology and events, we can better understand the dynamics of change.

In closing this chapter, I caution readers against interpreting these conclusions as stating that all of the Andean concepts under discussion will disappear. What I am saying is that they will be transformed. In describing the transformations of the key concept of "we" versus "they" effected by migrants in Lima, I have proposed three logical possibilities for the transformation of the same concept in the village. The basic assumption is that the two ideological systems—the urban and the traditional—are self-regulating systems that interact with one another as well as with the events and flow of activity. It is within these dimensions that a dialectical and structural point of view is most profitable.

9. A Final View Through the Andean Kaleidoscope

9.1 Major Structural Themes and Principles

In the introduction to this book I stated that in retrospect my first field experiences in Chuschi seemed as though I had been viewing structural shapes and patterns through a kaleidoscope in a dimly lighted room. However, with time and increased understanding I was able "to shed light" on the structural relationships Chuschinos utilize to interpret their experiential world.

The analogy of a kaleidoscope is a very appropriate one for Chuschino society and cosmology. Like the patterns of a kaleidoscope, the experiential world of this Andean community appears to be rearrangements of structural shapes and forms. One's first impression is that Chuschino society is in constant motion within a conceptually enclosed spatial domain. The civil-religious hierarchies move through their vertical world to ritually define pertinent ecological boundaries in order to begin the agricultural year. Other formalized ritual actions dramatize and reaffirm shared values and beliefs as well as redefine social categories. Many of the structural themes to be discussed in this chapter were discovered by studying ritual processes, to use Victor Turner's well-known phrase. By concentrating on ritualized activities I was able to isolate recurrent themes and values as they were expressed in different ritual contexts.

I have come to view each chapter of this book as another turn of a structural kaleidoscope, providing another perspective of the major structural themes and principles operating in the Chuschino social, political, spatial, temporal, and cosmological spheres. I have adopted the definition of structure as a self-regulating, transformational system, and, in order to uncover the relationships operating between discrete structural units within a system, I have dissected Chuschino ideal models to reveal the underlying principles of structural organization. Moreover, I have examined the dialectic between ideal systems and the events of history and activities to elucidate the processe of transformation.

Unlike the many anthropologists who construct structural models as if the were isolated from activities on the ground, I take the position that we must include in our analyses the struggle of activities and historical events with str tural systems to be able to understand the dynamic process of emerging syntheses. Change is a reality and static equilibrium is a culturally engineered fiction: the dialectic between ideologies and activities can increase our under standing of the mechanisms of change. Ideology is used to interpret events, but sometimes events overpower and change ideologies because ideologies no longer adequately explain the events.

This chapter is a discussion of the structural themes and principles operati to sustain Chuschino social and ideological closure, which in turn strengthens economic autonomy—the major concern of Chuschino society.

9.2 The Economic Basis of the *Varayoq* Structures

In chapter 2 we found that the Chuschino conception of ecology involves bounded ecological niches for diversified exploitation that ensures economic autonomy. The nucleated village, with its dual structures, Upper and Lower Barrios, is located in the middle of the vertical zones. The village is conceive of as the civilized center opposed to the uncivilized puna lands where the omnipotent mountain deities reside. Chuschino social space is further divide by the opposition of the traditional moieties to the central plaza, where foreigners such as schoolteachers, merchants, the church, and governmental bureaucracies have invaded Chuschino social space. This zone of foreigners is opposed to the two moieties where the communal members of the traditional closed corporate society reside.

Residence is the criterion for membership in the moiety *taksa varayoq* structures, the civil-religious hierarchies described in chapter 4. These dual and mirrored structures perpetuate the conception of the bounded ecological zones through a series of ritual enactments at all of the boundaries during the harvest festival in May, called Santa Cruz (described in 6.3), and again during the cleaning of the irrigation canals, the Yarqa Aspiy, in September (6.2). The members of the dual civil-religious prestige hierarchies literally walk through the vertical ecological space, reaffirming the essential information of diversified exploitation by delimiting the boundaries with ritual payments to Earth Mother and the mountain deities. The dual prestige organizations, representing the barrios, move out from the civilized center simultaneously to the distant dual sources of irrigation water in the puna and back to the center again, where they are met by the *hatun* members. The unified community then descends to the juncture of the irrigation canals below the village boundary adjacent to the cemetery, the place of the dead. This all-important fertility rite culminates with the entire village population drinking together at the expense of the moiety *varayoq* and *hatun varayoq* to celebrate the dual forces of regeneration—fertility and death. The moiety *varayoq* have established spatial and ecological order; they have made the appropriate ritual offerings to the mountain deities and to Earth Mother; and they have purified the village. The *hatun varayoq's* participation symbolizes the union of the two moieties into the complete whole. And, now dressed in new clothing, the members of the community drink with their ancestors to initiate the agricultural cycle once more.

After the ritual cleaning of the irrigation canals and the irrigation of the fields, Earth Mother is believed to be in gestation during the long rainy season, which is the time of hunger and disease. At the beginning of the dry season in May, the harvest festival, Santa Cruz, is celebrated by gathering into the village the crosses that delineate each agricultural zone. The crosses are decorated with the first fruits of each zone and are offered to the village priest. The crosses remain within the civilized center under the protection of the moiety *varayoq* in each of their chapels until they are returned to the respective productive zones by the newly initiated unmarried boys of the *taksa varayoq* during the Yarqa Aspiy in September, the equinox celebration summarized above.

The crosses are the icons of fertility and productivity. The movements of the moiety *varayoq* through their bounded ecological space begins in September with ritual payments to initiate the agricultural year; it terminates in May with the gathering of the symbolic first fruits of the harvest. The *varayoq*'s movements in September and May are like one full turn of the structural kaleidoscope, expressing the village's hegemony over its varied and far-flung productive zones. The dual *varayoq* organization establishes order at the outset of the agricultural year by making ritual payments to Earth Mother and the mountain deities, the female and male supernatural forces necessary for regeneration. As the irrigation water is ushered into the village, the women of each moiety circle in opposite directions around the plaza and sing that they too are cleansed and ready. As the *hatun* members receive the moiety members in the civilized village, social order is solidified by the union of the two moieties and the center. Cosmological order established once more, the cyclical nature of agricultural time can take its natural course.

It is interesting that neophytes, the young boys initiated for the first time into the *varayoq* organizations of the moieties, must, as their first act of office, return the crosses to their appropriate zones, thus perpetuating the ongoing articulation between economic production and the civil-religious hierarchies of the moieties. An abundant harvest is taken as evidence that the moiety organizations have fulfilled their obligations. Conversely, natural disasters causing crop failures are taken as signs that they have not performed their ritual duties well.

Given the economic function of the *taksa varayoq* of the moieties, the abolition of the *hatun varayoq* (see 4.5), which served the district officials and the church, comes as no surprise. Faced with the economic necessity of reducing their civil-religious hierarchical structures, the community chose to abolish that organization that served "foreign" institutions, namely the church and the district bureaucracy. Furthermore, the *hatun varayoq*'s principal ritual obligations were to sponsor the culminating unification ritual of the Yarqa Aspiy and to observe Christmas, Easter, and carnival, religious holidays imposed on the indigenous community by the Catholic church. Whether the *hatun* organization had economic functions in the past is unclear but its role as unifier of the two moieties was an important one. Nevertheless their functions in 1970, the date of abolition, were primarily as arms of foreign control. By preserving the moiety organizations the community is striving to perpetuate the mode of diversified exploitation of its vertical environment and to ensure the solidarity of the group's control over its territory, elements essential to its economic autonomy.

Now that we know that the dual civil-religious prestige systems of the barrios function to maintain hegemony over the community's vertical zones and ensure autonomy through diversified exploitation, we must examine the economic function of the *sallqa varayoq,* dedicated to the care of the church' cofradía herds. During the dramatic events of 1970 the village decided to retain the *sallqa varayoq* along with the moiety dual organizations. Also during that year litigation was brought against the church by a group of returned migrants to remove the cofradía herds from the church's control and form a co-operative (see 8.6). This conflict had not been resolved when I left the field in 1970, but the migrants realize the economic potential of 250 head of cattle and 1,500 head of sheep if controlled by a cooperative and oriented toward the national market. The community thinks of these herds as communal property, but the priest and departmental bishop argue that the animals belong to the church. Whether the community will accept the formation of a cooperative is open to question, for they are reluctant to orient their economic activities to the national market. Moreover, they express the fear that agrarian reform workers will gain control of this vast wealth, so important to the ceremonial fund that helps finance many of the community's rituals and public works.

In chapter 3 I stated that a household's wealth is based on size of herds rather than number and size of agricultural plots. Herding is the other principal economic activity in Chuschi. Privately owned herds are maintained on the puna communal lands by extended households. Membership in the *sallqa* prestige system requires one to own animals and to have served in several positions of the village civil-religious hierarchies (4.3). The cofradía herds are the responsibility of the *sallqa* herders, who must leave their agricultural plots in the care of family members to serve one year in the puna (see 4.3.4).

The *sallqa* prestige system performs important symbolic functions for the community. The members dramatize the opposition of savage *(sallqa)* versus civilized by descending on the village on horseback as a savage horde during Corpus Christi, celebrated at the end of May or early June, before the June solstice. As might be expected, the December solsticial celebration, which has been syncretized with Christmas, is also related to herding: it is a fertility rite for llamas, performed in the village center by one of the village prestige hierarchies. Before 1970, this ritual was sponsored by the *hatun varayoq;* after the abolition of this organization, the ritual sponsorship was assumed by the moiety organizations. The major actors of the fertility rite are a group of women dancers and one male dancer. Costumed with a llama skin over his head, the lone male repeatedly enters the group of female dancers. The women carry long poles with colored streamers attached to a circle at the top. The poles are held erect as the women dance their peculiar, vibrating dance, in which tiny hop-like steps are taken. From a distance the women dancers resemble a large, colorful, vibrating U. The male dancer, or *macho* (meaning male or old man), repeatedly enters the U configuration of the women, giving the appearance of a symbolic act of copulation. This interpretation is clarified by the antics of the *macho*, who breaks away from the dancers to mount from behind an unexpecting woman in the crowd, as the crowd laughs and comments that the *macho* has copulated. To the delight of the crowd, I was often such a target. In 6.4.3 I described a mock wedding ceremony that is part of the Herranza, in which a young bull was "put to bed" with a young cow that had not calfed. The two animals are tied together in ventral to ventral position simulating human copulation. After this is performed, the male participants announce that they "need their cows." They approach women and enact symbolic animal copulation. The two rituals express the mutual interdependence of animal and human fertility.

However, the most critical interdependence is between agriculture and herding, the two fundamental economic activities of the community. Ritual complementarity between the two is enacted throughout the year. There are two major agricultural rituals, in September and in May. Conversely, there are four rituals dedicated to herding. Moreover, we find that the ritual specialists associated with each of these activities enact rituals for one another, or perform their rituals in the other's specialized space. For example, agricultural rituals are performed in the puna, fertility rites for the herds are performed in the village. Sacred objects are moved from the agricultural to the herding zone and vice versa to underscore the economic interdependence of the two activities. The moiety civil-religious hierarchies ascend to the puna to make their most important ritual offerings to the mountain deities at the sacred sources of irrigation water. They leave crosses at these offering places during the rainy season to ensure agricultural success. The crosses are brought into the village in May to symbolize the first fruits of harvest.

The four points of the year associated with herding are all extremely important in Andean cosmology. June and December are the solstices and February and August are the dangerous months when the earth opens up and receives offerings. The significance of solsticial observances during Inca time will be discussed in 9.3. Today the Catholic celebrations of San Juan and Christmas have been superimposed on the solsticial dates. Nevertheless, we can see that the economic content of the solstices, symbolic of key aspects of herding, has remained intact. In June the herders descend into the village as a savage horde invading from the puna. Duviols (1973) provides evidence from documents that in many parts of the Andes pastoralists were of different ethnic origin and foreigners to the nucleated agricultural settlements. It is a common belief that herders are uncivilized as opposed to civilized agriculturalists. Thus the annual invasion has a long tradition. When the herders descend from the puna in June they also bring the two small female saints that are guardians of the herds. These two saints are miniatures of the effigies of Saint Rosa and Saint Olimpia that are housed in the church and said to be the mothers of the puna guardians. They are brought into the village to be blessed by and "to visit their mothers." The descent of the *sallqa varayoq*, the savage herders, corresponds also to the time when animals are brought into the agricultural zone to fertilize and feed on the harvested fields.

The two small saints remain in the civilized center, the village, until the synthetic ritual of the Yarqa Aspiy, the cleaning of the irrigation canals during the September equinox, when the saints and the crosses are returned to their appropriate places. The Yarqa Aspiy establishes order throughout the diversified territory, and the cycle can begin once more.

The *sallqa varayoq* return to the village in December again with their guardian saints, but this time they are the benefactors of the fertility rite sponsored by the village civil-religious hierarchies. Both saints are returned to the puna in January when the new members of the *sallqa varayoq* organization take office for the year. Saint Olimpia is venerated in December but Saint Rosa is given homage in August, during that dangerous time of the year when vapor escapes from the inner earth to cause disease and death. August and February are the most propitious times to make offerings to the Wamani the mountain deities believed to be the owners of all animals. Personal encounters with the Wamanis during the Herranzas have been set forth in 6.4. The Herranzas are fertility and protective rites for the herds, observed both by individual households and the community as a whole. The *sallqa varayoq* perform this ritual for the community's cofradía herds.

Duviols (1973) documents not only that pastoralists and agriculturalists were of different ethnic origins but also that they venerated separate idols believed to be their ancestors. He argues that the common mixed subsistence and settlement pattern we know today resulted from the invasion of herders from the puna into the nucleated settlements of agriculturalists, causing a synthesis of economic and religious practices. With this data, the symbolic invasion of the *sallqa varayoq* is better understood as a continuing synthesis of power relations and economics established long before the Spanish arrived. Chuschinos are utilizing an ancient economic and ritual complementarity to preserve their autonomy and hegemony over their territory. The movement of saints and the reciprocal ritualism discussed above has played a large role in sustaining the interdependence of pastoralism and agriculture, the basis of Chuschino economics.

9.3 The Structural Order of the Annual Cycle

In the above discussion, I have alluded to some of the relationships expressed in Chuschino time and space. I have also argued that one of their principal concerns is to maintain equilibrium and order in a world in which dual forces are balanced against one another. The best example of such equilibrium is the cyclical order of the annual round governed by the dichotomy of the dry and rainy seasons, which in turn shapes the rhythm of the agricultural and pastoral activities and rituals. Natural dichotomies are found: the two equinoxes in March and September and the two solstices in December and June. The equinox observances in March appear to have declined greatly through syncretization with Christian Lent and Carnival celebrations.

By comparing an early account of the annual ritual cycle with modern ethnographic data we can examine what has been retained and what has been transformed. In a chronicle written between 1587 and 1613 by Guamán Poma de Ayala (1936: 235-260), the year is divided into twelve months, with the major ritual activities for each month described in detail. I have set them out in table 7 by opposing the two natural seasons in Chuschi.

In the calendar described by Guamán Poma, the dry season was the time of state activities—the census and distribution of land, and the observances of the minor Inti Raymi, sacrifices to the visible sun. In April, the transitional month between the two seasons, the Inca displayed his generosity by supplying

TABLE 7

THE ANNUAL CYCLE ACCORDING TO GUAMAN POMA

Dry Season	Rainy Season
	October—*Uma Raymi* 100 white llamas sacrificed to pri pal *wakas*. Black llamas tied in pl Dogs also tied. A great plea for ra (women are shown weeping).
May—*Aimoray Quilla* The harvest feast. Produce brought to *collcas*. Abundance symbolized by double-eared corn or double potatoes. The Inca offers multicolored llamas.	November—*Ayamarcay* Month of the dead. Food and drin given to mummies, which are rem from their *pucullo*. Women chose for *aclla wasi*. Rites of first hair cutting, ear piercing, first shoes, fi menses, and donning adult clothin
June—*Cuzqui Quilla* Moderate *Inti Raymi*. 500 children, gold, silver, and shells buried. Census of the entire empire.	December—*Cápac Inti Raymi* The great sacrifice to the sun. 500 children buried alive with gold, silver, shells.
July—*Chacra Conacuy* 100 brown llamas and 1,000 white guinea pigs burned in plaza so that produce will not be ruined by sun or water. Pestilence. Distribution of land.	January—*Cápac Raymi* Month of penitence. Sacrifices to sun and moon. Processions from mountain to mountain, to Wanacauri and Pacritambo. Sexual activity prohibited.
August—*Chacra Yapuy* Corn is planted. Sacrifice to the *wakas* of the poor and commoners. Some offer own sons and daughters; usual sacrifice includes chicha, guinea pigs, shells, and ground corn.	February—*Paucar Varay* Heaviest rain, sickness, hunger. C sums of gold, silver offered to su moon, and all *wakas*. Vapor leav the inner earth. Rites of first hai cutting and donning adult clothi
September—*Coya Raymi* Grand fiesta of the moon. Impor- tant women host the celebration. Villages are cleansed with irrigation water. Men arm themselves as if to go to battle and purify their villages with fire.	March—*Pacha Pucuy* Black llamas offered to *wakavilc* and *orcocuna*. Sorcerers talk to the demons (of the underworld) Great hunger. Salt forbidden. Fruit forbidden to women. Earth is "full."

April—*Inca Raymi*
Multicolored llamas offered by Inca to
the *wakas* of the commoners. Public
feasting at the expense of Inca. Food
is ripe. Time of games. Ear piercing
ritual.

abundant food for public feasting from the state storehouses, thus demonstrating the economic and political power of the state during this time of scarcity before the harvest.

As the Inca model became transformed under Spanish rule, public feasting at the expense of the state was abandoned. Nevertheless, in Chuschi, the *hatun varayoq,* before the 1970 abolition of this organization, sponsored public feasting and celebrations, thereby displaying their generosity during Easter and Carnival. Their other duty was to sponsor the Christmas festivities, which correspond to the great sacrifices for the "real," invisible sun to ensure its return from its journey through the underworld. We see that the major state celebrations from Inca times became transformed into localized Catholic celebrations corresponding to the same periods of the year and sponsored by the *varayoq* hierarchy associated with the church and the state. However, these celebrations and the sponsoring *varayoq* institution were finally abandoned due to lack of articulation with the economic functions of the other civil-religious prestige hierarchies.

We have seen that within the memory of informants the community maintained a *varayoq* organization dedicated to the care of planted fields (the *qichwa* or *campo varayoq,* 4.4). In addition, female informants claimed that thirty years ago Coya Raymi as described by Guamán Poma was celebrated as the great feast of the moon on August 30 by the women *varayoq* to begin the Yarqa Aspiy in September. Women tied up their dogs and prayed and wailed to the moon, the Coya or queen and wife of Inti, the sun, begging her to send rain. Their descriptions remarkably resembled that of the noble chronicler, Guamán Poma, except that Santa Rosa has become identified with the moon.

Comparing this description with Guamán Poma's, we find that during the colonial period the equinoctial celebrations in September were sponsored by "important women" and, as in the modern Yarqa Aspiy, men symbolically cleansed their villages with irrigation water. But the women of Chuschi clearly state that the function of their ritual activities during the Santa Rosa festivities was to secure rain, which corresponds to Poma's description of Uma Raymi in October. In other words, the modern equinoctial celebrations have compressed the Inca observances for September and October into one, the Yarqa Aspiy. Furthermore, a continuing process of transformation has meant that women have lost their important ritual role in the initiation of the new annual cycle. The pressure of Spanish influence and syncretism have transformed ritual activities, preserving essential economic and ecological information while causing the abandonment of women's roles, human sacrifice, and to some degree sorcery.

There are other correspondences between Guamán Poma's depiction of the annual cycle and modern rituals. The harvest feast in May and its logical opposite, the month of the dead in November, are still important elements in Chuschi's organization of the year. However, November no longer includes the rites of initiation into adulthood such as first menses, first hair cutting, and receiving adult clothing. Nevertheless, the logical construction of death and renewal rites has been incorporated into the Yarqa Aspiy when the community drinks to the ancestors as the final act of this condensed initiation of the agricultural year.

Guamán Poma describes February as the month when dangerous vapors escaped from the inner earth, as is believed today. Likewise, February is the month of heaviest rain, sickness, and hunger and the time when the mountain deities are propitiated with offerings. In Guamán Poma's time offerings were made to the sun, the moon, and all *wakas,* or sacred stones and objects. Today, when Chuschinos perform the Herranza during February and August they say that it is the time of their little mothers and little fathers, suggesting that they are involved in the vestiges of an ancestor cult. This interpretation is in agreement with Duviols's analysis of localized ancestor cults in which *wakas* were believed to be the petrified ancestors of specific groups.

Note that in Guamán Poma's calendar, August was dedicated to sacrifices to the *wakas* of the poor and commoners to initiate the planting of corn. In Chuschi, August is the time of cattle fertility rites as described above. The initiation of corn-planting has been condensed into the great synthetic celebration of the Yarqa Aspiy. However, in the nearby community of Cancha-Cancha, the corn-planting ritual called Chacra Yapuy is still observed in August. Many Chuschinos attend this important corn ritual, which is also a rite of sexual reversals. A man dresses as a woman, blackens his face, and "plants" the plaza with the remains left in the bottoms of the brewing pots used to prepare corn beer. This is a reverse portrayal of actual planting. The plaza is planted instead of fields; a transvestite with a reverse-colored face performs the task using "that which is thrown away" as seed. People from many near villages attend the ritual, and, once it has been completed, planting begins in earnest.

It appears to me that Andean men are balancing the scale of procreative power between males and females. As mentioned in 2.7, only women can place seed in the ground. Once this is done, the new annual cycle can begin again. As Bateson suggests in Naven (1958), without such equalizing techniques social units would explode with tensions and pressures.

The fact that women are perceived as more powerful in the procreative process necessitates a rite of reversal to reestablish order. The ritual described above functions to equalize the apprehension of the inequality of power between the sexes in order to maintain social and cosmological equilibrium.

Balancing the sexual forces of the social and cosmological world is one of the major concerns of Andean people. The complementary nature of the synthesis between sexual powers is considered necessary for regeneration and procreation. This synthetic process can best be seen in the elements of the Andean Cosmos.

9.4 The Andean Cosmos

Again let us compare an early account of the Andean cosmological order with modern beliefs of Chuschinos. Perhaps the most famous description was written sometime between 1513 and 1520 by an indigenous nobleman named Joan de Santa Cruz Pachacuti Yamqui (1950: 204-281), who included a drawing of the temple of the sun in Cuzco (ibid.: 226) as a kind of map of the cosmos. See figure 6.

The drawing is in the shape of a house within whose outline masculine elements are depicted on the right side and feminine elements on the left (Zuidema, 1969: 21). In the center of the drawing is a vertical series of figures interpreted by Zuidema as representing the neutral axis of the cosmos. However, I believe the central figures depict the realization of the combination of male and female elements—the necessary synthesis for procreation and regeneration.

The major elements of the drawing with their associated elements are set out in table 8. The generative process begins with Viracocha, the supreme creator god, represented by a golden oval plaque with the five stars of Orion above it. Zuidema (1977b) interprets Viracocha as a bisexual supreme creator god, father-mother of the sun, moon, man, woman, and all creation.

Below Viracocha lies the Southern Cross with two of its four stars designated as *saramanca* and *cocamanca*, "cooking pot of corn" and "cooking pot of coca." These two stars form one of the arms of the cross and are obviously feminine concepts: the other arm of the cross is not named, but must be the concept of male energy necessary for reproduction. Zuidema (ibid.) interprets the Southern Cross as a female symbol, but I see it as the manifestation of the union of male and female contributions to ongoing life.

Man and woman are clearly shown below the cross, and below them are depicted the *collcampatas*, the storehouses and their terraces. The creator god is the origin and generator of all and the *collcas* represent abundance in the real world, the end product of the procreative process. Together they form a closed system—the beginning and the end of the reproductive cycle.

The constellation of male elements to the left (but to the right as one faces out—right is generally associated with males, left with females) has the sun as the apex with Venus of the morning, the grandfather, directly below. A group of stars with the words *verano* and *suchi* appear below the morning Venus. *Suchi* perhaps refers to a species of fish; *verano* means "summer" but is more

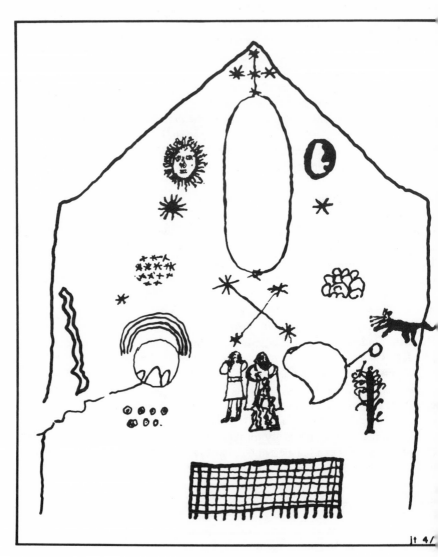

FIGURE 6
TEMPLE OF THE SUN IN CUZCO, AFTER PACHACUTI YAMQUI

TABLE 8

MAJOR ELEMENTS IN THE DRAWING BY
PACHACUTI YAMQUI

	Viracocha	
Sun		**Moon**
Morning Venus (as Grandfather)		Evening Venus (Grandmother)
Stars of Summer	Southern Cross	Clouds of Winter
Lightning		Cat
Lord Earth (with a rainbow)		Mother Sea (fed by a spring)
"eyes of abundance"	Man Woman	Young tree
	The terraces of the storehouses	

commonly applied to the dry season. The world with an arching rainbow is
pictured next, as Cámac Pacha, Lord Earth. Inside the earth are mountains
and the words Pacha Mama, Earth Mother. Exiting from the earth is the
river Pillcumayo, the legendary place of origin of the Incas. Cámac Pacha
refers to the world in its totality, while Pacha Mama denotes the inner earth
or Earth Mother. The last entry in direct line of descent from the sun in the
"eyes of abundance," *ymaymana ñauraycunañawin,* which also can be trans-
lated as the "eyes of generosity of all things." Off to the side is the lightning,
chuqqlla yllapa.

On the opposite side is the moon, sister and wife of the sun. Grandmother
Venus, star of the evening, is beneath the moon, with the words *choquechinchay
o apachi* (grandmother) written below. A cloud cluster with the words for
winter, hail, wind, and mist is depicted below morning Venus. Off to the side is
a black cat, *choquechinchay,* a supernatural cat or dragon that ascends to the
heavens to secure wealth from the Upper World (Zuidema 1977b). Mother
Sea (or Mother Lake) (Mama Cocha), fed by a spring *(puqyo),* and a young
tree *(mallqui)* are the last entries of the feminine side of the cosmological
ledger.

Zuidema (ibid.) discusses three mediators in Pachacuti Yamqui's structural
model: (1) the rainbow that mediates between the sky and the earth; (2) the
supernatural cat, *choquechinchay,* that mediates between the Underworld

and the Upper World, and (3) the lightning that descends from the Upper World to the earth. I would like to add that the rainbow originates at one point on the earth, reaches the sky, and terminates at another point on the earth. The Inca is often depicted under a rainbow, his means of communication with the Upper World. The lightning flashes down, but the cat springs from inside the Underworld. According to modern informants, the dangerou vapor believed to rise up when the earth opens in February and August is also called *choquechinchay*. We can therefore conclude that male elements are associated with downward movement and female with upward. I further suggest that the color white is a masculine symbol and black is its feminine counterpart. Also, it appears to me that the movement of the lightning is a manifestation of male energy, while a still body of water such as a lake or the sea and the inside of the earth are feminine concepts related to nurturing (6.2).

If we were to attempt to extract social concepts from Pachacuti's drawing we would see state origins and functions on the masculine side of the drawing and familial origins and functions on the feminine. The Inca is a direct descen dant of Inti, the sun; his symbol of power is the sun, and the rainbow is his means of communication with the visible sun and Viracocha, the real sun. In a common scene depicted on *qeros,* wooden ceremonial drinking vessels, the Inca is seen kneeling in the sun temple (probably before the great oval image) while two attendants blow conch shells that presumably form a rainbow over the Inca's head. The principal social characteristic of Inca rule, abundance redistributed through state control and conceived of as personal generosity of the king, is symbolized by the "eyes of great abundance and generosity." On the right we see the symbols of nurture (Mama Cocha and *puqyo*) resulting in the growth of a young sapling or branch *(mallqui)* that grows upward from the earth. Today in Chuschi, *mallqui* signifies both sapling and ancestor (6.3). Elsewhere Pachacuti Yamqui (1950: 218) uses trees to symbolize the parents, roots, and trunk of the Inca dynasty. This royal dynasty had a stron agnatic component—directly from the sun—while commoner status could be explained as the union of two complementary and equal kin groups. Zuidem (1977a) analysis of Inca kinship in terms of *panatin* (a group of men and thei sisters) and *turintin* (a group of women and their brothers) reflects the same principle of sexual complementarity. The model drawn by Pachacuti Yamqu captures the dynamic aspects of the masculine and feminine forces of the uni verse whose combination is necessary for regeneration and procreation.

By comparing this sixteenth-century explanation of Andean cosmology with modern concepts we once more can study continuity and change.

I found no evidence that the concept of a bisexual progenitor is an integra part of the modern syncretized Chuschino pantheon. Nevertheless, the conce is still an important one. It is believed that hermaphroditic animals are progenitors of the herds. They are called *wari* (or *mari*) and are believed to be the symbolic fathers-mothers of the herds, even though the astute pastorialists realize that the animals are in fact sterile. If one is born to a herd it is guarded and displayed during the fertility rituals in August and February.

The modern synthetic nature of sexual complementarity is expressed in a drawing executed by a seven- or eight-year-old girl when she was asked to draw the Upper World, Hanan Pacha, as part of an experiment I conducted in 1967 with some fifty children to attempt to capture their ideas about cosmological entities. (See figure 7.) The results of this research have been published in Spanish (Isbell: 1976).

Compare the elements of this child's drawing with Pachacuti Yamqui's. Her description closely parallels his own words. She sketched the sun, Inti, with his wife the moon, Coya, directly opposite to his right. Note that the orientation is the opposite of that in Pachacuti Yamqui's drawing, which is presented from a participant's point of view, whereas the girl's is presented from an observer's point of view. Below the sun and the moon are two stars, which she called grandfather (*abuelo*) and grandmother (*abuela*). At the bottom she drew a figure of a woman identified as her mother; to the side is Kay Pacha, "the earth we live on," divided into moieties, one white and one black. The fact that she omitted her father might be a reflection of the extreme sexual parallelism whereby women identify with women and men with men in so many aspects of social, ritual, and supernatural life. The black and white world might also be associated with sexual symbolism, white-male versus black-female dichotomy.

The child's version of the Upper World is a simplified version of Pachacuti Yamqui's elaborate model. The children were asked to draw various cosmological entities, among them the mountain deities (Wamanis) and non-Christian ancestors called *gentiles*. Interestingly, many children combined these two concepts to express a synthetic model much like Pachacuti Yamqui's.

One ten-year-old boy produced a drawing combining a cross and a condor as manifestations of the Wamanis and a cat and a tree (or *mallqui*) as the non-Christian ancestors. (See figure 8.)

As mentioned above, *mallqui* signifies both sapling, or branch, and ancestor. The boy is expressing the duality of the forces of the ancestors, the non-Christian *gentiles* of the Underworld, and the procreative energy of the Wamanis that results in progeny (the sapling). Although the elements are somewhat transformed, the dual concept of the masculine and feminine forces drawn by Pachacuti Yamqui is shown in the boy's drawing. The boy's cat (*choquechinchay*) in its role as the mediator of the Underworld, the residing place of the ancestors, and his tree are clearly related to the dual

FIGURE 7
THE UPPER WORLD, HANAN PACHA

FIGURE 8
THE UPPER WORLD, HANAN PACHA

concepts of ancestors and progeny shown by the noble sixteenth-century chronicler. The guitar symbolizes the mediator role of music as a communicator between opposing concepts.

The substitution of the Wamanis for one of the male entities in Pachacuti Yamqui's drawing is understandable when we examine the detail on the masculine side of his depiction of the temple of the sun. Note the mountains inside of his rendition of Pachacámac, Lord Earth. The cult of the Wamanis is an ancient one related to specific mountains in specific locations. Just as different ethnic groups had their own *waka*-ancestors, they also venerated specific mountains in their locality. When the Incas imposed the state cult of the sun, the localized cults of mountain deities remained intact. The Spanish likewise imposed a new state religion on conquered populations, and Christianity was smoothly syncretized with local indigenous and Inca beliefs.

The cross has been discussed throughout this book as an excellent example of the multivocal character of symbols. Here we see the cross identified as the Wamani, along with the condor as one of his manifestations in modern folklore. I think we can easily argue that the condor is one of the mediators between the Real World (Kay Pacha) and the Upper World (Hanan Pacha).

An eleven-year-old girl drew a series of mountains with two condors and a white bird with black spots hovering overhead. See figure 9. She said the birds and the mountains were Wamanis. The non-Christian ancestors (the *gentiles*) were represented as a series of lakes inside the mountains, with brightly colored flowers and plants growing inside the lakes. I would like to argue here that she is expressing the union of male energy from the mountain deities and the nurturing of the lakes as still bodies of water.

Taken as a totality, the children's drawings embody the same symbols of sexual complementarity necessary for fertility, procreation, and regeneration as expressed in the sixteenth-century drawing by Pachacuti Yamqui. This same concern for sexual complementarity and equilibrium is mirrored in social relations.

9.5 The Symmetry and Asymmetry of Social Relations

The clearest expression of sexual complementarity is found in the belief that one is not an adult until one marries. Chuschinos say that a male and a female are not complete until they have been united with their "essential other half." Once married, a person can assume the role of a productive social member. The preference for parallel inheritance discussed in 3.5 reflects the dual symmetry of the sexes. Males ideally inherit from their fathers and women from their mothers. In 5.3 I discussed how this same parallel principle operated in the inheritance of names in the seventeenth century.

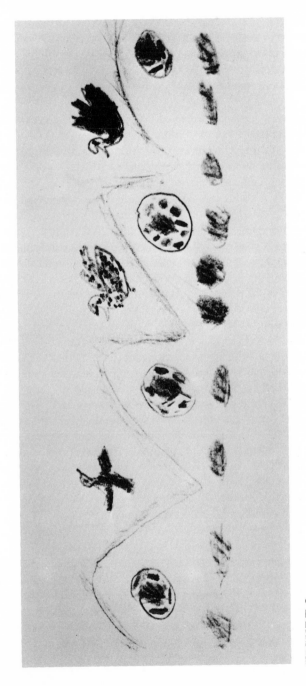

FIGURE 9
THE UPPER WORLD, HANAN PACHA

The balance of power between the sexes is a cultural artifact. Chuschino women have more symbolic procreative power than men, as evidenced by the fact that women own all seed and only they can place seed in the ground. Men do the plowing. In 9.3 I discussed the rite of reversal performed by men during the first planting ritual that functions to redress this conception of inequality of power.

Nevertheless, it appears that women are losing symbolic power in Chuschi as well as social power. For example, their independent civil-religious hierarchy which was described as a mirror image of the male institutions, has disappeared. However, the economic balance between the sexes is stable as long as women control their lands, animals, and property. In addition, partners are essential to the household's production. Division of labor is complementary.

Another enlightening symbolic drama of sexual complementarity is enacted during a wedding ceremony when the *ramo apay* (5.6.8 and 5.7) is performed. Symbolically a girl child and a boy child are baptized to signify the creation of the essential elements of a new kindred—the male and female issue that are the minimal unit necessary for Chuschino marriage exchange. A stated marriage preference is to exchange generation mates (5.2) to ensure continued alliances between two kindreds.

The relationship between two kindreds united through a marriage alliance is ritually defined as symmetric in the *perdonakuy* ceremony (5.6.9). Through this ritual act the bride's and groom's kindreds redefine their relationships to one another as formal and "compadre-like," prohibiting sex and insults and conversely establishing obligatory bonds of mutual aid and reciprocity.

Within this symmetric relationship between the members of the two kindreds, there exists the ritualized expression of asymmetry in the roles of the *masas* and *llumchuys* (5.4.2), who personify the relation of the outsiders (the affines) to the kindred performing the ritual. The *masa* plays the role of a clown, a servant, and sometimes assumes the role of a woman, serving food and drink to the congregation. Two *masas* are always necessary actors in all ritual situations (see chapter 6). The *llumchuys* must serve their female affines, preparing food and drink for the festivities. In 7.2 we discovered that the reciprocal obligations of affines, especially *masas*, exceed all other social categories.

The complex network of reciprocity and mutual aid (chapter 7) provides one of the basic social mechanisms by which a closed corporate peasant community is able to ensure the perpetuity of a closed endogamous society. In 5.8.1 I demonstrated that Chuschi is more endogamous today than it was during the colonial period between 1661 and 1685. Furthermore, Chuschi's population is declining due to outward migration (3.2), creating alliances and bonds of reciprocity between Chuschinos living in urban Lima and the village.

The impact of out-migration has been discussed in chapter 8, but I want briefly to summarize the dialectic between migrants and villagers in terms of symmetric versus asymmetric relationships.

Over time Chuschinos have increasingly closed in on themselves socially, economically, and symbolically in order to strengthen their defenses against the encroachments of the outside world. Their overriding concern is to preserve their autonomy. Nevertheless, the out-migration that began in the early 1940s has transformed many symmetric relationships into asymmetric ones. As migrants have increased their access to ready cash, their power and status have also increased. The community has become dependent on the migrants for their ability to facilitate the processing of papers through the maze of centralized bureaucracies in Lima. An example was given in 8.2 in which the migrants were responsible for presenting the documentation to the Ministry of Indigenous Affairs to have Chuschi recognized as a corporate community. Political influence became augmented to the point that today the migrant club has the authority to audit the village books, supervise elections, and call the peasant community's administrative authorities into Lima to account for their decisions. Individual Chuschinos have become dependent on their relatives residing in Lima for a wide range of aid. They send their children to the capital city to be educated. They rely on their employed relatives in Lima to help them get jobs and provide housing. Finally, mutual aid is provided for sponsorship of fiestas and rituals both by the migrants to their peasant relatives and vice-versa.

The most important development that has occurred in the past thirty years is that the migrant association in Lima has come to exercise a great deal of control over the politics of the village due to its position as cultural mediator between the national bureaucracies in Lima and the village corporate community. The migrants' sophisticated urban knowledge and new values are both suspect and considered beneficial. This area of ambiguity is a cause of tension between the village and the Lima migrant settlement.

It is possible that if the migrants' power of decision grows and if they continue to control economic resources in Chuschi and have access to cash in the urban environment, then the closed corporate community of Chuschi could become a satellite of the urban invasion settlement instead of the administrative and ceremonial center that it is today.

To close my discussion of symmetric and asymmetric social relations let me say that there are obviously many types of unequal relationships in Chuschi that are contrary to the ideal of maintaining equilibrated relationships. There are differences in wealth even among the comuneros (chapter 3) and important differences in power (chapter 4), as well as differences in power between the sexes. Women have very little direct influence in the political life of the community except to have an equal voice in elections. There are also disputes within families over inheritance, armed battles over land boundaries between villages, theft, and fraudulent misuse of public funds and property, all of which threaten to cause chaos in a community whose major strategy for social survival is somehow to persuade people to uphold the ideal values of harmony, consensus, reciprocity, and social and cosmological balance. These values are repeatedly reinforced in codified symbols and icons within obligatory ritual activities. Some dramatize dual forces of fertility. Others continually contrast that which is ideal with that which is disdained.

Perhaps the most powerful social opposition is the dichotomy discussed in 3.1 between comuneros, members of the closed corporate community, and the *qalas*, the naked or peeled ones, defined as outsiders and foreigners. In ritual dramas, outsiders are depicted as nonparticipants in the maintenance of social institutions. They never sponsor the key rituals discussed in chapter 6. In 6.2, in the description of the foreigners such as the priest, the soldiers, and the tropical forest savages, the last, the *chunchus,* appear as exploitative and threatening beings who epitomize antisocial behavior. Moreover, they are classified together with the powerful foreign herbalists, the *hamites,* and the dreaded *naqaq,* the supernatural being who steals body fat, eats babies, and castrates men. By ridiculing these negative powers in their midst, the villagers are attempting to neutralize their power and balance the scales once more. Furthermore, by ritualizing the representational images of the threatening "forces of evil," the community is annually reminded who its enemies are, a common social mechanism for the maintenance of social solidarity.

9.6 Impending Dangers

In the preceding discussion I have outlined the structural principles I believe to be fundamental to Chuschinos' ideology of social and economic closure. We found that ecological and social boundaries are delineated in ritual "walks" through physical space. And we found that the maintenance of these boundaries is the function of the moiety and puna civil-religious hierarchies. Thus the civil-religious hierarchies are the guardians of Chuschino territory and diverse vertical exploitation.

The symbolic nature of the annual cycle was described, and I concluded that many key concepts have been condensed and compressed into the great synthetic ritual called the Yarqa Aspiy, the cleaning of the irrigation canals, during the September equinox. Those festive holidays that do not relate to economic activities have been abandoned. The Andean cosmos was described as a synthesis of male and female forces essential to fertility and regeneration. Finally, the symmetry and asymmetry of social relations were explored.

Abstracting the relations operating in each of these systems, we repeatedly find that Chuschinos are drawn to dual conceptualizations. They see the world as a force field that must be balanced: the civilized center versus the savage puna, the comuneros struggling against the *qalas,* the rainy season opposed to the dry season. Regeneration and death are both necessary to the life process, as are men and women. In addition, the potential animosity between kindreds is neutralized in obligatory reciprocity and repeated marriage alliances, an expression of the ideal symmetric relationship expected between two kindreds joined in marriage.

Nevertheless, the asymmetric position of the *masa* is a necessary part of *all* rituals. His role reversal as a clown, a woman, and a thief (he often feigns a comic act of stealing the corn beer or the meat from his affinal relatives' celebration) continually reminds his affinal relatives that he is a wife-taker who has married one of their women and removed her from her own kindred. In contrast, the role reversal of the male actor in the corn-planting ritual *(chacra yapuy,* 9.3*)* is an effort by the male-dominated society to diminish the exalted symbolic power of women, who own seed and place seed in the ground. By initiating the annual cycle, men are attempting to balance the scales between the sexes before beginning another agricultural cycle.

What are the impending dangers to this dualistic Andean world view? Chuschi, as a recognized peasant community (see 2.4), does not contribute significantly to the national economy. The village is going to come under increased pressure from governmental agencies to orient itself toward the national market and national identity. One of the proposed plans is to organize multi-community production cooperatives. Chuschinos will have to make critical choices in the near future, and many pressures are at work. Increased education brings with it an awareness of what the outside world has to offer, and more and more of Chuschi's youth are making the decision to leave the community in search of "a better life" than the arduous existence of an agriculturalist-pastoralist. The national program of propaganda tells the peasants that the government is striving to open the doors of national participation and self-determination for the peasant masses. The government wants the peasants to share in the process and responsibility of propelling the country into the industrialized twentieth century. These factors are enhanced by the ever-growing need for cash in the community. If Chuschi continues to lose population as members leave the community in search of salaried jobs, and if Chuschinos continue to send their children to Ayacucho and Lima to be educated, the traditional values that maintain social and economic closure will be greatly undermined.

The continual flow of out-migration has meant that the traditional peasants are made aware of new values of individual and community progress. The migrant association in Lima is oriented toward the improvement of the village They are currently agitating to have electricity installed. A health center and a secondary school are under construction. Migrants and governmental agenc are frustrated by the amount of time, energy, and resources that are expende in supporting traditional rituals. However, we have seen how essential these ritual activities are to the perpetuation of values with which Chuschinos have defended themselves for centuries. This closed corporate peasant community is attracted by the promises of the revolutionary government that the peasant masses will have self-determination, but they suspect that they will lose contr over their resources. They also fear that bureaucrats will benefit at their expense. Chuschinos will have to predict the consequences of their choices as the pressure to become an open community mounts higher and higher in the future. They are not opposed to better education and better health care, nor are they averse to a higher standard of living. However, they are fearful of losing what they have controlled for so long. From their point of view, their most valuable asset is their autonomous control over their communal and private holdings. Becoming a part of the national society might mean the loss of that control. When Chuschinos perceive a threat they respond, "We must defend ourselves." The dialectic between traditional ideologies and events is an ongoing process. The purpose of this book has been to analyze the nature of Chuschinos' systematic mechanisms of defense and to outline some of the events and factors currently impinging on their closed corporate peasant community.

10. Postscript–Four Years Later

10.1 A Return to Chuschi, 1974-1975

In July of 1974 I returned to Peru after a four-year absence. I taught at Catholic University in Lima as a Fulbright professor from August to December of 1974. In April of 1975 I returned to Chuschi to investigate children's acquisition of symbols by videotaping their enactments of rituals utilizing dolls and a miniature house as props for the dramatizations. My research team included two North American students and two Peruvians: a Quechua-speaking student of linguistics and a socio-linguist who had studied in the United States. Arriving with a five-member research team and expensive video equipment intensified some of the problems we encountered (see 10.2).

In July of 1974, my husband, my daughter, and I returned to Chuschi for the July 28 independence day celebrations. Before leaving Lima, I notified the migrant community in the invasion settlement of our planned visit to Chuschi, and the news was quickly carried to the village by the constant flow of travelers between the urban and rural settlements.

This third trip to Chuschi stands out in sharp contrast to our initial field-work in 1967, when the comuneros were suspicious and silently reticent (see 1.1). We were graciously received and housed by our compadres and friends. We noted that stories about our past visits to the village had become greatly exaggerated. For example, we overheard a woman say to a group of other women that our daughter had been born in the village and was thereby a Chuschina. In 1967, when we first arrived in the village, she had been under three years of age, and during 1969-1970 she celebrated her fifth birthday in the village. On our return in 1974 she was ten years old. Many people felt that they had "watched" her grow up. Compadres and friends were concerned about the well-being of my mother, their "abuelita" (little grandmother), who had been with us in 1967. She had not returned to the high altitudes of the village for health reasons, but did visit Lima for five months in 1975.

I returned to Chuschi for Christmas, which I hypothesized would be dedicated to herding rituals (this indeed was the case: see 9.2), and then again the first week of April to begin my research on what Quechua-speaking children of different cognitive age groups know about their cultural concepts. During this field period I reached a high point in my anthropological career. One of my compadres held the position of *taksa* alcalde. Santa Cruz, the harvest festival beginning on May first, was his final obligation for the year. He asked me to be his *dispensera,* the person who distributes all food and drink.

My duties began when I was solemnly taken into the storeroom of my compadre's house and shown the quantities of coca, trago, and grains that had been accumulated for the festivities. He explained to me that the other alcaldes had to be served the most generous portions and the regidores next, and that the alguaciles had to be served along with their superiors but I had to be careful that they did not drink too much. I had to attend to the wives of the civil-religious officials in the same ranking order.

I was totally in charge because my comadre was confined with false labor pains. On the night of the first of May, she almost miscarried and was experiencing severe pains. Nevertheless, the next morning, when the officials returned from the puna with the crosses (see 6.3), she demanded that she be propped up under the portal and between pains served all of her husband's subordinate officials the required morning meal.

Her pains continued through the next two days, and I assumed her duties as well as mine. I became very worried that the fetus had died in the womb and that my comadre would also die. I rushed around the village attempting to find someone who could help. A group of male schoolteachers were playing cards outside of one of the teacher's rooms in the small path. I explained our plight. Without showing much concern or stopping their card game, they said yes, these Indian women often die in childbirth. There was no medical help at all in the village at the time, because the village health worker had been moved to another locality due to lack of an adequate place to treat patients. He had been working in the municipal building, but the municipal mayor announced that he could no longer receive patients there. The village health post had been under construction for five years but was not completed, therefore the provincial health officials transferred the health worker to another village. In the three months we were in Chuschi in 1975, four women died in childbirth.

I finally found a mestiza midwife who was visiting her family. After examining my comadre, the midwife said that she had another month before the baby was due. She gave her medicine to stop the false labor pains. The entire incident underlines my relationship with some of the comuneros in contrast to the growing tension we experienced with the mestizo school-teachers. I found myself incorporated into the ritual life of the comuneros and ostracized by the mestizo schoolteachers—an exact reversal of my relationship in 1967, the first year I worked in Chuschi.

On the evening of May 2, formal visitation began. I followed the barrio's civil-religious officials and their wives as they made the rounds to all of the other officials' houses. We received a shot of trago and coca at each house. When we returned to my compadre's house, I was instructed to begin serving as the officials and their wives arrived. In hierarchical order, I served the *varayoq*, being careful to follow my compadre's instructions. However, I had not been instructed how to refuse a drink from each official and each wife as I served them. There were twenty-odd officials of the civil-religious hierarchies who participated in Santa Cruz, and I repeatedly had to drink with each one as well as toast each woman there.

After each alcalde and his subordinates complete a round of visits to the houses of other alcaldes, the congregation settles down in the alcalde's house to drink all night. At about twelve midnight, my compadre called for his *dispensera* (me) to serve hot trago. I rushed to the cooking hut, instructed the women to stoke the fires under the cooking pots, and filled my teapot with hot cane alcohol. I ran to the portal area, where my compadre was seated with his regidores to his right and left. My comadre was enduring her diminishing pains silently on a pallet of animal skins. I served the men first, in appropriate order, only to be told that the trago was not hot enough. I stumbled back to the cooking hut to reheat the huge vat of drink. The second serving met with his approval, but nevertheless I was reproached by my compadre. By this time, I could hardly stand, because each time I served anyone, I had to drink with them. Shortly thereafter, I collapsed in a heap with a group of other sleeping women. My head was spinning and my stomach did not feel too well. In a fog I heard my compadre yell, "Where is my *dispensera*? I want my soup." It was dawn. There was no feasible way that I could muster the fortitude to be able to serve a congregation of some fifty people their morning soup. The women around me announced that I was drunk and asleep. Then my compadre named my North American female research assistant to take my place, and she heated and served the meal while I slept fitfully.

I want to explain that during the evening of drinking the atmosphere was quiet, solemn, and religious. The desired goal is to unify the group through communal obligatory drinking. One certainly feels the solidarity of such a group after three days of such intensive interaction. The only comic relief was provided by me, the *dispensera* who stumbled around and could not perform her duties. The women bedded me down on the floor with animal skins and blankets, and my compadre good-naturedly chided me about my lack of strength. Even my comadre, whose false labor had weakened her, managed to drink, eat, and interact with the congregated comuneros. Only I, the gringa passed out.

On the morning of May 3, the crosses were taken to the plaza and into the church, even though there was no priest present to bless them (see 10.3.2). I stole away and hid in my own house because by this time I was very sick from drink. I missed the entire day and refused to respond to all pleas. My assistant performed my duties for me. Just as one can nominate one's family to take over one's ritual duties, I had to nominate other foreigners to take over mine. My compadre arrived at my house in the evening with more cane alcohol "to cure my head." He sympathized with my lack of ability to withstand marathon drinking. Moreover, he expressed his gratitude for my services and said that now I was truly one of his *kuyaq* (see 7.2), "one who loved him."

In typical Andean reciprocal terms, I had repaid him for his services to me during my birthday party the month before, when he had assumed a servile position to me as I had done during his important ritual obligations. Our prestige and statuses were reversed in accordance with the special events we each sponsored.

Other compadres and comadres had donated produce, beer and wines, and labor for my three-day birthday party. I spent the equivalent of about seventy-five dollars preparing the feast, which featured a *pachamanca,* a traditional meal of llama and mutton roasted in the village baker's earthen oven with potatoes, ears of corn, cheese, and broad beans. The gathered guests numbered over thirty, including village officials; however, only two of the village school-teachers attended. The majority declined my invitation, as an expression of disdain for the "Yankee imperialist capitalist exploiter," whom they also firmly believed to be a CIA agent. Most conspicuous was the absence of the municipal mayor, who is also a primary school teacher.

10.2   The Foreign Anthropologist—A Convenient Enemy

10.2.1   Prelude to a Conflict

The ease with which I became integrated into comunero activities contrasts sharply with the boycott organized against me and my research team by the majority of the teachers in Chuschi. At the time of my visit in July of 1974, a minor incident should have warned me of the events to come. During the festivities for independence day on July 28, an employee (not a teacher) of the secondary school drunkenly told my husband that "Yankees" had no business being in Chuschi and asked why we did not stay home where we belonged. We explained that we were there to visit our compadres. We also insisted that we had been invited to Peru by the government to teach and to do research. However, later events made it clear that governmental support was not sufficient for unified support from the dual segments of Chuschino society.

In April, when we returned to begin our investigations, I presented our research plan to the directors of the schools, the municipal mayor, and the district governor, as well as to the president of administration of the peasant community, who is my compadre. I also presented our credentials from the Ministry of Education, the departmental Director of Education, and Catholic University. On presenting our credentials, I explained to all of the officials that we had the institutional support of the Ministry of Education and Catholic University of Lima. I outlined a plan to organize a bilingual center in Chuschi, financed by Catholic University, in which the community, teachers, and students would develop and experiment with their own Quechua-Spanish materials. I argued that such a project would be of great benefit to the community and to the education of the children. I also argued that Chuschi would benefit financially from the support from Catholic University, which would provide the funds and technical support for Chuschinos to develop their own curriculum with cultural materials relevant to the locality rather than having bilingual materials imposed upon them from Lima. Furthermore, I explained that on completion of the videotaping of the children I would leave a portable generator to the community powerful enough to provide lights for the plaza and the municipal building.

The comunero leaders were favorably disposed to the proposal of a bilingual center and were enthusiastic about acquiring a generator for lights. Moreover, my presence in the past had not caused any calamities to befall the community. The municipal mayor, a primary teacher who was not a native of Chuschi, politely listened to our research plans and the proposal for a bilingual center and thanked me for the generator. With a smile he examined our papers and said, "You have always been generous to the community in the past." However, in the subsequent months it became clear that he was violently opposed to our intrusion into the community. The reasons are complex and have only become clear to me after a great deal of reflection. I will follow the example of June Nash (1974: 498) and explore the structural factors that culminated in organized opposition to my research, opposition from a segment of Chuschino society (the *qala* teachers, see 3.4) who had in previous years given me support that I had declined to use. I had not wanted to be associated in the minds of the comuneros with the "foreign" schoolteachers, who have generated a great deal of ill will in the community.

In large part the ill feelings that are generated are due to the fact that only three teachers out of nineteen are from Chuschi, and one of those three lives alone in the community while his wife lives in the departmental capital of Ayacucho. The majority are either single or are separated from their families. The attitude of the teachers is that they cannot maintain their families in such a backward place, nor do they want their children attending village schools. The normal career of rural schoolteachers is to "serve time" in a remote rural community and then be advanced to a larger population center, where they can maintain a higher living standard and be united with their families. Therefore, the turnover of teachers in rural communities is constant which diminishes the likelihood of teachers' becoming integrated into a community. In a closed corporate community like Chuschi, the comuneros are suspicious of the teachers and say they are only employees, whom they can fire at will. Moreover, the teachers are impatient with the peasants' reluctanc to adopt the progressive reforms they advocate. Very little interaction occurs between the two groups.

When I returned in 1974 I found that two of the native Chuschino teacher were still there; a third had finished college and had begun teaching in the secondary school. Two of the non-native teachers had been there for over five years and the rest were new. One, who had been transferred, had been returned to Chuschi as a disciplinary action for drunkenness. Many of the new teachers and a couple who had been in the community for over three years were not advanced due to their political opposition to the government and their membership in a vocal national teachers' union called SUTEP. Several of the national leaders of the union have been jailed in an effort to break the unity and power of the union, which opposes the educational reforms recently put into effect by the military regime. The most important demands of the union are increased salaries (an average salary for a rural scho teacher is 6,000 *soles*, or about 150 dollars a month), job security in the form of long-term contracts, and decentralized education. With the passage of the educational reforms, teachers were granted one-year contracts, renewable eac year. Furthermore, a program for training university students includes one-year internships in rural communities, which means that the established teachers have lost a great deal of their bargaining power. There are three cate gories of teachers: those with a university degree, those with a teacher's training degree, and those who have not completed such training. Obviously, teachers in the last category are the most vulnerable. However, increasing numbers of university-trained teachers are drawn to the union, which has mounted unified opposition to the government. They believe that by unifying their ranks on a class basis, they can accomplish greater reforms for their own benefit and for the education of the communities they serve. The local leaders of the union are never advanced to administrative positions and are often banished to rural places and not transferred. Resentment runs high. Education is the most popular vehicle for upward mobility, and these teachers find that their avenue for improvement of personal status has been blocked. I think that the latter issue played a large part in the opposition I found present in 1974-1975—opposition I had never experienced before.

I had arrived in Chuschi in 1967 as an impoverished student, returned in 1969 to conduct doctoral research, and returned in 1974 as a full professional, a *doctora* in one of their own universities. The contemplation of the upward mobility granted me by their own society, which denied the same mobility to them, caused a great deal of frustrated resentment. Furthermore, the explanation of my success by the newly politicized teachers was in terms of "Marxist dogma." I was viewed as a capitalistic exploiter. Not that I had exploited the comuneros' labor; rather, I had exploited their information for my personal gain. The repayment I wished to make to the community, in the form of helping to organize a bilingual center and the gift of the generator, was rejected by the teachers. They also believed that either I was a CIA agent or I was spying for the Ministry of Education.

Opposition from the teachers first took the form of silent avoidance and actions like declining the invitation to the fiesta organized in my honor for my birthday. Later, however, they took more active measures to hinder our research. One such action was to find reasons for the socio-linguist not to accomplish the goals of surveying attitudes concerning bilingual education and investigating the feasibility of organizing a bilingual center for curriculum development in Chuschi. They accomplished this by repeatedly questioning the research plan and demanding a day-by-day account of the socio-linguist's activities. Also, they demanded more credentials, which meant trips to Lima and the department capital, a time- and money-consuming demand. Finally, the teachers conceded that they would consider working with a socio-linguistic survey if the investigator signed a notarized statement renouncing all association with the "gringos" and moved out of our house.

The Peruvian Quechua-speaking student from Catholic University suffered different consequences, because he was working directly on my research project, which was independent of the socio-linguistic one. He experienced continual harassment, which culminated in conflict. One afternoon, a group of teachers who had been drinking heavily most of the day called him "the running dog of the capitalistic CIA agents." The incident ended in a fist fight with appropriate apologies and resumed decorum when everyone sobered up the next day. The president of administration of the community severely reprimanded my research assistant for engaging in open conflict. He explained that that was not the way to win a battle. A comunero rule of behavior is never to display open hostility but rather to operate behind the scenes to amass consensus and support for one's position. Later we will see this same principle operating when the comuneros advise me as to appropriate strategies during or "day of conflict" (10.2.2).

On Mother's Day, 1975, at a celebration held in the boys' primary school, one of the radical teachers gave an impassioned speech in Quechua about our presence and activities in the community. I was not present. The Peruvian socio-linguist and a North American doctoral candidate working in a nearby village were asked to leave by the president of the parents' association (who was a returned migrant from Lima). They feared that the North American was taping the speech, to be used later by bureaucratic officials in the Ministry of Education against the teacher. The student was carrying a bundle of vegetables, which had been a gift. The bundle was mistakenly identified as containing a hidden tape recorder. When I asked a monolingual Quechua-speaking woman friend who had attended the meeting what the teacher had said, she replied that she did not know because he must have been speaking Spanish. What had happened is that she did not understand the words capitalists, agents of the CIA, and so forth, nor did she understand the concepts. The gulf between the political realities of the majority of the comuneros and the teachers widens as the two groups become more polarized. The teachers experience greater and greater frustration when the comuneros do not perceive the danger of capitalistic exploitation, and the comuneros become annoyed when the teachers do not support their political maneuvers against their familiar enemies, the hacendados and governmental officials who encroach on their encapsulized world (see 10.3.3).

In spite of the efforts of the teachers, our taping of various age groups of children was successfully completed. Rather than experiencing a lack of willing participants, we experienced the reverse problem, with too many children wanting to participate at any given time. We maintained an open door policy and showed all the tapes that we filmed to anyone interested, but only three of the teachers viewed the tapes: one was a Chuschino compadre and two were university-trained secondary teachers, one of whom was collaborating with us in the collection of oral literature taped in his classes. The most unfortunate aspect of the situation was this lack of willingness on the part of the teachers to interact with us. By maintaining their distance they were able to sustain the image of their "convenient enemy," the stereotype of the exploiting capitalists, without directly entering into a dialogue about our own political views.

10.2.2   The Day of Open Conflict

The culmination of our increasingly conflict-ridden situation with the opposing faction of teachers occurred during the fiesta of Corpus Christi, the first week of June. We were videotaping the procession of the *sallqa varayoq* as they came into the village from the puna with the *santas menores* on the first day of the celebration. The municipal mayor, who is a primary school teacher and not from Chuschi, participated in the celebration by sponsoring a scissors dance. Participation by a teacher in an indigenous celebration is unusual, and the appearance of scissors dancers, who cut social and cosmic order into bits and pieces as they dance, is not commonly a part of Corpus Christi. Their inclusion was an attempt to symbolize the danger we foreigners represented to the community. The opinion of many friends was that the teacher had participated in order to confront us directly. One of the frequent complaints of the teachers was that we were constantly in the company of one group of comuneros or another during fiestas. We were studying the aspects of Andean culture (i.e., traditionalism) about which they felt most ambivalent. They believe that the maintenance of traditional practices and ritual observances impedes progress and change, which, as we have seen in the body of this book, is in fact true. What the advocates of rapid change do not perceive or value is the importance of the mechanisms of defense and solidarity that are built into such traditional practices.

During the first day of Corpus Christi the municipal mayor was obviously very annoyed about our filming activities. The procession had arrived at the chapel that marks the outermost boundary of the village and is where the participants traditionally stop to drink communally and play music before proceeding into the village. As people congregated in front of the chapel, the municipal mayor gathered the *sallqa varayoq* inside the structure, by virtue of his power as a bureaucratic official (see 4.3.1). Later I learned that he had told the indigenous officials that we had not paid a "filming tax" of fifty *soles* (a little over a dollar) and that without that payment it was prohibited to film by law. We had never been told of such a tax and it does not exist. The *sallqa varayoq* left the chapel, approached us, and asked us to stop filming because it was prohibited. We stopped videotaping, but one of my research assistants continued to film with a small super-8 camera.

We were invited to the house of the mayordomo, the principal sponsor of the fiesta, and were told that in a private house we could film if we wanted. During the procession to the mayordomo's house with the band that he had hired, one of my North American assistants (a woman) decided to relieve the tense situation by asking if she could play with the band. She did so, to the delight of the band and onlookers. We were served as honored guests and then drank and danced most of the night with the congregation gathered in the mayordomo's honor.

The next day is traditionally the culmination of the religious celebration, when the puna *santas menores* are brought into the church to "visit their mothers" (as described in 9.2). I decided that we should film with the super-8 because of its small size, instead of risking harm to the video unit, which was essential to my research. I also made the resolution that we would not give in to the mayor's unreasonable claim that we had refused to pay a tax that did n exist and that we were not told about. As the procession came into the plaza, the two North American assistants began filming and I took still shots. I hear the municipal mayor drunkenly yell to one of the *sallqa varayoq* to "hit the gringos" with his *chicote* (a three-pronged leather whip). I saw the *varayoq* drunkenly stagger over to where the two assistants were stationed. The man raised his arm and hit one of my assistants on the back. The blows were not very hard and they fell on a down jacket, which protected him. He pushed the whip-wielding *varayoq* away and continued filming. The *varayoq* then turned to the woman assistant and hit her once lightly on the back, whereupo she stopped him by keeping him away with her outstretched arm. The man gave up and staggered away.

Meanwhile, I slowly crossed the plaza and joined the congregation in the churchyard, where the municipal mayor was in a rage. He threatened to have his people kill us and burn not only our house but all my compadres' houses as well. He pointed to my compadre, who had just terminated the office of alcalde *varayoq*, and claimed that he was going to jail for collaborating with the CIA spies. He would shout that we did not have a license (I suppose a permit to film) and I would keep referring to our documentation. He would repeat again and again, "No tienen licencia," and I would answer that of cours we had appropriate papers. A drunk comunero was standing at our side, and after each objection put forth by the mayor, he would say, "No, no, you don' have it" (referring to the license). And each time I answered, "Yes, we do," the man would echo, "Yes, yes, she does."

As the municipal mayor shouted, "Yankee imperialists! Spies!" we gathered ourselves together and slowly walked up the street to our house. A few young boys jeered but the adults remained silent, and the teachers looked on from the balcony of the municipal building. The mayor attempted to incite the crowd to grab our cameras to "sell them for the benefit of the community." As we left, several people patted me on the arm and said, "Don't pay attention to him, he's drunk."

Later in the evening, several comuneros came by the house to apologize for the mayor's behavior. I also had broken a comunero rule by engaging in public conflict, especially during a ritual occasion. My compadre, with whom I had exchanged reciprocal *kuyaq* obligations (described in 10.1), came by drunk, crying and saying he did not want to be put in jail. We assured him that the municipal mayor could not do that. He calmed down and began to plan our strategies to combat the municipal mayor. My compadre is a very respected comunero; he is one of the renowned ritual specialists of the village and also an excellent musician. He suggested that I sponsor him and his brother-in-law as *waqrapuku* (curled cattle-horn trumpet) players as my contribution to the mayordomo's fiesta. I agreed and we joined the festivities in the village plaza, where the mayordomo was displaying his generosity to the community by providing band music and alcohol for all to enjoy.

The last thing that any of us felt like doing was to appear in public and join in the festivities. We had to make several turns around the plaza with our musicians playing in front of us. We were extremely nervous, as all eyes were upon us. But as we approached the gathered throng of celebrators in front of the municipal building, the mayordomo thanked us with a hearty embrace for the contribution to his fiesta. We joined the procession to his house, where we drank, ate, and danced until the early hours of the morning.

I had previously made a cash contribution to the mayordomo, or rather to his daughter, a nineteen-year-old who worked for me in Lima. She was footing most of the bills for the fiesta because she was employed. Such a heavy financial burden on a young offspring is expected, even though she was single with a two-year-old child to support. Her parents considered the child their own and disputes often arose over who was going to keep him.

Even though she was locked in a bitter dispute with her parents over the custody of her child, it was inconceivable to her even to consider not providing the necessary cash for her father's ritual obligation. The fiesta consumed all of her savings and all of the family's surplus. In five days of feasting, 5 llamas, 1 cow, and 8 *urpos* or 320 liters of chicha and 3,000 *soles* worth of trago were consumed. They also spent 600 *soles* for the harpist, and the daughter sponsored the first bull of the bullfight, which involved buying a case of beer for the band. The band was donated by the mayordomo's brother. I provided the cow-horn trumpeters. The event that was most applauded by the crowd was the daughter's sponsorship of the bullfight, because it was a public display of support of her father's and mother's ritual obligation to the community.

Likewise, I realized that my public sponsorship of musicians for the fiesta was appreciated to a greater extent than my private donations in cash, because it, too, demonstrated publicly my esteem for the mayordomo. I also realized that such a public display was beneficial to our position in the community. My compadre was right: the way to win a battle is to display generosity and to gain support for one's position by collecting one's reciprocal debts. My compadre and his brother-in-law provided music continually for four days with little sleep. He said that he did not want to run the risk of criticism by anyone that our contribution was not a good one. By the end of the four days, their cheeks were swollen, their lips were cracked, and they were exhausted from lack of sleep and over-drinking. However, my compadre main tained that our actions could only gain us praise. We were now a part of the mayordomo's *kuyaq*, which made him and his household indebted to us. Thu in the minds of comuneros, conflicts are resolved by utilizing the strategies of reciprocity. Through my first-hand experience of conflict I discovered anothe dimension of Andean reciprocal behavior.

The next day we videotaped the bullfight, which was sponsored by the mayordomo, from the balcony of a store owned by a mestizo friend. The municipal mayor scowled but did not bring up the matter of the "film tax" again. His strategies took a different turn—and so did mine. While I had dis covered that comuneros utilize displays of generosity and reciprocal exchange: to resolve conflicts, I also discovered that mestizos concentrate on bureaucrati means to defeat their opponents.

A few days after the fiesta, I was informed that the municipal mayor had sent a telegram to the Peruvian Investigatory Police (PIP) in Lima claiming that a network of CIA spies were operating out of Chuschi with "sophisticatec electronic spying equipment." I countered with a 153-word telegram to the departmental prefect outlining all of our grievances against the municipal mayor. I ended the telegram with a statement that he was not conducting himself in accord with the spirit of the Peruvian revolution.

The PIP came to investigate a couple of days later. We had been called into their headquarters in Cangallo, the province capital, to be fingerprinted and to have our documents checked. On my arrival in June I had visited Cangallo to inform the bureaucratic officials and SINAMOS of our presence in Chuschi and to explain our research to the provincial director of education. However, I did not know that it was necessary to register with the PIP. I was informed that all foreigners had to do so. Therefore, when the PIP investigato came to Chuschi, he already knew us. He was cordial and assured us that the matter would be cleared up. He questioned us about the incident during Corpus Christi and asked for the name of the man who hit the members of my research team. Then he began to ask questions that I did not want to answer concerning the politics of the teachers, including the municipal mayor. I did not want to be cast in the role of an informer. However, I did mention that I considered it peculiar that the mayor was able to construct a fourteen-room hotel on his teacher's salary. The local rumors alleged that he was using munic ipal materials and funds. The investigator said he would look into it. I had decided that perhaps the mayor had used us as a diversionary tactic to keep attention away from himself. Several leaders of the community had previously petitioned to have him removed from office.

An uneasy calm prevailed. We returned nervously to our work. I accelerate our timetable so that we could collect as much videotaped material as possible.

I anticipated that we might have to leave the community before our scheduled departure in July. While daytime activities had the appearances of normalcy, we had nighttime visitors who informed us of the mayor's activities. The situation took on the aspects of an intrigue. If the mayor sent a telegram, we were informed of its contents. If I countered with a telegram, I am sure he was informed as well. Therefore we both adopted the strategy of mestizos whereby appeals are made to higher bureaucratic authorities rather than the traditional ritual displays that we both had engaged in the week before. Interestingly, some of our nighttime visitors were a few of the very same teachers who had been most vociferous in their opposition. However, while they would discuss politics in private, they would not readily exchange greetings in public. We all waited for a solution to the situation. The day after the investigation by the PIP official, I thought that a solution would be arrived at when a delegation from the province capital arrived to hold a formal hearing. It was Friday the thirteenth.

10.2.3 An Official Hearing

The delegation from Cangallo included the provincial sub-prefect, the municipal mayor from Cangallo, and two lawyers. They called a meeting that the president of administration of the community (my compadre), the president of vigilance, the district governor, the municipal mayor, and my research staff were requested to attend. Three schoolteachers also attended. The proceedings began with the municipal mayor of Chuschi giving his deposition.

The municipal mayor alleged that we had never presented our documentation to his office and had refused to show him our passports and visas. He accused us of evading Peruvian income taxes. He stated that he had not threatened our lives, nor had he commanded the *varayoq* to hit the members of my research team, neither had he threatened any of my compadres. All he had asked was that we pay the small "filming tax" required by the municipality. The final blow was when he said that he had heard that I and my female research assistant had joined *vida michy,* the adolescent sexual activities described in 4.6.1.

I had to answer his accusations by providing evidence that we had a legitimate reason for our presence in Chuschi. I began by showing the investigation commission our numerous authorized documents along with our research plan and several of my publications in Spanish. I emphatically stated that we had presented the same documents to the mayor's office on arrival as well as to the community's officials and to the district governor. I argued that we could produce witnesses to his violent behavior during the fiesta when he sent the *varayoq* to strike two of my staff members and threatened to have his people kill us. Furthermore, he had refused to issue legal papers to my compadre so he could travel and to register his recently-born son. I asked the committee if it was reasonable to believe that we had refused to pay a 50-*soles* filming tax when I had donated a 16,000-*soles* generator to the community. In a closing statement I declared that alleging that my assistant and I had participated in sexual activities with adolescent boys was pure slander.

The thing that surprised me was that the commission did not ask for any other witnesses, nor did they ask the community leaders to speak. I later learned that they had spoken to other people, the community leaders included, in private.

One of the teachers asked for the floor. He argued that we were exploiting the village and that I had bought off several people by manipulating compadrazgo relationships. He claimed that my presence had brought no benefit to the community, only tension.

I countered that the major obstacle to the community's deriving benefit from our work was the teachers' attitudes and opposition. I claimed that the community had lost the opportunity for educational advancement through the proposed sponsorship by Catholic University of a bilingual center in Chuschi. Such a center needed the cooperation of the teachers, and that was not forthcoming. I asked why the teachers had not used the history of Chuschi that I had prepared and why they opposed our research when they refused to talk to us about it or to view the tapes. My Peruvian assistant became angry and declared that the teachers did not interact at all with the comuneros. To that, one native son rose to his feet and shouted that he was a son of a comunero and proud of it. The sub-prefect demanded order and closed the meeting. I was surprised that no summary "verdict" was given. But bureaucracies move slowly everywhere and the solution I expected was not forthcoming that day.

When I asked my compadre, the president of the community, why he had not spoken up in our behalf, he said that he had filed a complaint against the mayor and that was sufficient. He declared that open confrontation would get us nowhere. Not being able to predict the outcome of our situation and being very tired of the whole affair, we returned to our house to eat the birthday cake one of my assistants had baked for himself. Over our cake and coffee we decided to send the taped materials out with a member of the research team who had to leave within two days.

We packed up the video equipment and tapes into trunks and put my assistant on the bus to Ayacucho. I was afraid that someone would get the brilliant idea of destroying the equipment and tapes or demand that they be impounded. I had no fears that the content of the tapes would be considered subversive, but I was afraid of their being ruined in the hands of someone who did not know how to care for them. I also had visions of all my taped material rotting for months somewhere in a ministry warehouse in Lima, where one has to scrape the mold from one's shoes during the damp coastal winter.

My assistant's account of her trip into Ayacucho is worth repeating. She boarded the bus and tried to appear inconspicuous, which is difficult for a blond woman who is five feet ten inches tall. Unfortunately, the municipal mayor and several other teachers were also traveling on the same bus. During the first part of the trip, she recounts, a drunk comunero took to his feet unsteadily and clapped her on the shoulder and said in a loud voice, "The mayor is a thieving dog. I put my money on this gringa." At the national police control stop, the mayor got out of the bus and talked to the officer in charge, waving his hands excitedly while pointing to our trunks of equipment and film. The officer made a gesture with his hands as if to say, "What can I do?"

She arrived in Ayacucho without further incident and transported our materials to the home of one of my compadres.

A few days later I received a telegram demanding my appearance on a specific day at the national police post in Pampa Cangallo. I reasoned that we were not under arrest, because they come and take you away for that, they do not request your appearance at their post. But I was not at all sure what was in store for us. We packed up our remaining belongings and decided to continue on from Pampa Cangallo to Ayacucho. I arrived at the national police post to discover that the officer in charge wanted me to file a formal complaint against the municipal mayor. My compadre, having been threatened with jail, refused traveling papers, and denied a birth certificate for his new-born son, also filed a complaint. The officer was sympathetic and said that anytime we experienced further trouble we were to telegraph him because he was responsible for our safety. He said that he understood how it was to be a *blanco* (a white person) in this foreign land—he was from the coast. It was pointless to explain that I did not feel that I was in a foreign land. We arrived in Ayacucho and I filed another formal complaint with the prefect's office. Unfortunately, I was again questioned about the counter-revolutionary activities of the teachers. I declared ignorance. Although I had experienced difficulties at the hands of the teachers, I was sympathetic with their position and demands.

The day I visited the prefect's office I received a message that I was invited to accompany him to Cangallo the next day at 5:00 A.M. to attend the 120th anniversary of the province capital. The prefect's note maintained that it would be beneficial for me to attend so that we could talk to all of the provincial officials and resolve my difficult situation. To my chagrin, the manner in which a couple of officials decided to resolve my political problems involved receiving sexual favors. This is one of the unfortunate aspects of fieldwork faced by female researchers. I lost my temper after being under so much pressure for so long and called the bureaucrat involved an old fool. The scene was an unfortunate one that took place at mid-afternoon on the dance floor during the town's celebration. At that point I could not tolerate that kind of abuse of political power. I returned to Ayacucho exhausted and wondering exactly what position foreign anthropologists have in the third world.

10.2.4   The Position of Foreign Anthropologists in the Third World

During my visit to Cangallo I was offered several explanations as to why I had experienced difficulties during 1974-1975 and never had before. One of the most interesting was offered by a SINAMOS official who explained that several years ago two foreign anthropologists supposedly had been conducting research in the Pampas River area with a group of Peruvian students. However, he maintained that their goal was to motivate peasants to take over land forcibly. He even claimed that the group sold machine guns to villagers. I registered my dismay when he named several of the Peruvians and reminded him that many of the people he had named were now working for SINAMOS. Nevertheless, he claimed that his was a true story and that I was paying for their revolutionary activities. What I did not tell the official was that I had been a part of the research team along with the Peruvian students. Selling machine guns and organizing violent land take-overs had been the furthest thought from our minds. Another theory was that the teachers' opposition was a counter-revolutionary movement—a phrase that has become the catch-all for any event that is not to the liking of bureaucrats. Yet another attributed my difficulties to plain ignorance. I do not think that any of these simplistic explanations is adequate. The situation was much more complex.

I mentioned earlier that the development of political consciousness among teachers had greatly increased since 1970. A class consciousness has arisen that has moved the political realities of teachers further away from those held by comuneros. Both groups see different issues before them, and communication between the two groups, which was not good to begin with, is declining.

Teachers are often impatient with the peasants' reluctance to change. Moreover, peasants are suspicious of the teachers' motives when they advocate change. Politicized teachers belong to the larger world, while the comuneros deny that that world is rapidly beginning to affect their lives. I found that the one aspect of proposed change that comuneros perceive as critical is any effort to encroach upon their autonomy and their territory (see 10.3.3).

By concentrating on the defense mechanisms utilized by Chuschino comuneros to protect the closed corporate nature of their community, I came to believe that I too was protected by their defense mechanisms from the outside world. June Nash (1974: 498) has come to the same conclusion in analyzing the political difficulties she experienced in the field in Bolivia. She states: "I realized that the defensive insulation of the people against the outside world protected me from coming to grips with the political issues just as it seemed to protect the people from the conflicts of the wider world. In Bolivia it was not possible to choose the role of an impartial observer. . . . The polarization of the class struggle made it necessary to take sides or to be cast by them on one side or the other. In a revolutionary situation, no neutrals are allowed."

I had not taken any sides on any issues because I too felt that I was somehow protected by peasant ideology from the outside world. Therefore, for the teachers I was defined as a capitalist CIA agent, and for the SINAMOS official I was a potential revolutionary. I became a potential "convenient enemy" for everyone. One of the teachers explained to me that he was willing to talk to me about my political position in the privacy of my house but that in public I was his ideological enemy. In order to explain failures and frustrations, all movements, especially revolutionary ones, need convenient enemies. Anthropologists are extremely convenient targets.

As class polarization continues and groups define their needs and begin to articulate their demands, the position of the anthropologist will become increasingly more difficult because factionalism will increase. It appears that in Peru's current revolutionary climate, class polarization will continue to increase as various segments of the society become aware of the potential benefits a rapidly changing social system under economic development has to offer them. One of the serious problems is that economic development cannot keep pace with the expectations of the various self-interested classes. The incidences of violence described in chapter two demonstrate the rising tensions in Peru's effort to propel the country into the industrialized world. As reforms are enacted without adequate funds to make benefits available to all segments of the society, class struggles will increase. The peasants of Chuschi have chosen a strategy of protecting what they have, while the radical teachers of Chuschi have chosen strategies to gain what they do not have—better wages, increased social mobility, and the power to influence decisions. In part, this explains the lack of involvement of the teachers in the current struggles of the comuneros against their old familiar enemies— the government, the church, and hacendados.

10.3 Changes in Chuschi since 1970

All of the major changes that I found on my return to Chuschi were

concentrated in the areas centered in conflicts with the above-mentioned institutions: the government, the church, and the only hacienda on Chuschi's
borders. These conflicts will be briefly described below. One of the most
interesting changes that I found when I returned to Chuschi in 1974 was that
the community had reinstituted the *hatun varayoq* organization that had been
abolished in 1970 (described in 4.5). The reason for the reestablishment of
this traditional organization was to protect the community's cofradía animals
from becoming incorporated into a cooperative.

10.3.1   An Attempt to Form a Cooperative

In chapters 2, 4, and 8 I have discussed the impact of migrants on their
community. Two returned migrants became the first presidents of administration and of vigilance. One of their concerted efforts was to take over the
church's cofradía of 250 head of cattle and 1,500 head of sheep. The battle
with the church had been a long one and several migrants had been repeatedly
jailed before the migrants' power became legitimized.

The agrarian reform officials supported the migrants' efforts but never
directly intervened in the conflict. When the migrants successfully expelled
the village priest in 1972 (to be discussed in 10.3.2) they realized the plans
they had formulated in 1970 to organize a cooperative of the cofradía animals
(see 8.5). The agrarian officials from Ayacucho inaugurated the new cooperative. However, the venture lasted only two weeks.

Comuneros asserted that the migrants had acted unilaterally without the
consent of the community. Membership in the cooperative was based on a
fee of 50 or 100 *soles* (reports differed). The community members maintained
that the cofradía animals belonged to them and could not be incorporated into
a cooperative that outsiders, such as bureaucratics and technicians, would
control. They closed the cooperative and reinstituted the *hatun varayoq* to
protect the community's animals.

I interviewed several other people about the failure of the cooperative and
got varying stories. Many people told me that one migrant had absconded
with eight head of cattle the first week the cooperative functioned. A returned
migrant told me that outsiders had come to ruin the cooperative. An agrarian
official said that he was not sure what had happened, but he stated that
Chuschi had always been a difficult place into which to introduce new ideas
and changes. The priest's version was quite different.

10.3.2   The Expulsion of the Village Priest

In February of 1972, the migrants led a movement in the community to expel the village priest. The conflict over the animals and property controlled by the church had been going on for several years. But with the support of the community, the migrants were successful. Such disputes were common in the region at the time. The church usually lost due to the support given by the agrarian office in the peasants' efforts to take control of the wealth in land and animals held by the church. Usually such take-overs were thereafter organized into cooperatives under the direction of the agrarian reform office. However, in Chuschi, we have seen that such efforts to form a cooperative directed toward the national market failed. The community feared loss of their communal wealth at the hands of outsiders. The cofradía animals were under direct community control when I left in 1975. However, a disease had depleted the herds considerably. The Agrarian Reform Office was putting pressure on the community to form a cooperative so that the community could take advantage of the technical assistance they had to offer. Some favored doing so, but the majority prevailed in their conservative position. They preferred to sell a few animals at a time when a consensus decided that cash was needed for some communal project.

When I interviewed the priest, he was mystified by his expulsion from Chuschi. He had been there for fifteen years and felt that he had served the community well. He realized that new ideas and forces were at work but could not exactly understand them. He felt that the action of the community was like stealing from the church. He argued that the cofradía had belonged to the church since early colonial times, and he had the documents to prove it. However, comuneros felt that the church had illegally taken what had belonged to their ancestors. The community was therefore receiving what had been rightfully theirs all the time.

People said that the priest had worn a pistol the last few months he was in Chuschi. He told me that he had feared for his life. In 1974 he was serving the community of Pomabamba, which is in the district of Chuschi. However, he refused to officiate at any religious functions in Chuschi, and very few people traveled to Pomabamba to seek out his services. Most people waited until a priest passed through to contract masses for the dead, weddings, or baptisms.

I attended a meeting of the migrant association in Lima in August of 1975 when a special commission reported on its findings after a special visit to Chuschi. The migrants were petitioning for electricity to be installed in Chuschi, and they were also searching for ways to finance the completion of the health center and the secondary school. However, one of their central concerns was to monitor the progress of the litigations over the cofradía animals and the case of the disputed land occupied by an hacendado (see 10.3.3).

One of the investigation delegates reported on a conversation that he had had with a visiting priest who had arrived to preside over the special mass to inaugurate the newly instituted district educational nucleus. The priest asked when the community was going to return the parish house to the church. At that time the parish house was being used for the vocational school. The occupation of the parish house has been a bone of contention because the bishop argues that a priest cannot be sent to Chuschi until he has somewhere to live. The migrant replied that he had kept an account of how much the priest had collected during his two-day visit in charges for masses. He calculated that the priest had collected over 15,000 *soles.* He replied to the priest that with such revenue the church could well afford to build a new parish house. He also asserted that the church could use its portion of the cofradía to finance its needs. Evidently an agreement had been reached by which the community was to keep 70 percent of the confiscated cofradía and the church was to receive 30 percent. However, the agreement was not to be enacted until a new priest was installed in the village. The migrant association feels that the church exploits their home community to an extreme. In Lima, fewer services are charged for, even though the migrant population has greater access to cash.

One of the side effects of the absence of a local priest is that the small Protestant sect that was brought to Chuschi by migrants has grown since 1970. They claim some three hundred members. Rivalries between Protestants and Catholics were also on the increase. I noted that two extremes of comuneros—the wealthiest and the poorest—were being attracted to Protestantism. With the Protestant ideology of personal advancement, comuneros can escape the obligations of participation in the complex of reciprocity and displays of generosity that consume so much of their economic surplus.

Nevertheless, even though a schism is developing in the religious ideology of the community, Catholics and Protestants alike presented a solid front against their common foe—the one hacendado within the district's territory.

10.3.3   The Invasion of an Hacienda

On April 6, 1975, the comuneros held a public meeting and decided that the cofradía animals would be moved onto the land of the only hacienda bordering on Chuschi's communal lands. A twenty-year old dispute over the land that the hacendado was occupying was finally coming to a head. The consensus of the community was that if they invaded the hacendado's land, the agrarian reform office would take quicker action in deciding the case. I believe that this tactic of invasion was borrowed from their migrant relatives' experiences in Lima. In fact, several migrants participated in the organization of the invasion.

It was agreed that the invasion would take place on April 16 and that any household that did not send one male to participate would be fined 3,000 *soles*. The hacienda is located near Niñobamba and adjacent to the communal lands of Chuschi, which are called Inga Wasi. The invasion was well organized, and over fifty men accompanied the movement of the herds. The hacendado's potato crops were damaged. One of his men shot and killed a dog, but that was the only act of violence.

The invasion did indeed speed up the review process of the litigation. On May 28 the agrarian reform office sent a national land judge to inspect the boundaries in dispute and hear formal arguments presented by both sides. We asked the community if we could accompany them and videotape the proceedings. They agreed, believing it would be advantageous to have such an event recorded.

Before May 28, we journeyed to Ayacucho to request permission from the office of the agrarian reform and from SINAMOS to film the proceedings. At first SINAMOS officials were reluctant, but we invited them to view some of our tapes and argued that such a document would be good public evidence of the workings of the revolution. They arranged an appointment with the national land judge and suggested that we secure his permission as well. He not only granted us permission but felt adjudication of land disputes was a public matter.

Over two hundred men rode a full day's hard ride from Chuschi across the cold puna to attend the hearing. We traveled by road to Ayacucho with our equipment and then on to Niñobamba, where we were housed for the night with a number of Chuschinos from the village and from Lima. The next morning the judge began the hearing and inspection of boundaries at 7 A.M. It was a most impressive sight to see all of the mounted peasants unified to protect their territory. The hacendado was a very lonely figure with his handful of men and his lawyer.

The judge worked continuously from 7 A.M. until dark. He first heard the arguments from both sides while a secretary typed the depositions, using the hood of a truck as his desk. Each side presented evidence for its claim. The president of administration of Chuschi offered documents dating back to the seventeenth century as evidence of the legal boundaries of the community including the hacendado's land. The lawyer for the hacendado argued that the land had been sold to the present owner's great-grandfather. He presented an impassioned argument concerning the capitalistic exploitation by the comuneros in their effort to deprive one man of his land and livelihood. I was amazed to hear the term capitalistic exploitation extended to a recognized peasant community's attempt to recuperate its communal land. The lawyer for Chuschi argued that the bill of sale was false and that the ancestor of the present owner had illegally occupied the land.

We returned to Ayacucho in the back of the land judge's truck in the pouring rain and then on to Chuschi, where the comuneros were celebrating certain victory, although when I left Peru in August of 1975 a decision had not yet been handed down. However, given the current attitude of the government in favor of returning land to recognized communities, I believe that if Chuschi can prove the land will be utilized, the community stands a very good chance of recuperating a part of its communal herding land that has been alienated from the community for three generations.

I want to add one final note to my discussion of the changes I had found in Chuschi. In looking at the conflicts that the comuneros became engaged in during the four-year period between 1970 and my return, I found that all of their activities were directed toward protecting their autonomy and closed corporate status. The ideology of the military reformist government lent support for the community's position against the church and the hacendado. However, while government planners probably see these activities as consisten with increasing integration into the national culture, I am sure that Chuschinc perceive their activities as protecting their isolation.

Migrants have an interesting structural position vis-à-vis the community. They provide tactical support from Lima by handling most of the legal paper-work for the community. However, they are attempting at the same time to introduce important changes, such as improving education and health. Even so, the migrants have a vested interest in helping to protect the community's communal land. They also value the degree of isolation the village maintains from outside interference from bureaucrats, because most of them still control privately-held agricultural plots in the community.

In 8.5 I discussed the structural position of returned migrants and offered three logical possibilities for resolving their ambiguous position vis-à-vis the community. When I returned in 1974-1975, I found that indeed two of these predicted possibilities had occurred serially. The traditional moieties opposed the migrants' attempt to organize a cooperative in 1972. They reinstituted the *hatun varayoq* in an effort to protect the community's interests. In 1975, however, when the village invaded the only hacienda on its frontiers, the migrants and the traditional moiety members united to confront a common foe—the hacendado. When I left in August, the migrant association had pledge to handle all of the necessary legal paper work in Lima for the litigation with the national Agrarian Reform Office. The migrants demanded that the president of administration of Chuschi appear at one of their formal meetings in Lima to explain his handling of the case. They exert considerable political power in village affairs.

I see little indication that the community of Chuschi is losing its closed corporate status. Rather than perceiving the possibilities of national integration favorably, the comuneros appear to be attempting to strengthen their mechanisms of defensive isolation. Nevertheless, new ideologies are being developed in the Lima migrant settlement that will ultimately have great effects on the traditional community.

10.4 Migrants' Manipulation of Symbols to Construct an "Upper Class"

In August of 1974 I attended the festivities dedicated to Santa Rosa, the patron saint of the Chuschino invasion settlement. Comparing the 1974 celebration with the one I attended in 1970 (see 8.5), I noted that several important symbolic elements had been added.

The most striking addition to the celebration was organized by a group of the most economically successful and upwardly mobile families among the migrants. Several of these families no longer live in the settlement, but they remain active in the migrant association. All of them have mobilized compadrazgo ties and other important social links with persons outside of the migrant community. The group consisted of only about four or five families who sponsored what is called a *qaru chullay*. One of the sponsors explained to me that this was an annual custom of Ayacucho hacendados, in which the land owners would ascend to their balconies and throw gifts to the gathered laborers who lived on their land. *Qaru* means distant and *chullay* signifies to clarify, to sanctify, or to cleanse. Therefore, the celebration sanctified and clarified the *social distance* between the hacendados and their subjugated laborers. The handful of upwardly mobile migrants consciously emulated the landed classes' actions in an effort to likewise separate themselves from the other migrants. They were attempting to place social distance between themselves and the migrants who have not been so successful in the capitalistic urban economy.

The *qaru chullay* sponsors wore costumes depicting the dress of hacendados, cotton ponchos and wide brimmed straw hats. They festooned themselves with red ribbons with money tied to them. As the procession of Santa Rosa made its way through the invasion community from the nearby church, these affluent members of the migrant community marched in front of the saint. The procession stopped to pay homage at three houses owned by one of the sponsors on its way up the hill to the Chuschino club. In front of the sponsors of the *qaru chullay,* the various familiar caricatures of foreign dominators and invaders paraded and performed their comic antics: the *chunchus* shot their miniature arrows into the crowd, the *naqaq* pretended to castrate men with his wooden sword, and the *hamites* sold magical herbs and potions. As in the

1970 celebration described in 8.5, the representation of the military was abse
However, the caricature of the priest had been changed to represent a bishop.
The dancer playing this role wore a large red plastic bishop's hat and a white
plastic cape. He performed mock baptisms and marriages along the route of
the procession. The contrasts afforded by the solemn procession of the patro
saint and her devoted followers, the sponsors of the *qaru chullay* with their
airs of an "upper class," and the comic antics of the dancers leading the procession were extraordinary. While the traditional order of social power was
ridiculed in front of the procession, a new order immediately followed, with
the devoted crowd bringing up the rear.

When the procession reached the club, the sponsors of the *qaru chullay*
ascended to the roof and threw their gifts to the crowd below. They held
their own celebration on the roof of the club, with their own band, while the
masses celebrated below, inside the club. Perhaps the most interesting facet
of this conscious manipulation of symbols to construct a class structure is tha
the sponsors of the *qaru chullay* literally separated themselves spatially. They
raised themselves above the other migrants spatially in their effort to establish
their social distance. Throughout this book we have noted the use of space a
a framework in which Chuschinos act out their important cultural concepts.
It therefore is not surprising that these affluent migrants also used the metap
of space in codifying their new concept of themselves. Upward mobility had
been codified on the familiar Andean cognitive map of spatial relationships to
communicate a new structure—class differentiation.

10.5   What Does the Future Hold?

Not wishing to play the role of a soothsayer, but nevertheless realizing tha
an examination of the dialectic between structures and activities and events
can enable us to understand some of the dynamics of change, I am going to
offer a few predictions concerning the direction of change for Chuschi in the
near future.

We have seen that the community has rejected the formation of a cooperative that signified interference from the outside world, which would in
turn endanger autonomy and social closure. Given the current situation in
Peru, I believe that such efforts to resist incorporation into the national
economy and culture will continue in the immediate future.

The migrants continue to play an important role as cultural brokers, but
given the events of 1972, when the attempt to form the cooperative failed,
the community will probably be more cautious about accepting any further
drastic changes proposed by the migrants.

The impact that the radicalized teachers will have on the community will be minimal because, as discussed earlier, they do not share the political concerns of the comuneros, who are attempting to protect their cultural isolation. However, the teachers exert considerable influence on their students, and if the development of class consciousness continues to be the teachers' ideology, we can expect changing attitudes to be acquired by the younger generations.

The community's positive experience with the Agrarian Reform Office in regard to their litigation with the neighboring hacendado could predispose them toward accepting further cooperation from governmental offices. However, I predict that Chuschinos will retain their conservative attitudes in regard to becoming incorporated into the national structure of cooperatives. One possible event could change that position, however.

My Peruvian research assistant returned to Chuschi in February of 1976. He reports that no one in the community wants to accept the position of caretaker of the suspension bridge that connects Chuschi with the villages across the Pampas River. The salary for the position is 1,500 *soles* a year, and people feel that it is too low for the work involved. The community is not maintaining the bridge, which means that villagers from across the river cannot reach the weekly Chuschi market. There is talk of moving the market up the valley to Pomabamba, where another village maintains a suspension bridge in good repair.

Many of the comuneros cannot imagine that the market would ever be moved from Chuschi; they say, "But it has always been here." However, the market vendors feel differently because the larger part of their business comes from members of other communities, who often travel a day's walk or further to reach the market. If Chuschi loses its market, an economic decline could force the community to search for other sources of cash to augment its subsistence economy. It might then reconsider its position concerning the formation of a cooperative.

Consumerism and new cultural values due to increased out-migration and education may in time cause changes in the perspective of the community. Although the pressures for change have increased since 1970, we have seen that traditional defenses have also increased. The return to traditionalism in the form of reinstituting the *hatun varayoq* structure and rejecting the cooperative is an attempt by the comuneros to protect their economic autonomy. The close integration of ecological exploitation and political and social organization with ritual processes is both a strength and weakness in the defenses of the community against the encroachments of the outside world. As long as the structural relationships, the variations on the themes of dualism, are functioning to maintain economic and social closure, the community will withstand change. But, with such an integrated system, a change in one structure will cause changes in all of them. The comuneros say: "To defend ourselves is to defend our traditions." Whether they will be able to do so in the future depends on the outcome of the dialectical process between structural principles and historical events.

Appendix

Decree by Blasco Núñez de Vela, Corregidor of the Province of Vilcas Huamán, 1593, from a Copy in the Village Records of Quispillaqta

En el pueblo de San Cristóbal de Putica, a 31 dias del mes de marzo de 1593 años ante Blasco Núñez de Vela, Corregidor y Justicia Mayor de la provincia de Vilcas, pareció un indio que digo llamarse don Garcia Yanqui Tanta, principal del pueblo de Chuschi y presentó este Real Provision y pedió cumplimiento de ella . . . y la puso en precio su cabeza . . . i por don Antonio Asto Cabana, Cacique principal del pueblo de Chuschi e indios Aymaraes, mitmas de la encomienda de Juan Mañueco me fue hecho relación diciendo que ciertos indios de la encomienda de Pedro de Rivera que vivan en el dicho pueblo de Chuschi el rio en medio Canas mitmas les tenían ciertas tierras usupadas de poco tiempo acá habiendolas quitado forzosamente contra su voluntad con negros de Pedro de Rivera, vecino de la ciudad de Humanga, en quienes están encomendados los dichos indios que me pedian las adjudicase las dichas tierras i por mi orden fue al dicho pueblo de Chuschi i vistas las dichas tierras que están de la parte donde están poblados los dichos indios comarcanos i hallé que decían que los indios Canas de la encomienda de Pedro de Rivera hace muchos años que poseen las dichas tierras, los cuales dichos indios Canas me mostraron un Auto de Damián de la Bandera, Corregidor que fue de la dicha ciudad de Guamanga, en el cual declara pertenecer las dichas tierras que los dichos Indios Aymaraes piden a los dichos Canas en estos cinco topos que manda y señale á los dichos Aymaraes y más me mostraron una Provisión Real en que mandan que estando en posesión los indios Canas de las dichas tierras parte un arroyo grande que está entre el pueblo de los dichos Aymaraes y el pueblo de Canas . . . i por mi visto que los unos y los otros dicen y alegan e informandome de muchos indios antiguos de las del rededor hallé que estos dichos indios decían que en los tiempos de Tupac Inga Yupanqui, habian oido decir que los dichos indios Aymaraes estaban poblados en aquellas tierras por mandato del dicho Topa Inga Yupanqui i que decían ser suyas, pero que después de los dichos indios Canas, vinieron allé la tienen y poseen labrándolas y sembrándolas, porque dicen que Wayna Capac se les dió i mandó poblar ahí por lo cual todo y para los quitar de pleitos y diferencias mando a los dichos indios Aymaraes y Canas guarden y cumplan el auto y autos hechos por Damián de la Bandera.

Glossary

NOTE: The common variations in orthography appear in parentheses adjacent to the main entries, which conform to modern conventions. For example: *puqyo (pukyo), waka (huaca)*.

Achita: *Chenopodium pallidicaule*, a grain related to *quinua*.

Albadukay: Ritual display of authority by the alcaldes to their subordinates (the regidores and alguaciles) in the indigenous prestige hierarchies *(varayoqkuna)*.

Alcalde: Mayor; the top rank in any of the indigenous prestige hierarchies *(varayoqkuna)*.

Alcalde menor: Lit., lesser mayor. See *Taksa* alcalde.

Alguacil: Lit., constable. In Chuschi, the lowest rank of all in the *varayoq* organizations. Single youths are initiated into the barrio *taksa* prestige hierarchy as alguaciles. Only after marriage can they progress up the hierarchy.

Amaru yarqa: *Amaru*—snake, bull, rooting of a pig; *yarqa*—irrigation canal. The convergence of the canals from Upper Barrio. *Amaru yarqa* runs the length of the village and becomes *hatun yarqa*. See map 6.

Apu: Great, eminent, rich.

Arroba: Weight of 25 pounds; liquid measure varying from 2.6 to 3.6 gallons.

Awra: Reciprocal term for affines. In Chuschi, used by members of two kindreds united by a marriage tie. The marriageable members of the group are excluded from the *perdón* ritual that defines the *awra*.

Ayllu: Generic term signifying a corporate group with a head. Within the domain of Chuschino kinship, the *ayllu* is a bilateral kindred with sexual bifurcation and genealogical distance as principles of structure.

Ayni: Form of private reciprocity whereby persons who respond to a call for aid (see *Minka*) are "lending *ayni*" and expect repayment in kind. This may be a localized meaning.

Barrio: District, quarter, ward. In Chuschi, one of the two halves of the village, one of the moieties.

Caja: Lit., box. Also, cash register or place where one pays for goods or services received. In Chuschi, the place(s) where ritual payments to the mountain deities, the Wamanis, are made.

Calvario: Calvary. In normal Spanish usage, the road marked with altars or crosses that is traveled, with stops to pray at the altars or crosses, in memo of Christ's journey to Calvary. In Chuschi, *calvario* has come to designate the large crosses, nine to twelve feet tall, brought down to the village durin the harvest festival, Santa Cruz (lit., Holy Cross).

Cámac Pacha (Kámaq Pacha): Lit., Lord Earth. The earth in its totality.

Campo envarados: See *Qichwa varayoqkuna*.

CAPS: Cooperativas Agrarias de Producción Social (Social Agrarian Productic Cooperatives). Under the 1969 Agrarian Reform Law, the sugar haciendas on the coast were cooperativized and came under state management.

Chacra Yapuy: Lit., to plant the field. The ritual first planting of the agricultural year, performed during the latter part of August in the community of Cancha-Cancha. Chacra Yapuy is performed in Chuschi generally after the Yarqa Aspiy.

Chicha: Corn beer.

Chinlili: Small, guitar-shaped instrument played by men in Chuschi. It has six strings, tuned to the following (relative) pitches: E, B, G, D, B, G. The fourth (drone) string is often doubled in octaves.

Chirisuya: A wooden reed instrument. The ideal reed is from the tailfeather of a condor.

Cholo, chola: A person of recent upward social mobility. Characteristically, a cholo participates in both the indigenous culture of the Andes and the national or mestizo culture without being fully incorporated into either. This social ambiguity means that leaders of peasant movements are often cholos. Their ability to break the caste-like quality of Indian and mestizo relationships is due to new economic potentialities found in the urban environment or acquired through increased education.

Chonta: Hard, dark palm wood from which Chuschi's *varayoq* make their staffs of office. Genus *Guilielma,* with at least three species, *G. ciliata, G. gasipaes, G. insignis.*

Choquechinchay: According to Pachacuti Yamqui, a fierce, multicolored animal revered by the Otorongo (lowland) Indians, who were bisexual. Modern informants say that the term refers to the vapor that escapes from the earth in February and August.

Chunchu: Generalized term for all indigenous people of the tropical forests.

Cirse: Type of reed used in the Herranza (branding) ritual. Botanical identity unknown.

Coca: *Erythroxylon coca, E. novogranatense.* Two closely related species utilized as a mild stimulant by chewing the leaves with the ash from certain plants, which releases the alkaloid. When coca is processed, cocaine alkaloi is obtained. However, the indigenous use of coca was, and is today, as a stimulating mascatory to relieve hunger and fatigue. The leaves are important in various rituals.

Cofradía: Brotherhood. In Chuschi, the term is used to refer to the land belonging to the saints and to the animals belonging to the church.

Comadre: Lit., co-mother. See Compadrazgo.

Compadrazgo: Lit., co-parenthood. System in which adults contract fictive or spiritual kinship through ritual sponsorship of a child or object.

Compadre: Lit., co-father. See Compadrazgo.

Compadres de ramo: Lit., co-parents of the branch. Men and women who offer their services as future co-parents for future children, usually in a parallel form, men to men and women to women. See *Ramo apay*.

Comunero: Communal member of a recognized peasant community. The term Chuschinos use for participating members of the community. The 1969 Agrarian Reform Law defines full and associate comunero status.

Comunidad indígena: Indigenous community locally recognized in 1925. The 1969 Agrarian Reform Law changed the name to comunidad campesina (peasant community). See Peasant community.

Condenados: Persons who engage in incestuous relations. They are transformed into animals and condemned to wander at night with bells around their necks.

Corte monte: Lit., cut the undergrowth. A ritual in the Lima invasion settlements that involves planting a grown tree festooned with gifts and then ceremonially cutting it down. Most often practiced during Carnival.

Curato: Parochial territory comprising several communities.

Corregidor: Spanish administrator during the later colonial period in Latin America. The *corregidores de indios* replaced the *encomenderos* (see *Encomienda*) in the late sixteenth century.

Dispensera: Lit., dispenser. Woman in charge of serving cane alcohol, chicha, and food to guests at a fiesta.

Ecónomo: Accountant. In Chuschi, the accountant for the church's cofradía possessions.

Encomienda: An early system of Spanish administration whereby conquerors were granted Indians as a labor force in return for performing military and religious obligations. The early *encomiendas* were often called *repartimientos*.

Envarados mayores: See *Hatun varayoqkuna*.

Faena: Obligatory public communal labor.

Gentiles: Souls of the dead believed to reside in burial caves. Usually associated with bones or mummy bundles that cause illness and death. Non-Christian ancestors.

Guardia: Policeman, guard.

Hacendado: Owner of a large ranch or estate. See Hacienda.

Hacienda: Landed estate. An outgrowth of the *encomienda* system.

Hamites: Long-distance herb traders who originated near Lake Titicaca and journeyed throughout the Andes selling and collecting herbs.

Hanan Pacha: Upper World.

Hatun: Great, large, big.

Hatun varayoqkuna: Also called *varayoq mayores, envarados mayores.* Lit., major staff-bearers or the bearers of the great staffs. Before 1970, those members of the indigenous prestige hierarchy subordinated to the governor of the district and associated with the church. This organization represents the apex of the prestige hierarchy. It was abolished in 1970 by communal vote, only to be reestablished in 1972 to protect the cofradía animals both from the church and from attempts to form a cooperative.

Hatun yarqa: Great irrigation canal. It is the continuation of the *amaru yarqa* at the *qonopa.* See map 6.

Hectare: One and one-half acres.

Herranza: Ritual that involves the branding or marking of herds and ceremonial payments to the mountain deities, the Wamanis.

Illas: Small stone effigies of cattle, sheep, and horses. They are said to be the animals belonging to the mountain deities, the Wamanis, and are of a sacred nature.

Junta comunal: Community government or council.

Karu ayllu: Distant, marriageable relatives. See *Ayllu.*

Karu pani: Distant sister. A female generation mate sufficiently far removed to be marriageable.

Kay Pacha: Lit., this earth. The earth we live on, the here and now.

*Kimsa pawsa: Kimsa—*three; *pawsa—*double scroll design. Name given to the ceremonial bundle used in the Herranza.

Kindred: Bilateral kinship structure of shallow genealogical depth, usually defined as ego-centered. In Chuschi, the *ayllu* is a sibling-centered kindred of first cousin range and only two generations in depth.

Kuraka: Indigenous chief.

Kuyaq: Lit., those who love me. A wide network of consanguineal, affinal, and spiritual relatives who participate in reciprocal exchanges such as helping a person who is in charge of a fiesta.

Lampa: Indigenous hoe.

Latifundio: Large landed estate with broad expanses of land under cultivation

Llampu: Special powder used in the Herranza, made from ground corn and other ingredients.

Lliklla: Rectangular or square wool cloths used as a sort of backpack to carry babies, food, etc.

Llumchu: Woman who married ego's brother or son. Daughter-in-law, sister-in-law. Term is also extended to collateral affines, i.e., cousin's wife.

Machka: Toasted ground corn or *quinua* that is sprinkled on top of chicha.

Mal aire: Harmful air, thought to cause sickness.

Mallki (mallqui): Sapling. Ancestor.

Masa: Man who marries ego's sister or child. Term is also extended collaterally to include cousin's husband.

Masamasi: Two *masas* who share an affinal relationship to a particular person i.e., two men who have married sisters or cousins.

Mashua: Tropaeolum tuberosum. Tuber widely believed to be anaphrodisiac and medicinal, but major use is as a food staple. Also called *anu* in southern Peru.

Mayopatan: Mayo—river; *pata*—plain or level place. Riverbottom. Lowest named ecological zone in Chuschi, at 2,300 meters at edge of Pampas River. Exploited for cactus fruit, some fruit trees, and squash and other products demanding warmer climates. Some corn also grown there.

Mayordomo: Sponsor of a fiesta. Tenure usually lasts a year.

Mestizo: Generally, a person of mixed Spanish-Indian ancestry. In Peru, however, usually refers to the segment of the Andean population that identifies with the national culture, is bilingual, and, most important, dominates the Indians politically and economically. From another perspective, mestizos are usually dependent on Indians for labor because they do not command networks of mutual aid and reciprocity. In Chuschi, mestizos are politely called vecinos (neighbors) and derogatively *qalas*. Besides the numerous schoolteachers, merchants, and bureaucrats, there are only four mestizo families in the village. The relationship between mestizos and Indians is generally rigid and often described as caste-like in character. This social rigidity contrasts with the social mobility of the class known as cholos.

Minifundio: A small farmstead. The mass of Andean peasants are owners or users of extremely small plots, less than five hectares per family.

Minka: Collective labor for public works, usually repaid with food, alcohol, chicha, and cigarettes. In Chuschi, *minka* is a request for labor, which is responded to with *ayni.*

Mita: From *mitay*—to take turns. Originally instituted as a form of taxation on indigenous communities. In Chuschi, *mita* was used in the past to provide the priest, military officers, and prominent mestizos with household servants and field labor. The community has rebelled against such servitude.

Mitmaq: Person or village moved from one place to another. The Incas used this method of colonization to assure their conquests, prevent uprisings, and propagate their culture.

Moiety: One of two parts into which a social group is divided. Chuschi is divided into two localized moieties called barrios.

Naqaq: The dreaded supernatural being that extracts one's body fat, castrates men, and eats small children.

Ñawin: Ñawi—eye. *Ñawin* indicates third person—his or her eye. However, it also means initial, best, or principal. It is an abstract notion.

Ñawin taytacha: Name for the sacred springs. *Taytacha* means "god." Hence the springs are called "god initial," referring to the source of the water, or "god eye."

Oca: Oxalis tuberosa. Several varieties of this tuber are grown throughout the puna region of the Andes. *Ocas* are often sun-dried and stored.

Pacha Mama: Lit., Earth Mother. The inner earth.

Pagapu: A ritual payment made to the mountain deities, the Wamanis.

Pampa: Plain, field. Often corrupted in place-names to *bamba*, e.g., Calcabamba–stony plain.

Pani: Lit., sister or female cousin (male speaking). *Paniy* (male speaking)–n sister or cousin. Also, a ritual that formally separates a girl who is to be married from her home.

Peasant community: The 1969 Agrarian Reform Law modified the name an status of recognized indigenous communities (comunidades indígenas). T are now called peasant communities (comunidades campesinas). Private property was abolished, administrative and vigilance councils were establis and criteria for membership and usufruct rights were delineated.

Perdón (perdonakuy): Lit., mutual pardon. Ritual in the marriage process that redefines relationships between the kindred of the bride and groom a establishes the *awra*.

Personero: Member of the junta comunal of recognized communities who w responsible for documents and land litigation. The 1969 Agrarian Reform Law replaced the junta with administrative and vigilance councils.

PIAR: Proyecto Integral de Asentamiento Rural (Integral Rural Settlement Project). Intermediate form of rural organization that incorporates different agricultural enterprises within a geographical area. These organizations are designed to provide profit-sharing by members.

Pichqa: Lit., five. Divination and purification rite involving washing the deceased's clothing and cutting and burning the funeral participants' hair.

Pukllay: Singing and dancing contests on the puna between young, unmarrie males and females that culminate in group sexual activities.

Puna: Extensive high region of the Andes, divided into lower (*urin*) and upp (*hatun*) zones. The zone that supports tubers such as potatoes, *ullucos, o* and *mashua* and grains such as wheat, barley, and *quinua* is the *urin sallqa,* lower puna, which begins at the upper limit of corn production at about 3,000 meters. The *hatun sallqa,* upper puna, begins at 3,600 meters and extends beyond 4,000 meters; it is utilized for grazing. The altitudinal limits given are for Chuschi and vary in other parts of the Andes. *Sallqa* also means savage, uncivilized.

Puñukuy: Lit., to sleep together. Ritual symbolizing the consummation of marriage.

Puqyo (pukyo): Spring generally associated with the mountain deities, the Wamanis.

Puyñu: Small clay bottle. See *Takyachiy puyñu.*

Qala: Lit., naked or peeled one. Foreigner, person without social identity within the community due to lack of participation in reciprocal aid and the civil-religious hierarchy. Plural, *qalakuna.*

Qaru chuyay: *Qaru (karu)*–distant, far; *chuyay*–to clarify. Ritual that clarifies and affirms the social distance between hacendados and laborers.

Qichwa (kichwa): Valley lands important for corn production. In Chuschi this zone begins at about 3,300 meters at its upper limit, where it conjoins with the *sallqa* or puna. The nucleated community is located in the center of the zone at 3,154 meters. The lower boundary, where the *mayopatan* begins, is not clear. The altitudinal range of this zone varies somewhat throughout the Andean region.

Qichwa varayoqkuna: Organization, no longer extant, in the prestige herarchy, comprising a mayor (alcalde) and two unmarried youths as his subordinates, who guarded the agricultural zone of the village.

Qonopa (qoñupa): Chapel in Lower Barrio where the Yarqa Aspiy celebration terminates with repetitive drinking. It is on the site of the convergence of the irrigation canals (see map 6).

Quinua: Chenopodium quinoa. A grain common in the Andes, grown in the lower *sallqa* or puna.

Ramo apay: Lit., bringing of the branch. One of the ritual steps of marriage, in which the couple to be married acquire their first and principal compadres, who baptize bouquets of flowers representing children and who ideally serve as the real baptismal godparents of all the couple's children.

Reducción: The practice of forceably congregating Indian populations into communities in order to Christianize them. These populations were generally controlled by religious orders.

Regidor: Lit., alderman, council member. Regidores are the second-ranking members of the *varayoq* prestige hierarchies and are called the "arms" of their alcaldes.

SAIS: Sociedades Agrícolas de Interés Social (Agricultural Societies for Social Interest). Large conglomerates under state management, consisting of indigenous communities and expropriated haciendas and directed toward improved cattle production for the national market.

Sallqa: See Puna.

Sallqaruna: Uncivilized or savage people; also, people who live on the puna.

Sallqa varayoqkuna: Traditional prestige organization of herders dedicated to the care of the cofradía herds that belonged to the church prior to 1970. In that year the community took possession of the herds. The *sallqa varayoqkuna* had to own animals and to have passed at least to *hatun* alguacil before holding a position in the herding hierarchy.

Santa Cruz: Lit., the Holy Cross. The harvest festival, which takes place in early May.

Santas menores: Minor female saints.

Señor cesante: Retired lord. Respectful term for those who have completed the positions of the civil-religious hierarchy.

SINAMOS: Sistema Nacional de Apoyo a la Movilización Social (National Support System for Social Mobilization). Governmental organization created in 1972.

Sol: Monetary unit of Peru (plural, *soles*). Also, the sun.

Taksa: Small, lesser.

Taksa alcalde: Highest rank in the dual barrio prestige hierarchies. The two mayors are the second rank from the apex of the civil-religious hierarchy, the *hatun* alcalde.

Taksa varayoqkuna: Lit., the lesser staff-bearers or the bearers of the lesser staffs. The dual prestige hierarchies that serve the two village barrios. Membership is determined by residence.

Takyachiy puyñu: Takyachiy—to be sustained in equilibrium; *puyñu*—small clay bottle used for carrying water. The ritual purification of the bride and groom in equilibrium with one another throughout life is symbolized by the two pottery drinking bottles kept in the rafters of the house. The ritual preparation of the two bottles is part of the wedding ceremonies.

Tiyapakuq: Lit., he who sits on the land of others. A person who does not own land. Most persons in this situation act as herders for more wealthy comuneros.

Topo (tupu): Indian measure of one and one-half leagues.

Trago: Cane alcohol.

Tunku: Small basket of *cirse* reeds.

Ulluco (olluco): Ullucus tuberosus. Plant with tuberous roots used for food

Usupa: Child born to parents before they are married.

Vara: Lit., staff. In Chuschi, also refers to a member of the indigenous prestige hierarchy. See *Varayoq.*

Varayoq: Lit., he who possesses the staff. A member of the indigenous prestige hierarchies. The plural is *varayoqkuna,* but *varayoq* is often used as the plural. See *Hatun varayoqkuna, Taksa varayoqkuna.*

Varayoqkuna: See *Varayoq.*

Varayoq mayores: See *Hatun varayoqkuna.*

Vecino: Lit., neighbor. Resident of Chuschi who is a Spanish-speaking, Western-dressed, foreign non-participant in communal life. See *Qala,* Mestizo.

Viracocha (Wirakocha): Supreme creator god of the Incas. Symbolized by a golden oval and the five stars of Orion, according to Pachacuti Yamqui.

Visitador: Official royal inspector during the colonial era. Inspections were called *visitas.*

Waka (huaca): A sacred place, stone, or object.

Wakcha: Orphan. By extension, poor, unlucky.

Wallqa: Collar, necklace, chain hung around the neck. The bread and fruit *wallqas* worn in Chuschi during the Herranza and other fiestas are worn over one shoulder and under one arm.

Wamani: Localized mountain deity who provides water and is owner of all animals. The Wamanis are hierarchically organized according to power as reflected in the size and prominent characteristics of the mountain peaks.

Waqrapuku: A hunting-horn-shaped instrument made of cattle horns nested into one another to achieve its considerable curved length. It is played like a brass instrument, by producing vibrations with the lips. The harmonic scale range is anywhere from an octave to two octaves.

Warmi urquy: Lit., to remove or take out the woman. Marriage ritual in which the terms of marriage are negotiated between the parents and godparents of the groom-to-be and the bride-to-be's parents.

Watan misa: Lit., anniversary mass. Final ceremony following a person's death. A mass marking the first anniversary of a death.

Watankuy: "Having a year together." Period of cohabitation, theoretically one year, before marriage.

Wayluru (wayruru) seeds: Cytharexylon herrerae. Red and black bean-like seeds used in ritual payments to the mountain deities, the Wamanis, during the Herranza.

Willka (vilca, villca) seeds: Dark brown, flat, tear-shaped, bean-like seeds, identified as *Anadenanthera colubrina,* used in the lowlands for the manufacture of hallucinogenic snuff. Used in the highlands in divination rites and as part of the payment to the mountain deities, the Wamanis, during the Herranza.

Yarqa Aspiy: *Yarqa*—irrigation canal; *aspiy*—to dig, to scratch. Ritual cleaning of the irrigation canals, which takes place around the September equinox. This fiesta marks the beginning of the planting season. See *Chacra Yapuy.*

Yaykupakuy: The "formal approach" before a wedding, when delegates from the groom ask for the bride.

Yugada: Amount of land that can be ploughed in one day with one pair of oxen.

Bibliography

Adams, Richard N.
    1959   *A Community in the Andes: Problems and Progress in Muquiyauyo.*
              Seattle: University of Washington Press.
    1962   "The Community in Latin America: A Changing Myth." *The
              Centennial Review* 6 (3): 409-434.
Alberti, Giorgio, and Mayer, Enrique, eds.
    1974   *Reciprocidad e intercambio en los Andes peruanos.* Perú Problema
              No. 12. Lima: Instituto de Estudios Peruanos.
Albó, Xavier
    1972   "Esposos, suegros y padrinos entre los Aymaras." Paper presented
              at the Symposium on Andean Kinship and Marriage, 71st Annual
              Meeting of the American Anthropological Association, Toronto.
Alcántara, Elsa, and Vásquez, Arturo
    1974   *Dinámica poblacional y estructura agraria en el Perú.* Lima:
              Pontificia Universidad Católica.
Altschul, Siri Von Reis
    1967   "Vilca and Its Use." In *Ethnopharmacologic Search for Psycho-
              active Drugs,* edited by D. Efron, pp. 307-314. Public Health
              Service Publication No. 1645. Washington, D.C.: U.S. Government
              Printing Office.
Avila, Francisco de
    1939   "Damonen und Zauber in Inkareich, Aus dem Ketschua ubersetzt
              und eingeleitet," translated by von Hermann Trimborn. *Quellen
              und Forschungen zur Geschichte de Geographie und Volkerkunde*
              (Leipzig), Band IV.
    1966   *Dioses y hombres de Huarochirí.* Translation of the original
              (1598) by José María Arguedas. Lima: Museo Nacional de Historia
              y el Instituto de Estudios Peruanos.
Barthes, Roland
    1972   "The Structuralist Activity." In *The Structuralists from Marx to*

Lévi-Strauss, edited by R. T. DeGeorge and F. M. DeGeorge, pp. 148-154. Garden City, New York: Doubleday and Company.

Bateson, Gregory
1958 *Naven.* Stanford, California: Stanford University Press.

Belote, James, and Belote, Linda
1977 "The Limitation of Obligation in Saraguro Kinship." In *Andean Kinship and Marriage,* edited by R. Bolton and E. Mayer, pp. 10₵ 116. Washington, D.C.: American Anthropological Association Special Publication No. 7.

Bolívar de Colchado, Fanny
1967 "El distrito de Chuschi." In *Los Distritos de Vischongo, Chusch. Concepción y Ocros,* by V. H. Sarmiento Medina, F. Bolívar de Colchado, C. Ramón Córdova, and G. Colchado A., pp. 1-22. Lima: Instituto Indigenista Peruano.

Bolton, Ralph
1977 "Qolla Marriage Process." In *Andean Kinship and Marriage,* edit by R. Bolton and E. Mayer, pp. 217-239. Washington, D.C.: American Anthropological Association Special Publication No. 7

Bonavia, Duccio, et al.
1972 *Pueblos y culturas de la sierra central del Perú.* Lima: Cerro de Pasco Corporation.

Bonilla, Heraclio, and Spalding, Karen
1972 "La independencia en el Perú: Las palabras y los hechos." In *La independencia en el Perú,* Perú Problema No. 7, pp. 15-64. Lima: Instituto de Estudios Peruanos.

Bourque, Susan C., and Palmer, David Scott
1975 "Transforming the Rural Sector: Government Policy and Peasan₁ Response." In *The Peruvian Experiment,* edited by A. Lowenth₂ pp. 179-219. Princeton, New Jersey: Princeton University Press.

Brush, Stephen B.
1973 "Subsistence Strategies and Vertical Ecology in an Andean Community: Uchucmarca, Peru." Ph.D. dissertation, University of Wisconsin-Madison.
1976 "Man's Use of an Andean Ecosystem." *Human Ecology* 4 (2): 147-166.
1977 "The Myth of the Idle Peasant: Employment in a Subsistence Economy." In *Peasant Livelihood,* edited by Rhoda Halperin an₁ James Dow, pp. 60-78. New York: St. Martin's Press.

Buechler, Hans, and Buechler, Judith Marie
1971 *The Bolivian Aymara.* New York: Holt, Rinehart and Winston.

Burchard, Roderick E.
1974 "Coca y trueque de alimentos." In *Reciprocidad e intercambio ₁ los Andes peruanos,* edited by G. Alberti and E. Mayer, pp. 209-251. Lima: Instituto de Estudios Peruanos.

Bustamante B., Alberto
1974   *Legislación sobre reforma agraria y cooperativas agrarias.* Lima: DESCO.
Catacora A., Sergio
1968   "Organización social de la comunidad de San Ildefonso de Chuqui Huarcaya." Tesis para optar el grado de Bachiller en Ciencias Antropológicas, Universidad Nacional de San Cristóbal de Huamanga, Ayacucho, Perú.
Cohen, A.
1974   *Two-Dimensional Man: An Essay on the Anthropology of Power and Symbolism in Complex Society.* London: Routledge and Kegan Paul.
Concha Contreras, Juan de Dios
1975   "Relación entre pastores y agricultores." *Allpanchis Phuturenqa* 8: 67-102.
Cotler, Julio
1969   "La mecánica de la dominación interna y del cambio social en el Perú." In *Perú Problema,* Perú Problema No. 1, edited by J. Matos Mar and F. Fuenzalida, pp. 145-188. Lima: Moncloa-Campodónico.
1970a   "Traditional Haciendas and Communities in a Context of Political Mobilization in Peru." In *Agrarian Problems and Peasant Movements in Latin America,* edited by Rodolfo Stavenhagen, pp. 533-558. Garden City, New York: Doubleday.
1970b   "Crisis política y popularismo militar en el Perú." *Revista mexicana de sociología* 31, no. 3: 737-784.
1972   "Bases del corporativismo en el Perú." *Sociedad y política* 2: 3-11.
1975   "The New Mode of Political Domination in Peru." In *The Peruvian Experiment,* edited by A. F. Lowenthal, pp. 44-78. Princeton, New Jersey: Princeton University Press.
Custred, Glynn
1974   "Llameros y comercio interregional." In *Reciprocidad e intercambio en los Andes peruanos,* edited by G. Alberti and E. Mayer, pp. 252-289. Lima: Instituto de Estudios Peruanos.
1977   "Peasant Kinship, Subsistence and Economics of a High Altitude Andean Environment." In *Andean Kinship and Marriage,* edited by R. Bolton and E. Mayer, pp. 117-135. Washington, D.C.: American Anthropological Association Special Publication No. 7.
Davies, Thomas M.
1974   *Indian Integration in Peru.* Lincoln, Nebraska: University of Nebraska Press.
Dávila, Mario
1971   "Compadrazgo: Fictive Kinship in Latin America." In *Readings in Kinship and Social Structure,* edited by Nelson Graburn, pp. 396-406. New York: Harper and Row.

De la Puente Uceda, Luis F.
1966   *La reforma del agro peruano.* Lima: Ediciones Ensayos Sociales.
Delgado, Carlos
1971   "Tres planteamientos en torno a problemas de urbanización acelerada en áreas metropolitanas: El caso de Lima." In his *Problemas sociales en el Perú contemporáneo,* Perú Problema No. 6, pp. 119-158. Lima: Campodónico Ediciones.
Dobyns, Henry F.
1964   *The Social Matrix of Peruvian Indigenous Communities.* Ithaca, New York: Cornell University Press.
Dobyns, Henry F., and Vásquez, Mario C.
1963   *Migración e integración en el Perú.* Lima: Editorial Estudios Andinos.
Doughty, Paul L.
1968   *Huaylas: An Andean District in Search of Progress.* Ithaca, New York: Cornell University Press.
1970   "Behind the Back of the City: 'Provincial' Life in Lima, Peru." In *Peasants in Cities,* edited by W. Mangin, pp. 30-46. Boston: Houghton Mifflin Company.
Duviols, Pierre
1973   "Huari y Llacuaz: Agricultores y pastores. Un dualismo prehispánico de oposición y complementaridad." *Revista del Museo Nacional* (Lima) 39: 153-193.
Earls, John
1968   "Categorías estructurales en la cultura andina." Tesis para optar el grado de Bachiller en Ciencias Antropológicas, Universidad Nacional de San Cristóbal de Huamanga, Ayacucho, Perú.
Escobar, Gabriel
1973   *Sicaya: Cambios culturales en una comunidad mestiza andina.* Lima: Instituto de Estudios Peruanos.
Fajardo, Jesús V.
1960   *Legislación indígena del Perú.* Lima: Editorial Mercurio.
Firth, Raymond
1973   *Symbols, Public and Private.* Ithaca, New York: Cornell University Press.
Flores Ochoa, Jorge A.
1968   *Los pastores de Paratía. Una introducción a su estudio.* Serie Antropología Social, No. 10. Mexico City: Instituto Indigenista Interamericano.
1975   "Pastores de alpacas." *Allpanchis Phuturenqa* 8: 5-24.
Fonseca Martel, César
1972   "Sistemas económicos en las comunidades campesinas del Perú." Tesis Doctoral en Antropología, Universidad Nacional Mayor de San Marcos, Lima.

Foster, George M.
1953   "Cofradía and Compadrazgo in Spain and Spanish America."
        Southwestern Journal of Anthropology 9, no. 1: 1-26.
Fox, Robin
1967   *Kinship and Marriage.* Baltimore, Maryland: Penguin Books.
Fuenzalida V., Fernando
1970a "La estructura de la comunidad de indígenas tradicionales." In
        El campesino en el Perú, Perú Problema No. 3, pp. 16-104. Lima:
        Moncloa-Campodónico.
1970b "Poder, raza y etnía en el Perú contemporáneo." In *El Indio y el
        poder en el Perú,* Perú Problema No. 4, pp. 15-86. Lima: Moncloa-
        Campodónico.
Geertz, Clifford
1968   "The Cerebral Savage." In *Theory in Anthropology,* edited by
        R. O. Manners and D. Kaplan, pp. 551-559. Chicago: Aldine
        Publishing Company.
Gillin, John
1947   *Moche: A Peruvian Coastal Community.* Washington, D.C.:
        Institute of Social Anthropology, Smithsonian Institution.
Goodenough, Ward H.
1970   *Description and Comparison in Cultural Anthropology.* Chicago:
        Aldine Publishing Company.
Greaves, Thomas
1972   "The Andean Rural Proletarians." *Anthropological Quarterly* 45,
        no. 2: 65-83.
Guamán Poma de Ayala, Felipe
1936   *El primer nueva crónica y buen gobierno.* Paris, France: Institut
        d'Ethnologie.
Guardia Mayorga, César A.
1967   *Diccionario Kechwa-Castellano Castellano-Kechwa.* Lima: Ediciones
        Los Andes.
Handleman, Howard
1975   *Struggle in the Andes: Peasant Political Mobilization in Peru.*
        Austin and London: Institute of Latin American Studies, The
        University of Texas Press.
Harding, Colon
1975   "Land Reform and Social Conflict in Peru." In *The Peruvian
        Experiment,* edited by A. F. Lowenthal, pp. 220-253. Princeton,
        New Jersey: Princeton University Press.
Instituto Indigenista Interamericano
1971   "Estatuto de comunidades campesinas del Perú." *Anuario Indi-
        genista* (Mexico City) 5, no. 3: 191-208.
Instituto Nacional de Planificación
1969   *Atlas histórico geográfico y de paisajes peruanos.* Lima: Instituto

Nacional de Planificación.
1973   *Estudio sobre la población peruana.* Lima: Instituto Nacional de
        Planificación.
Isbell, Billie Jean
    1972a   "Acquisition of Quechua Morphology: An Application of the Be
             Test." *Papers in Andean Linguistics* 1, No. 1: 79-129.
    1972b   "No servimos más: Un estudio de los efectos de disipar un sistem
             de la autoridad tradicional en un pueblo ayacuchano." *Revista d*
             Museo Nacional 37: 285-298. (Also in *Actas y memorias del 39ᶜ*
             Congreso Internacional de Americanistas, III, 285-298. Lima.)
    1974a   "The Influence of Migrants upon Traditional Social and Political
             Concepts: A Peruvian Case Study." In *Latin American Urban*
             Research, vol. 4, *Anthropological Perspectives on Latin America*
             Urbanization, edited by W. A. Cornelius and F. M. Trueblood,
             pp. 237-259. Beverly Hills, California: Sage Publications.
    1974b   "Parentesco andino y reciprocidad. *Kuyaq:* los que nos aman."
             In *Reciprocidad e intercambio en los Andes peruanos,* Perú
             Problema No. 12, edited by G. Alberti and E. Mayer, pp. 110-15
             Lima: Instituto de Estudios Peruanos.
    1976   "La otra mitad esencial: Un estudio de complementariedad sexu
             en los Andes." *Estudios Andinos,* año 5, vol. 5, no. 1: 37-56.
    1977   "*Kuyaq:* Those Who Love Me: An Analysis of Andean Kinship a
             Reciprocity in a Ritual Context." In *Andean Kinship and Marri*
             edited by R. Bolton and E. Mayer, pp. 81-105. Washington, D.C
             American Anthropological Association Special Publication No. 7
Isbell, Billie Jean, and Roncalla Fernández, Fredy A.
    1977   "The Ontogenesis of Metaphor: Riddle Games among Quechua
             Speakers Seen as Cognitive Discovery Procedures." *Journal of*
             Latin American Lore 3, 1 (Summer 1976): 19-49. UCLA Latin
             American Center.
Isbell, William H.
    1968   "The Interpretation of Prehistoric Site Location in Terms of a
             Modern Folk Model." Paper presented at the 67th Annual Meet
             of the American Anthropological Association, Seattle.
    1970a   "Las culturas intermedias de la sierra central." *El Serrano* (Lima
             19, no. 248: 16-19.
    1970b   "El horizonte medio y la unificación de los Andes centrales." *El*
             Serrano (Lima) 19, no. 249: 16-20.
    1972a   "Un pueblo rural ayacuchano durante el imperio Huari." *Actas*
             memorias del 39° Congreso Internacional de Americanistas, III,
             89-105. Lima.
    1972b   "Quechua Speakers and the Cultivation of Steep Hillsides." Pap
             presented at the 37th Annual Meeting of the Society for Americ
             Archaeology.

1977   *The Rural Foundation for Urbanism.* Urbana, Illinois: University of Illinois Press.

Jiménez de la Espada, Marcos
1965   *Relaciones geográficas de indias–Perú,* vol. 1. Madrid: Biblioteca de Autores Españoles.

Keatinge, Elsie B.
1973   "Latin American Peasant Corporate Communities: Potentials for Mobilization and Political Integration." *Journal of Anthropological Research* 29: 37-58.

Knight, Peter T.
1975   "New Forms of Economic Organization in Peru: Towards Workers Self-Management." In *The Peruvian Experiment,* edited by A. Lowenthal, pp. 350-401. Princeton, New Jersey: Princeton University Press.

Lambert, Bernd
1977   "Bilaterality in the Andes." In *Andean Kinship and Marriage,* edited by R. Bolton and E. Mayer, pp. 1-27. Washington, D.C.: American Anthropological Association Special Publication No. 7.

La Prensa (Lima). October 7: "Invaden tierras de cooperativa." October 8:
1963   "La caballería no pudo desalojar a invasores de Fundo Valdivieso." October 9: "Invadieron de nuevo el Fundo Valdivieso."

Leach, Edmund R.
1965   *Political Systems of Highland Burma.* Boston: Beacon Press.

Lévi-Strauss, Claude
1963   *Structural Anthropology.* New York, London: Basic Books.
1966   *Savage Mind.* Chicago: University of Chicago Press.
1969a   *The Elementary Structures of Kinship.* Boston: Beacon Press.
1969b   *The Raw and the Cooked.* New York: Harper and Row.

Long, Norman
1977   "Kinship and Entrepreneurship in the Peruvian Highlands." In *Andean Kinship and Marriage,* edited by R. Bolton and E. Mayer, pp. 153-176. Washington, D.C.: American Anthropological Association Special Publication No. 7.

Lounsbury, Floyd G.
1964   "Some Aspects of the Inca Kinship System." A paper read at the International Congress of Americanists, Barcelona.

Lowenthal, Abraham F.
1975   "Peru's Ambiguous Revolution." In *The Peruvian Experiment,* edited by A. F. Lowenthal, pp. 3-43. Princeton, New Jersey: Princeton University Press.

Lumbreras, S., and Luis, G.
1959   "Sobre los Chancas." In *Actas y trabajos del II Congreso Nacional de Historia del Perú,* I, 211-243. Lima: Centro de Estudios Históricos-Militares del Perú.

Malengreau, Jacques
  1972   "Kin, Compadres, Padrinos and Comuneros in Cusipata: A Conte
          porary Village in the Peruvian Andes." Paper presented at the
          symposium on Andean Kinship and Marriage, 71st Annual Meeti
          of the American Anthropological Association, Toronto.
Mangin, William
  1959   "The Role of Regional Associations in the Adaptations of Rural
          Population in Peru." *Sociologus* 9: 23-25.
  1960   "Mental Health and Migration to Cities: A Peruvian Case." *Anna
          of the New York Academy of Sciences* 84: 911-917.
  1964   "Estratificación en el Callejón de Huaylas." In *Estudios sobre la
          cultural actual del Perú*, pp. 16-36. Lima: Universidad Nacional
          Mayor de San Marcos.
  1967   "Latin American Squatter Settlements: A Problem and a Solutio
          Latin American Research Review 2, no. 3: 65-98.
  1970   "Urbanization Case History in Peru." In *Peasants in Cities*, edite
          by W. Mangin, pp. 47-54. Boston: Houghton Mifflin Company.
Maranda, Pierre
  1972   "Structuralism in Cultural Anthropology." In *Annual Review of
          Anthropology*, vol. 1, edited by Bernard J. Siegel, pp. 329-348.
          Palo Alto, California: Annual Reviews Incorporated.
Marka (Lima). Año 1, no. 5: "Cooperativas agrarias: La mala senda," pp. 16
  1975   20; no. 17: "Dos entrevistas: El movimiento campesino," pp. 18-
          19.
Martínez, Héctor
  1968   "Las migraciones internas en el Perú." *Estudios de población y
          desarrollo* (Lima) 2, no. 1: 1-15.
Martínez, Héctor; Cameo, M.; and Ramírez, J.
  1969   *Bibliografía indígena andina peruana (1900-1968)*. Lima: Centrc
          de Estudios de Población y Desarrollo.
Matos Mar, José
  1964   "La propiedad en la Isla de Taquile." In *Estudios sobre la cultur
          actual del Perú*, edited by L. Valcárcel, pp. 64-142. Lima: Unive
          sidad Nacional Mayor de San Marcos.
  1966   *Estudio de las barriadas limeñas*. Lima: Departamento de Antro-
          pología, Universidad Nacional Mayor de San Marcos.
Mayer, Enrique
  1970   "Mestizo e indio: El contexto social de las relaciones interétnicas
          In *El indio y el poder en el Perú*, Perú Problema No. 4, pp. 88-15
          Lima: Moncloa-Campodónico.
  1974   "Reciprocity, Self Sufficiency and Market Relations in a Con-
          temporary Community in the Central Andes of Peru." Ph.D.
          dissertation, Cornell University, Ithaca, New York.
  1977   "Beyond the Nuclear Family." In *Andean Kinship and Marriage*,

edited by R. Bolton and E. Mayer, pp. 60-80. Washington, D.C.:
American Anthropological Association Special Publication No. 7.

Mayer, Enrique, and Palmer, David Scott
1972   "They Won't Listen: Campesino and Government Relations in the
Central Highlands of Peru." Paper presented at the Northeast
Consortium for Andean Studies Conference, Pennsylvania State
University.

Middlebrook, Kevin J., and Palmer, David Scott
1975   *Military Government and Political Development Lessons from
Peru.* Beverly Hills, California: Sage Publications.

Mintz, Sidney W., and Wolf, Eric R.
1950   "An Analysis of Ritual Co-Parenthood (Compadrazgo)." *South-
western Journal of Anthropology* 6: 341-368.

Mishkin, Bernard
1963   "The Contemporary Quechua." In *Handbook of South American
Indians*, vol. 2, edited by J. H. Steward, pp. 411-470. New York:
Cooper Square Publications.

Mitchell, William P.
1977   "Irrigation Farming in the Andes: Evolutionary Implications." In
Peasant Livelihood, edited by Rhoda Halperin and James Dow,
pp. 36-59. New York: St. Martin's Press.

Montalvo, Abner S.
1965   "Chinchero Social Structure: A Mestizo Indian Community of
South Peru." M.A. thesis, Cornell University, Ithaca, N.Y.

Murdock, George Peter
1960   "Cognatic Forms of Social Organization." In *Social Structure in
Southeast Asia*, Viking Fund Publications in Anthropology 9,
edited by George P. Murdock, pp. 1-14. Chicago: Quadrangle
Books.

Murphy, Robert F.
1971   *The Dialectics of Social Life.* New York and London: Basic
Books.

Murra, John V.
1967   "La visita de los Chupachu como fuente etnológica." In *Visita
de la Provincia de León de Huánuco* [1562] by Iñigo Ortiz de
Zúñiga, I, 383-406. Huánuco, Perú: Universidad Hermilio
Valdizán.

1968   "An Aymara Kingdom in 1567." *Ethnohistory* 15, no. 2: 115-151.

1970   "Current Research and Prospects in Andean Ethnohistory."
Latin American Research Review 5, no. 1: 3-36.

1972   "El 'control vertical' de un máximo de pisos ecológicos en la eco-
nomía de las sociedades andinas." In *Visita de la Provincia de
León de Huánuco* [1562] by Iñigo Ortiz de Zúñiga, I, 428-468.
Huánuco, Perú: Universidad Hermilio Valdizán.

1975   *Formaciones económicas y políticas del mundo andino.* Lima:
        Instituto de Estudios Peruanos.
Nash, June
1974   "Ethics and Politics in Social Science." *New York Academy of
        Sciences: Transactions II,* vol. 36, no. 6: 497-510.
1975   "Nationalism and Fieldwork." In *Annual Review of Anthro-
        pology,* vol. 4, edited by B. J. Seigel, pp. 225-246. Palo Alto,
        California: Annual Reviews Inc.
Núñez del Prado, Oscar
1969   "El hombre y la familia: Su matrimonio y organización político-
        social en Q'ero. *Allpanchis Phuturenqa* 1: 5-27.
Oficina Nacional de Estadística y Censos
1973   *Perú: Crecimiento demográfico y desarrollo económico y social.*
        Lima: Oficina Nacional de Estadística y Censos.
Orlove, Benjamin S.
1974   "Reciprocidad, desigualdad y dominación." In *Reciprocidad e
        intercambio en los Andes peruanos,* edited by G. Alberti and
        E. Mayer, pp. 290-321. Lima: Instituto de Estudios Peruanos.
1975   "Surimana: Decaimiento de una zona, decadencia de un pueblo."
        Antropología Andina (Cuzco) 1-2: 75-110.
1977a   "Integration Through Production: The Uses of Zonation in
        Espinar." *American Ethnologist* 4: 84-101.
1977b   "Against a Definition of Peasantries: Agrarian Production in
        Andean Peru." In *Peasant Livelihood,* edited by Rhoda Halperin
        and James Dow, pp. 22-35. New York: St. Martin's Press.
Pachacuti Yamqui, Joan de Santa Cruz
1950   "Relación de antigüedades deste Reyno del Piru." In *Tres rela-
        ciones,* edited by M. Jiménez de la Espada, pp. 207-281. Asunció
        Editorial Guaraní.
Palomino Flores, Salvador
1968   "La cruz en los Andes." *Amaru* (Lima) 8: 63-66.
1970   "El sistema de oposiciones en la comunidad Sarhua." Tesis para
        Optar el Grado de Bachiller en Ciencias Antropológicas, Univer-
        sidad Nacional de San Cristóbal de Huamanga, Ayacucho, Perú.
1971   "Duality in the Socio-cultural Organization of Several Andean
        Populations." *Folk* (Copenhagen) 13: 65-88.
1972   "Dualidad en la organización socio-cultural de algunas poblacione
        andinas." *Revista del Museo Nacional* (Lima) 37: 231-260. (Also
        in *Actas y memorias del 39º Congreso Internacional de America-
        nistas* III, 231-260. Lima.)
Parker, Gary John
1969   *Ayacucho Quechua Grammar and Dictionary.* The Hague-Paris:
        Mouton.

Piaget, Jean
1970   *Structuralism.* New York: Basic Books.
Pinto R., Edmundo G.
1970   "Estructura y función en la comunidad de Tomanga." Tesis para
Optar el Grado de Bachiller en Ciencias Antropológicas, Universidad Nacional de San Cristóbal de Huamanga, Ayacucho, Perú.
1972   "Ecos del warachiku en la comunidad de Tomanga." *Revista del
Museo Nacional* (Lima) 37: 261-284. (Also in *Actas y memorias
del 39° Congreso Internacional de Americanistas,* III, 261-284.
Lima, Perú.
Quijano Obregón, Aníbal
1965a   "La emergencia del grupo cholo y sus implicancias en la sociedad
peruana." Tesis Doctoral, Facultad de Letras, Universidad
Nacional Mayor de San Marcos, Lima.
1965b   "El movimiento campesino peruano y sus líderes." *América
Latina* 8: 43-65.
1967   "Contemporary Peasant Movements." In *Elites in Latin
America,* edited by S. M. Lipset and A. Solari, pp. 301-340. New
York: Oxford University Press.
1971   "Nationalism and Capitalism in Peru." *Monthly Review* 23, no. 3:
3-122.
Quispe M., Ulpiano
1969   *La herranza en Choque Huarcaya y Huancasancos, Ayacucho.*
Instituto Indigenista Peruano, Monograph Series No. 20. Lima:
Ministerio de Trabajo.
Ramón C., César, et al.
1967   *La comunidad de Chuschi.* Instituto Indigenista Peruano. Ayacucho,
Perú: Sub-Proyecto de Investigación Zona Cangallo.
Ravicz, Robert
1967   "Compadrinazgo." In *Handbook of Middle American Indians,*
vol. 6, *Social Anthropology,* edited by Manning Nash, pp. 238-253.
Austin: University of Texas Press.
Raymond, J. Scott, and Isbell, William H.
1969   "Cultural Remains in the Pampas River Valley, Peru." Paper
presented at the Annual Meeting of the Society for American
Archaeology, Milwaukee.
Rowe, John H.
1963   "Inca Culture at the Time of the Spanish Conquest." In *The
Handbook of South American Indians,* vol. 2, edited by J. H.
Steward, pp. 183-330. New York: Cooper Square Publications.
Scheffler, H. W., and Lounsbury, F. G.
1971   *A Study in Structural Semantics: The Siriono Kinship System.*
Englewood Cliffs, New Jersey: Prentice-Hall.

Schultes, Richard E.
1972   "An Overview of Hallucinogens in the Western Hemisphere." In
        Flesh of the Gods, edited by P. T. Furst, pp. 3-54. New York:
        Praeger.
Soto Ruiz, Clodoaldo
1976   *Diccionario quechua: Ayacucho-Chanca.* Lima: Ministerio de
        Educación, Instituto de Estudios Peruanos.
Spalding, Karen
1972   *De indio a campesino.* Lima: Instituto de Estudios Peruanos.
Stein, William W.
1961   *Hualcan: Life in the Highlands of Peru.* Ithaca, New York:
        Cornell University Press.
Tarazona, Justino
1946   *Demarcación política del Perú: recopilación de leyes y decretos
        (1821-1946).* Lima: Ministerio de Hacienda y Comercio.
Toledo, Francisco de
1867   *Memorial y ordenanzas: relaciones de los virreyes y audiencias
        que han governado el Perú* [1575]. Lima: Imprenta del Estado.
Towle, Margaret
1961   *The Ethnobotany of Pre-Columbian Peru.* Chicago: Aldine Pub-
        lishing Company.
Troll, Carl
1958   *Las culturas superiores andinas y el medio geográfico.* Lima:
        Publicaciones del Instituto de Geografía, Universidad Nacional
        Mayor de San Marcos.
Turner, John C.
1970   "Barriers and Channels for Housing Development in Modernizing
        Countries." In *Peasants in Cities,* edited by W. Mangin, pp. 1-19.
        Boston: Houghton Mifflin Company.
Turner, Victor
1967   *The Forest of Symbols.* Ithaca, New York: Cornell University
        Press.
1969   *The Ritual Process: Structure and Anti-Structure.* Chicago:
        Aldine Publishing Company.
Van den Berghe, Pierre L.
1974   "Introduction" (pp. 121-131); "The Use of Ethnic Terms in the
        Peruvian Social Science Literature" (pp. 132-142). *International
        Journal of Comparative Sociology* 15, nos. 3-4.
Vargas Ugarte, S.J., Rubén
1951   *Concilios limenses,* vol. 1. Lima: A. Baiocco y Cia., S. R. Ltda.,
        Librería e Imprenta Gil, S.A.
Vásquez, Mario C., and Homberg, Allan R.
1966   "The Castas: Unilineal Kin Groups in Vicos, Peru." *Ethnology* 5:
        284-303.

Webster, Steven S.
1970   "The Contemporary Quechua Indigenous Culture of Highland Peru: An Annotated Bibliography." *Behavior Science Notes* 5, no. 2: 213-247. (Also in *The Condor and the Bull,* edited by P. T. Furst and K. B. Reed, pp. 491-585. Los Angeles, California: Latin American Center, University of California, 1971.
1973   "Native Pastoralism in the South Andes." *Ethnology* 12: 115-133.
1977   "Kinship and Affinity in a Native Quechua Community." In *Andean Kinship and Marriage,* edited by R. Bolton and E. Mayer, pp. 28-42. Washington, D.C.: American Anthropological Association Special Publication No. 7.

Wilson, Monica
1954   "Nyakyusa Ritual and Symbolism." *American Anthropologist* 56, no. 2: 228-241.

Wolf, Eric R.
1955   "Types of Latin American Peasantry." *American Anthropologist* 57, no. 3: 452-471.
1966   *Peasants.* Englewood Cliffs, New Jersey: Prentice-Hall.

Zuidema, R. Tom
1964   *The Ceque System of Cuzco: The Social Organization of the Empire of the Inca.* Revised edition. Leiden: E. J. Brill.
1966   "Algunos problemas etnohistóricos del Departamento de Ayacucho." *Wamani* (Ayacucho) 1, no. 1: 68-75.
1967   "Descendencia paralela en una familia indígena noble del Cuzco." *Fenix* (Lima) 17: 29-62.
1969a   "Hierarchy in Symmetric Alliances Systems." *Bijdragen* (The Hague) 125: 134-139.
1972   "Meaning in Nazca Art." *Göteborgs Ethnografiska Museum Arstryck* (Göteborg, Sweden) (1971), pp. 34-54.
1977   "Inca Kinship." In *Andean Kinship and Marriage,* edited by R. Bolton and E. Mayer, pp. 240-281. Washington, D.C.: American Anthropological Association Special Publication No. 7.

Zuidema, R. Tom, and Quispe M., Ulpiano
1968   "A Visit to God: A Religious Experience in the Peruvian Community of Choque-Huarcaya." *Bijdragen* (The Hague) 124, no. 1: 22-39.

Index

Adams, Richard: on corporate communities, 31
Adaptation: of migrants to urban environment, 177, 181, 183-191, 243-244
Administrative committee: establishment of, 30; election of migrants to, 192; research contacts with, 225
Adoption: of illegitimate children, 80; example of, 167-168
Affinal relations: in *kuyaq,* 13; subordinated to kindred of marriage, 14; sexual bifurcation in, 15; terms of address, 100, 104 (table 2); symmetric and asymmetric, 112-113; contributions to Yarqa Aspiy of, 171, 173 (fig. 5); reciprocal obligations of, 216. See also *Llumchu; Masa*
Agrarian leagues. See CCP; CNA
Agrarian Reform Law: description of, 25-31; purposes of, 27-28, 30; abolished personero and junta comunal, 30, 89; regarding peasant communities, 30-31; effects of, on research, 34; abolished private property, 38; effects of, on inheritance, 38-39; regarding vertical exploitation, 55; effects of, on village authority structures,

95-96; jurisdiction over migrant court actions, 192
Agrarian Reform Office: adjudication of land disputes, 240-242; community relations with, 245
Agricultural cycle: description of, 51-57; divided into halves, 163-164; represented in ritual, 165, 198-199; maintained by reciprocity, 176; and migration patterns, 181-182
Agricultural production: in Junín, 41; in Ayacucho, 43; in *sallqa,* 51; in *mayopatan,* 55; in *qichwa,* 55; prehistoric, 62; for market and subsistence, 73; and kin-based reciprocity, 76; importance of compadres in, 77
Agricultural zone: as mediation between village and *sallqa,* 57
Albadukay: description of, 146
Alcalde: definition of, 85; criteria for becoming, 87; responsibilities of, 139, 177; roles of, in Santa Cruz, 145-150 passim, 222-224 passim; ritual expenditures of, 171; as *masa* to affinal kin, 174
Alguacil: hierarchical position of, 86; initiation of, 139; roles of, in Santa Cruz, 145-150 passim